Electronics For Kids

FOR DUMMIES®
A Wiley Brand

by Cathleen Shamieh

FOR DUMMIES®
A Wiley Brand

Electronics For Kids For Dummies®

Published by: **John Wiley & Sons, Inc.,** 111 River Street, Hoboken, NJ 07030-5774, www.wiley.com

Copyright © 2016 by John Wiley & Sons, Inc., Hoboken, New Jersey

Published simultaneously in Canada

No part of this publication may be reproduced, stored in a retrieval system or transmitted in any form or by any means, electronic, mechanical, photocopying, recording, scanning or otherwise, except as permitted under Sections 107 or 108 of the 1976 United States Copyright Act, without the prior written permission of the Publisher. Requests to the Publisher for permission should be addressed to the Permissions Department, John Wiley & Sons, Inc., 111 River Street, Hoboken, NJ 07030, (201) 748-6011, fax (201) 748-6008, or online at http://www.wiley.com/go/permissions.

Trademarks: Wiley, For Dummies, the Dummies Man logo, Dummies.com, Making Everything Easier, and related trade dress are trademarks or registered trademarks of John Wiley & Sons, Inc. and may not be used without written permission. All other trademarks are the property of their respective owners. John Wiley & Sons, Inc. is not associated with any product or vendor mentioned in this book.

For general information on our other products and services, please contact our Customer Care Department within the U.S. at 877-762-2974, outside the U.S. at 317-572-3993, or fax 317-572-4002. For technical support, please visit www.wiley.com/techsupport.

Wiley publishes in a variety of print and electronic formats and by print-on-demand. Some material included with standard print versions of this book may not be included in e-books or in print-on-demand. If this book refers to media such as a CD or DVD that is not included in the version you purchased, you may download this material at http://booksupport.wiley.com. For more information about Wiley products, visit www.wiley.com.

Library of Congress Control Number: 2016931382

ISBN 978-1-119-21565-3 (pbk); ISBN 978-1-119-21572-1 (ebk); ISBN 978-1-119-21571-4

Manufactured in the United States of America

10 9 8 7 6 5 4 3 2 1

Contents at a Glance

Table of Contents

Introduction

Are you curious to know what really goes on inside your iPod, cellphone, tablet, or TV? Do you find it amazing that tiny electronic devices can do so many fun and interesting things? Have you ever wondered if *you* can build an electronic device that actually does something useful? If you answered yes to any of these questions, you've come to the right place!

Electronics is all about controlling *electrical current* — which you may know better as electricity — flowing in a complete path called a *circuit*. All electronic devices are made up of circuits, and every circuit contains a power supply, a path, and one or more parts (known as *electronic components*) to control current flow.

By using some basic electronic components to build projects that switch LEDs on and off, sound an alarm when light is detected, tune in a radio station, and more, you can begin to understand how your iPod, cellphone, and computer are able to do such incredible things.

About This Book

Electronics For Kids For Dummies introduces you to the incredible world of electronics in a fun way: by showing you how to build circuits that actually *do* something. As you build these circuits, you see for yourself how tiny electronic parts — resistors, capacitors, diodes, transistors, and integrated circuits — work together to control lights, sound, and timing.

The book walks you through 13 projects (plus a shopping "project") you can build and understand with just introductory knowledge. Each project includes a list of the parts you need, step-by-step circuit-building instructions (with colorful illustrations), and an explanation of how the circuit works.

By completing all the projects in this book, you will discover

✔ What it takes to make a complete circuit

✔ How to build circuits on a breadboard

✔ What series and parallel circuits are

✔ How to light an LED — without frying it

✔ Why switching electrical current between paths is so powerful

✔ How to pair a capacitor and a resistor to create a timer

✔ How to use a transistor to boost current

✔ What you can do with three different integrated circuits (ICs)

✔ How to create sounds at different frequencies

✔ Ways to control the sequencing of lights

✔ How to pull a radio signal out of thin air and amplify it

Although I can't promise that you'll be able to build a project as sophisticated as an iPod after reading this book, I can promise that you'll build some fun and interesting projects — and you'll be well on your way to expanding your knowledge so you can tackle more complex electronics projects.

This book is just a start. The rest is up to you.

Foolish Assumptions

In writing this book, I made the following assumptions about the interests and skill level of you and other readers:

- You don't know much — if anything — about electronics.

- You're interested in building projects that do something useful or fun.

- You'd like to learn the basic principles of electronics as you build your projects.

- You have some money to spend on project supplies and tools. With some smart shopping, $50 will get you most of what you need and $70–$100 will cover everything.

- You're able to place an online order for electronic components and get to a store or two (probably with help from an adult).

- You will carefully follow the safety tips in this book.

Icons Used in This Book

The tip icon flags time-saving shortcuts and other information that can make your circuit-building job easier.

This icon alerts you to important ideas or facts that you should keep in mind while building your electronics projects.

When you build electronic circuits, you're bound to run into situations that call for extreme caution. The warning icon reminds you to take extra precautions to avoid personal injury or prevent damage to your components or circuits.

This icon marks text that tells you technical details about the project you're building. If you choose to skip this information, that's okay — you can still follow along and build the project just fine.

Beyond the Book

In addition to the content in this book, you'll find some extra content available at the www.dummies.com website:

 ✔ **The Cheat Sheet for this book at** www.dummies.com/cheatsheet/electronicsfk.

 ✔ **Online materials covering additional topics are at** www.dummies.com/extras/electronicsfk.

 ✔ **Updates to this book, if any, at** www.dummies.com/extras/electronicsfk.

Where to Go from Here

As a project-based book, *Electronics For Kids For Dummies* is designed to allow you to choose what you want to work on when you want to work on it. You can build each project in order or skip ahead to a project that especially interests you. If specific information about, say, how to attach wires to a speaker appears in an earlier project, you'll find a reference to that earlier information in all later projects that use a speaker.

Even if you choose to jump into a later project first, you'd be wise to read Project 1 before you get started. Buying electronic components isn't like buying a laptop or a TV: You can't just walk into your neighborhood electronics store and pick up a few transistors and other parts. Project 1 lists everything you need to build the projects in the book and guides you through the shopping process to ensure that it's as easy, quick, and inexpensive as possible.

If you're new to electronics or have never built a circuit on a solderless breadboard, I recommend you read through Projects 2 and 3 before tackling the other projects. However, because each project walks you through the building steps in great detail, you don't have to master your breadboard to successfully build any of the projects in this book.

I hope you're as excited about electronics as I am. Have fun building the projects in this book!

Part I
Discover Basic Circuits

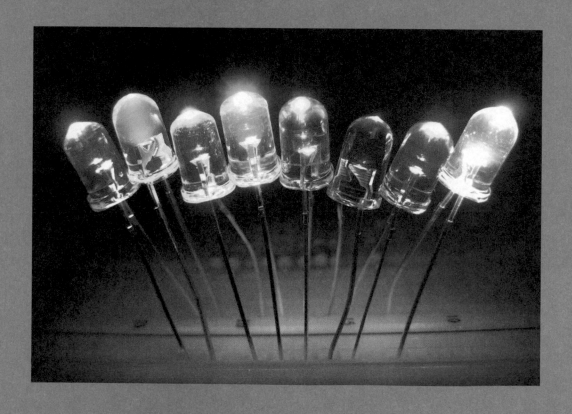

In this part, you'll build

For Dummies can get you started with lots of subjects. Visit www.dummies.com to learn more.

Go Shopping

To build the projects in this book, you need to buy a
bunch of *electronic components* (including resistors, capacitors,
diodes, LEDs, transistors, and integrated circuits), accessories
(such as alligator clips and wires), tools (such as wire strippers), and other supplies.

Plan Your Shopping Spree

I wish I could name a store in a shopping mall close to your house where you could just walk in, pick out all the parts you need, plunk down about $100, and go home and start building projects. Unfortunately, there is no such store (even RadioShack stores no longer carry a wide variety of electronic components).

So, you will need to order many of your supplies online, which means you have to plan to allow time for shipping. The good news is that you can save a lot of money by shopping online, and you can get most of the components you need in just one online trip (with an adult's assistance or, at least, an adult's credit card). You may still need to go to a couple of local stores to pick up some tools and other supplies.

Here are some recommended suppliers:

✔ **Tayda Electronics:** With warehouses in Colorado (US) and Bangkok (Thailand), Tayda ships worldwide. Allow 1–4 weeks for delivery, depending on where you live. The website, www.taydaelectronics.com, is easy to use. One visit to Tayda and you can order every electronic component and some of the accessories you need at reasonable prices (many for just pennies). I've provided Tayda part numbers for many of the components you need in the next section.

✔ **Fry's Electronics:** Between its stores (in several US states) and website (www.frys.com), Fry's stocks many of the electronic components and accessories you need. Fry's ships worldwide.

✔ **Farnell element14:** Start at www.farnell.com and select your country for the Farnell element14 company in your region. (The US company is branded Newark.) You'll find all the electronic components and many accessories you need. The website is geared toward industrial customers, so be prepared for highly technical product descriptions.

✔ **RadioShack:** RadioShack's online (www.radioshack.com) and in-store stock of electronic components seems to be dwindling, but if you really need a certain component right away, and your local store (US only) has it, it's worth the trip. Expect to pay significantly more at RadioShack than at other online suppliers.

You can also find most (or all) of the components, accessories, tools, and supplies you need on www.amazon.com or www.ebay.com. However, the product information is often spotty, so be sure you know exactly what you're ordering and be aware of shipping prices and delivery time frames.

Budget

If you're a smart shopper and order online, you can purchase all the electronic components and accessories you need for roughly $70 plus tax and shipping. (Of that $70, $20 is for two parts you need for Project 14, one of which is optional.) You may spend about another $30 (plus tax) on tools at local stores, if your family doesn't already have what you need. If you buy a lot of your components and supplies in a RadioShack store, budget another $25 or so.

Electronic Components and Accessories

This section provides a comprehensive list of the electronic components and related parts you need to complete the projects in this book. In the list that follows, I sometimes specify a product code (identified by #) and price (as of this writing, in January 2016) to give you an idea of what to look for and roughly how much you should expect to pay. Here's your shopping list of electronic parts, most of which are shown in Figure 1-1:

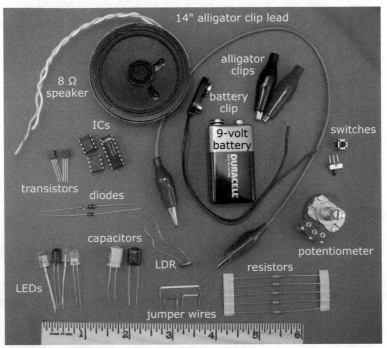

Figure 1-1

✔ **Batteries and accessories:**

- One (minimum) fresh 9-volt disposable (not rechargeable) alkaline battery ($2.50–$5.00).

- One 9-volt battery clip (sometimes called a snap connector). Tayda Electronics #A-656 ($0.10), RadioShack #2700325 ($2.99), or similar.

✔ **Wire, alligator clips, and switches:**

- Assorted precut, prestripped jumper wires (optional but highly recommended). Newark #10R0135 ($3.50), Newark #10R0134 ($6.00), RadioShack #2760173 ($7.00), or similar.

- 22-gauge solid wire, insulated, 15–25 feet (you only need 15 feet of wire if you purchase precut jumper wires). Multiple colors are preferable but not necessary. Tayda Electronics sells black (#A-4994), white (#A-4995), red (#A-4996), yellow (#A-4997), green (#A-4998), and blue (#A-4999) for $0.10 per foot.

- Alligator clips, fully insulated. Get 1 set of 10, preferably in assorted colors. RadioShack #2700378 (1 1/4-inch mini clips) or #2700356 (2-inch clips) or similar ($2.50–$3.50 per set). Also check online at Walmart, Amazon, or eBay.

- Alligator clip jumper wires (also called test leads). Get 1 set of 10. Tayda Electronics #A-2373 ($2.46) or similar.

- Two (minimum) 3-pin single-pole, double-throw (SPDT) slide switches. Make sure these switches are breadboard friendly with pins spaced 0.1 inch (2.54 mm) apart. Banana Robotics #BR010115 (5-pack for $0.99), Tayda Electronics #A-5102 ($0.78 each). Or look on Amazon.com or eBay for the 50-pack Amico #610256339894 (roughly $4.00).

- Eight 4-pin mini pushbutton (momentary-on, normally open) switches (also called tactile switches). Tayda Electronics #A-5127 or #A-5126 ($0.04 each) or similar.

✔ **Resistors:** You'll need an assortment of resistor values. Look for carbon film resistors rated at 1/4 watt (W) (or more) with a tolerance of 20 percent (or less).

Tayda Electronics sells individual resistors for just pennies each. Select RadioShack stores offer a variety pack (#2710312, $14.49), which contains 500 assorted 1/4 W resistors with 5% tolerance and includes all the values listed next.

Listed next are the resistor values, the color codes used to identify them, and the minimum quantities you need. Note that Ω is the symbol for *ohms,* the unit of measure for resistance. I recommend you get at least one extra of each of these values:

- One 10 Ω (brown-black-black)

- One 47 Ω (yellow-violet-black)

- Five 100 Ω (brown-black-brown)

- One 220 Ω (red-red-brown)

- One 330 Ω (orange-orange-brown)

- Two 470 Ω (yellow-violet-brown)

- One 820 Ω (grey-red-brown)

- Two 1 kΩ (brown-black-red)

- One 1.2 kΩ (brown-red-red)

- Two 1.8 kΩ (brown-grey-red)

- Two 2.2 kΩ (red-red-red)

- One 2.7 kΩ (red-violet-red)

- One 3 kΩ (orange-black-red)

- One 3.9 kΩ (orange-white-red)

- One 5.1 kΩ (green-brown-red)

- One 10 kΩ (brown-black-orange)

- One 22 kΩ (red-red-orange)

- One 47 kΩ (yellow-violet-orange)

- One 100 kΩ (brown-black-yellow)

- One 470 kΩ (yellow-violet-yellow)

- One 1 MΩ (brown-black-green)

- Optional: 1 4.7 MΩ (yellow-violet-green)

✔ **Potentiometers (variable resistors):**

Tayda Electronics has each value you need for just $0.50.
Expect to spend $3.49 each if you purchase potentiometers at
RadioShack stores. You need these rotary potentiometers:

- One 10 kΩ (linear taper). Tayda Electronics #A-1982 or similar.

- One 100 kΩ (linear taper). Tayda Electronics #A-1984 or similar.

- One 100 kΩ (audio/logarithmic taper). Tayda Electronics
  #A-1956 or similar.

- One 500 kΩ or 1 MΩ (linear taper). Tayda Electronics
  #A-1985 or #A-1658 or similar.

✔ **Capacitors:** When you buy the capacitors in the following list,
it's important to look for a voltage rating of 16 volts (V) or
higher. Prices range from roughly $0.01 to $1.49 each, depending on the size and supplier. Tayda Electronics sells each value
for just pennies. Always order at least one extra, especially
electrolytic capacitors. Note in the following list that F is the
abbreviation for *farad*s, the unit of measure for capacitance:

- One 2200 pF (which is 2.2 nF or 0.0022 μF) ceramic disc

- Two 0.01 μF Mylar (polyester) film

- One 0.047 μF ceramic disc

- One 0.1 μF Mylar (polyester) film

- One 4.7 µF electrolytic

- Two 10 µF electrolytic

- One 22 µF electrolytic

- One 47 µF electrolytic

- One 220 µF electrolytic

- One 470 µF electrolytic

- Optional: One 100 µF electrolytic

✔ **LEDs and other diodes:** Minimum quantities are specified in the following list, but I recommend you purchase at least a few more of each. (They're cheap — and they're fryable.)

- Ten diffused light-emitting diodes (LEDs), any size (3 mm or 5 mm recommended), any color. Buy at least one red, one yellow, and one green for the traffic light circuit in Project 13. Tayda Electronics sells 5 mm LEDs for $0.03 each in green (#A-1553), red (#A-1554), and yellow (#A-1555), as well as other colors and sizes for a few pennies each. (I suggest you buy ten red, ten yellow, and ten green.)

- Eight ultrabright clear LEDs, 5 mm, white. Tayda Electronics #A-408 ($0.05 each).

- Ten 1N4148 or 1N914 small signal diodes. Tayda Electronics #A-157 ($0.01 each) or #A-615 ($0.03 each).

- One 1N34/1N34A germanium diode. Tayda Electronics #A-1716 ($0.24).

✔ **Transistors:** Buy one or two more than the minimum specified quantity of each type, just in case you fry one. They cost pennies each online, or $1.49 each in RadioShack stores.

- Two 2N3904 general-purpose NPN bipolar transistors. Tayda Electronics #A-111 ($0.02).

- One 2N3906 general-purpose PNP bipolar transistor. Tayda Electronics #A-117 ($0.02).

✔ **Integrated circuits (ICs):**

- Two 555 timers (8-pin DIP). Splurge and buy four or five! Tayda Electronics #A-249 ($0.13 each).

- One LM386 audio power amplifier (8-pin DIP). Get two because they're so cheap. Tayda Electronics #A-206 ($0.23).

- One 4017 CMOS decade counter. Buy at least two because these chips are sensitive to static discharge. Tayda Electronics #A-020 ($0.30 each).

✔ **Miscellaneous:**

- One 8 Ω, 0.5 W speaker. Tayda Electronics #A-4140 ($1.28), RadioShack #2730092 ($3.99), or similar.

- One or more light-dependent resistor (LDR, or photoresistor). (any value). Tayda Electronics #A-1528 ($0.24) or similar.

- One spool (at least 50 feet) of 24 gauge (AWG) magnet wire. You need this expensive item if you choose to build the radio in Project 14. Temco #MW0190 or similar. ($6.00–$15.00 online at Amazon or eBay.)

- (Optional) One cheap ($10.00 or less) 3.5 mm audio headset. This headset is optional for Project 14. Check Walmart or your local dollar or other discount store.

Tools and Supplies

You need the following hand tools and other supplies to help you build your projects:

✓ **Solderless breadboard:** You use a solderless (pronounced "sodd-er-less") breadboard like the one shown in Figure 1-2 to build circuits. Purchase a breadboard that has at least 830 contact holes (also called tie points) and includes power rails (also called power lanes or bus lines), such as Tayda Electronics #A-2372 ($4.59) or RadioShack #2760001 ($22.00).

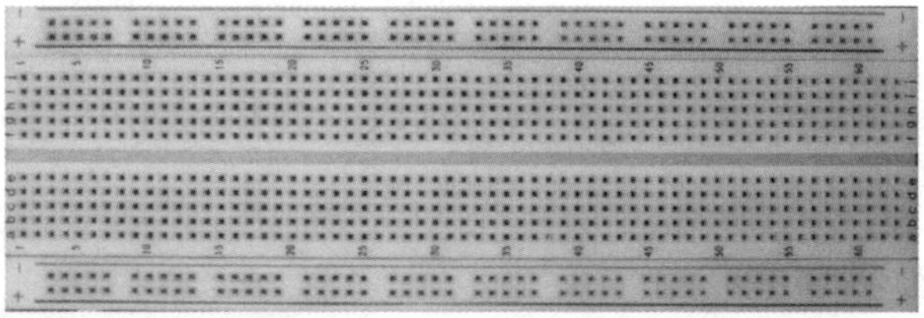

Figure 1-2

✓ **Wire stripper/cutter:** You use this tool to cut wires, trim component leads, and strip insulation from the end of wires. I recommend getting a gauged wire stripper/cutter (Figure 1-3, left), but you can use an adjustable wire stripper/cutter (Figure 1-3, right) instead. Make sure your wire stripper can be adjusted to strip 22-gauge

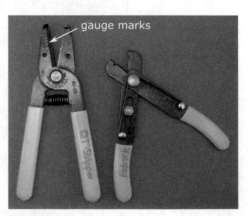

Figure 1-3

(22 AWG) wire. ($7.00–$20.00 at RadioShack, hardware stores, or Walmart.)

✔ **Needle-nose pliers:** Pictured in Figure 1-4, needle-nose pliers help you bend leads and wire and make it easier to insert and remove components from your solderless breadboard. (Check your family's toolbox or get a set of 5-inch pliers for $6.00–$12.00 at a hardware store or Walmart.)

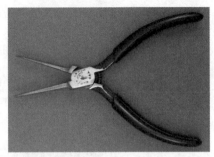

Figure 1-4

✔ **Antistatic wrist strap:** You use a strap like the one in Figure 1-5 to prevent the charges that build up on your body from zapping — and potentially damaging — the static-sensitive 4017 integrated circuit (IC) (used in Projects 12 and 13) during handling. Buy RadioShack #2762395, Zitrade #S-W-S-1, or similar. ($9.00 in select RadioShack stores; $2.00–$12.00 on Amazon.com, Walmart.com, and Newark.com.)

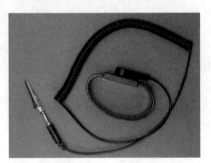

Figure 1-5

✔ **Safety glasses:** Okay, so you risk looking a bit geeky wearing safety glasses like the ones shown in Figure 1-6 while you work on your electronics projects. But better to look geeky than to not be able to look at all because the wire that you just clipped went flying into your eye. (3M #11228-00000-100 is actually attractive and costs about $1.00 on Amazon.com.)

Figure 1-6

✔ **Electrical tape:** You need about 4–6 inches of 3/4-inch electrical tape, such as Scotch #4218-BA-40. ($2.00 per roll at Walmart or any hardware store.)

✔ **Hot glue gun:** This item is optional for Project 14. You can purchase one at any craft store.

✔ **One 9-by-12-inch sheet of adhesive craft foam:** Check your local craft store (roughly $1.00). (Amazon and Walmart sell multipacks for $12.00–$15.00.)

✔ **One package of assorted grit sandpaper:** If you don't already have this, you can purchase it from any hardware store, Walmart, Amazon.com, and other suppliers ($5.00 or less).

✔ **Assorted household items:** One toilet paper roll, one paper towel roll, aluminum foil, one sheet of plain white paper, transparent tape, a ruler, a magnifying glass (optional), and one piece of cardboard or a plastic lid (optional).

LED Flashlight

One of the many fun things you can do with electronics is control lights. You can turn lights on and off, have them turn on only when the room gets dark, make them blink, change their timing, and much more.

For your first circuit-building project, you make your own flashlight using a special kind of electronic light bulb known as an LED (which is short for *light-emitting diode*).

So let's getting started making an LED flashlight!

Gather the Parts for the LED Flashlight

The main ingredients of your LED flashlight are a battery, an LED, and a resistor. They are the *components* of your circuit. Each component is like a piece of a puzzle: It has a certain job to do and it works with the other components to form the completed circuit.

Using electrical tape and craft foam, you can transform your three-component circuit into a portable, brightly colored device that you can show off — maybe even sell — to your friends.

Check out Project 1 for where to buy parts, tools, and other supplies. Grab a pair of scissors and your needle-nose pliers, then gather the items in the following list (shown in Figure 2-1):

- ✓ One 9-volt battery

- ✓ One ultrabright clear 5 millimeter LED

- ✓ One 470 Ω resistor (look for a stripe pattern of yellow, violet, brown, and then any color stripe)

- ✓ A roll of 3/4-inch wide electrical tape (you need roughly 4 inches in length from this roll)

- ✓ One 9-by-12-inch sheet of adhesive-backed craft foam (any color)

Before you start building your flashlight, you should know a few things about the three main circuit components (the battery, LED, and resistor).

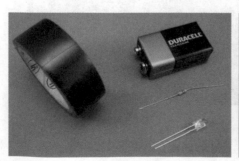

Figure 2-1

Energize Your Flashlight

Chances are you're familiar with 9-volt batteries like the one in Figure 2-1. The battery's job is to provide the electrical energy needed to power the LED in your flashlight circuit.

Explore your battery

Every battery has two *terminals*, which are the metal pieces that stick out from the top of a 9-volt battery (see Figure 2-2) or the metal ends of an AA, AAA, C, or D battery. One terminal is positive and is labeled with a +. The other terminal is negative and isn't labeled. Locate the positive and negative terminals on your 9-volt battery. Note that the two terminals look different.

Figure 2-2

When you connect your battery in a circuit, you connect the positive terminal to one part of the circuit and the negative terminal to another part of the circuit. The battery *voltage* is a form of energy (specifically, *potential energy)* that exists between the two terminals. Voltage is measured in *volts*, which is abbreviated *V*.

Voltage and current

When you connect a battery in a circuit, the battery's voltage forces electrons to flow out of the battery, through the circuit, and then back into the battery. But what are electrons, you ask?

Electrons are tiny particles that have a special quality known as negative charge. Electrons exist inside atoms, which are the building blocks of matter. When a bunch of electrons break loose from their atoms and travel together in the same direction, that flow of electrons is called *electric current*, or simply *current*.

In your LED flashlight circuit, electric current gives your LED the energy it needs to light up. And the 9-volt battery provides the energy (voltage) needed to push the current through the circuit. Batteries are one type of *voltage source*, providing voltage to force current to flow through circuit components.

Technically, what we call a battery is really a *cell*. A *battery* is really two or more cells connected together electrically. It's good for you to know that, but I still use the term *battery* to refer to a cell (as do most people).

Get to Know Your LED

You may be familiar with LEDs if you have an LED flashlight or use LED bulbs in your home. An LED, or *light-emitting diode*, is a device made of a special material known as a *semiconductor*. A *diode* is the simplest type of semiconductor device (meaning, component).

Diodes, LEDs, and other semiconductor devices have unique properties that make them useful. For instance, they don't always allow current to pass through them. Instead, they're picky about what's going on in the circuit and will allow current to flow only under certain conditions.

Diodes and bicycle tires

Have you ever pumped air into a bicycle tire? The tire contains a valve that allows air to flow into the tire, but not out of the tire. You have to apply enough pressure to the pump to force air through the valve.

A diode acts like a valve for electric current. Current flows only one way through a diode (like cars on a one-way street — we hope), and only when you apply a high enough voltage (like pressure) to the diode.

Seeing light from LEDs

A light-emitting diode is a type of diode that emits, or gives off, visible light. The light emitted from an LED can be red, orange, yellow, green, blue, violet, pink, or white, as shown in Figure 2-3. The color depends on the materials and processes used to make the LED.

Figure 2-3

LEDs also come in several shapes and sizes. The LEDs you use in the projects in this book have round, domed cases that are either 5 mm (millimeters) or 3 mm high.

There are two types of LEDs:

- *Diffused LEDs* have colored plastic cases (like tinted windows) to diffuse, or spread out, the light so it's easier to see. The color of the plastic case is usually the same as the color of the light.

- *Clear LEDs* have clear plastic cases but still emit colored light.

All the LEDs in Figure 2-3 are clear 5 mm LEDs. Figure 2-4 shows an assortment of LEDs, including a 5 mm clear LED that gives off an orange light. (It's the unlit version of the LED that is second from the left in Figure 2-3.)

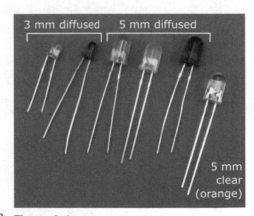

Figure 2-4

You can't tell what color a clear LED emits just by looking at it if it's not connected in a circuit. If you buy any clear LEDs, be sure to store them in a container or bag labeled with the color they emit.

Examine your LED

Take a good look at your LED and compare it to the LEDs shown in Figure 2-5. The actual semiconductor diode is tiny and is on a piece of metal inside the plastic case. The two stiff wires attached to the plastic case are leads that enable you to connect the tiny diode to a circuit.

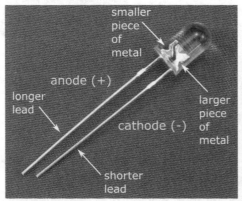

Figure 2-5

Because LEDs conduct current in only one direction, you need to know which way to connect the LED in your circuit. One side of the LED is the negative side (known as the *cathode*) and the other side of the LED is the positive side (known as the *anode*). Electric current flows from the anode to the cathode of an LED but not the other way around. You can tell which side of an LED is which in three ways:

- ✔ **Compare the lengths of the leads.** The shorter lead is the cathode (negative side) and the longer lead is the anode (positive side). (See Figure 2-5, left.)

- ✔ **Peek inside the plastic case.** The lead attached to the larger piece of metal inside the case is the cathode (negative side); the lead attached to the smaller piece of metal is the anode (positive side). (See Figure 2-5, left.)

✔ **Look (or feel) for a flat edge on the plastic case.** This flat edge is on the cathode (negative side) of the LED. (See Figure 2-5, right.)

Look at the leads of your LED. Can you tell which one is the shorter lead? Now look inside the case of your LED. (You may need to shine a flashlight on the case to see inside better.) Can you spot the larger and smaller pieces of metal? Finally, run your finger around the bottom edge of the plastic case. Can you feel a flat edge?

Being able to distinguish the anode from the cathode by peeking inside the case or finding the flat edge may come in handy when you do other projects in this book, because you may want to cut, or *clip*, the leads of an LED to create a neater circuit. After you clip the leads, you can't figure out which side is which by comparing the lengths of the leads.

Orienting an LED in a circuit

When you connect an LED in a circuit, you need to orient it so that current flowing from the positive terminal of the battery flows into the positive side (anode) of the LED. If you put the LED in backward, current will not flow. (I tell you which way to orient the LEDs you use in projects in this book.)

To conduct current and emit light, most LEDs require between 2.0 and 3.4 volts to be applied across the leads. The exact voltage needed depends on the color of the LED. A 9-volt battery is powerful enough to push current through any LED, but a 1.5-volt battery, such as an AA or AAA battery, isn't strong enough. For this reason, you use a 9-volt battery rather than an AA or AAA battery for your LED circuit.

Never, ever connect a 9-volt battery directly to an LED. If you do, you may damage the LED. LEDs can handle only a certain amount of current before they have a meltdown, and a direct connection with a 9-volt battery pushes way too much current through the LED. Chances are, the LED will light briefly and then go out for good, but the LED may also melt, make a mess, and smell up your house.

Protect Your LED with a Resistor

To limit the current that flows from your 9-volt battery through your LED, you insert a resistor in your circuit. *Resistors* slow down current, like a kink in a hose slows the flow of water.

Figure 2-6 shows you a variety of resistors. Every resistor has two leads, and it doesn't matter which way you insert a resistor into a circuit. Current flows either way through a resistor. (Resistors are not semiconductors, so they are not picky.)

Figure 2-6

Resistors don't require a minimum voltage like LEDs do (not picky!). Current flows through a resistor even with a tiny voltage applied. The higher the voltage you apply to a resistor, the higher the current that flows through the resistor — up to a point. Too much current can melt a resistor. (Don't worry. You won't melt any resistors for the projects in this book — as long as you follow the instructions!)

Understanding resistance

Every resistor has a value known as its *resistance* (what a surprise). The higher the resistance, the more the resistor restricts current. Resistance is measured in *ohms* (pronounced "omes"), and the symbol for ohms is Ω (which looks like an upside-down horseshoe and is the Greek letter omega).

Some resistances are measured in *kilohms* (pronounced "kill omes"), which means thousands of ohms. The symbol for kilohms is kΩ. Other resistances are so large they are measured in *megohms* (pronounced "meg omes"), which means millions of ohms. The symbol for megohms is MΩ. (You may be familiar with the prefixes, *kilo*, which means thousands, and *mega*, which means millions, from your math classes. And you've probably heard of measurements such as *kilometer,* as in the *k* in a 5k race, and *megabyte,* as in "My laptop has 4 *megabytes* of RAM.")

For your LED flashlight, you need a resistor with a value of 470 Ω. But resistors don't have their values stamped on their cases, so you need to know how to identify a 470 Ω resistor. You can tell what the resistance of a specific resistor is by looking at the colored bands on its case. Think of the colored bands as a code. The color and position of the bands tell you the value of the resistance.

 You don't have to decode resistor bands for the projects in this book because I tell you the color bands you need for the resistors in every project. But it's still a good idea to understand resistor color codes, so I recommend that you check out the information on reading resistor values at www.dummies.com/extras/electronicsfk.

For this LED flashlight project, look for a resistor that has a stripe pattern of yellow-violet-brown and then a fourth stripe of any color. That's a 470 Ω resistor.

Resistor power ratings

Resistors also come in different thicknesses. Generally, the thicker the resistor, the more electrical energy it can handle before having a meltdown. When resistors slow down current, a lot of heat is generated, and if too much heat is generated, the resistor will melt.

All resistors have *power ratings* measured in units of *watts* (abbreviated *W*). Ordinary resistors can handle up to 1/4 watt of energy, but you can also find 1/2-watt, 1-watt, and larger resistors for circuits that need to handle more power.

 You don't have to worry about resistor power ratings for the projects in this book. 1/4-watt or larger resistors will do just fine. And you won't see any marks on a resistor to indicate the power rating. When you purchase a resistor, the product information will indicate the power rating.

Make the LED Flashlight

To construct your LED flashlight, you build a circuit using the 9-volt battery, the 470 Ω resistor, the clear LED, some electrical tape, and some adhesive-backed foam. If you want, you can also make a case for your flashlight using some additional adhesive-backed foam. This section explains how to do both.

Build the flashlight circuit

Follow these steps to build the LED flashlight circuit:

1. Connect the 470 Ω resistor (yellow-violet-brown) to the positive battery terminal. (See Figure 2-7.)

Figure 2-7

   a. Bend the resistor lead around the positive battery terminal (using your needle-nose pliers may help make this easier).

   b. While gripping the positive battery terminal to hold the resistor lead in place, bend the body of the resistor down from the positive battery terminal and wrap the resistor around the battery.

   c. Press the unconnected resistor lead down against the short edge of the battery, under the negative battery terminal.

2. Make a foam cutout. (See Figure 2-8.)

   a. Cut out a 1-inch square piece of adhesive-backed foam.

   b. Bend the foam in half and use scissors to make two slits in the center of the square.

   c. Carefully cut out the foam between the slits so that there's a hole about 1/2 inch high and about 3/16 inch wide. (Don't agonize over the exact dimensions or making a neat slit.)

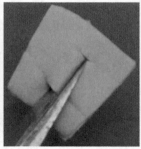

Figure 2-8

3. Place the foam cutout on top of the unconnected resistor lead. (See Figure 2-9.)

a. Remove the backing from the foam cutout so that the sticky side of the foam is exposed.

b. Place the foam cutout on top of the unconnected resistor lead, lining it up so that the lead is visible through the slit in the foam cutout.

Figure 2-9

c. Press the foam cutout down to make it stick to the battery.

4. Connect the cathode of the LED to the negative battery terminal. (See Figure 2-10.)

a. Using your needle-nose pliers, bend the shorter LED lead (cathode) and wrap it around the negative battery terminal.

Figure 2-10

b. While holding the LED lead in place against the negative battery terminal, bend the LED so that its plastic case is sticking up from the top of the battery near the edge.

Getting the LED positioned correctly (in this step and the next step) can be tricky. It may take you a few minutes to get it right.

5. Position the LED. (See Figure 2-11.)

While holding the LED's plastic case in place, bend the longer LED lead (anode) and position it so that it lies on top of the foam cutout.

The foam cutout should be sandwiched between the resistor lead and the LED lead, preventing the two leads from touching. There should be a small gap between the two leads.

small gap between leads

Figure 2-11

6. Secure the leads around the battery terminals using electrical tape. (See Figure 2-12.)

Cut two small pieces of electrical tape (each about an inch long). Press one piece of tape down onto and around the negative battery terminal, and press the other piece of tape down onto and around the positive battery terminal.

Figure 2-12

7. Tape the longer lead (anode) of the LED to the side of the battery. (See Figure 2-13.)

Cut a 2-inch piece of electrical tape. Use the tape to hold the end of the LED lead in place against the battery, but be careful not to cover the opening in the foam cutout with the tape.

8. Test the LED flashlight. (See Figure 2-14.)

Holding the battery in your hand, press down on the LED lead so that it makes contact with the resistor lead that is under the foam cutout. (Don't worry. You won't get hurt.)

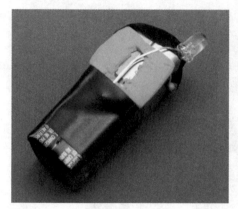

Figure 2-13

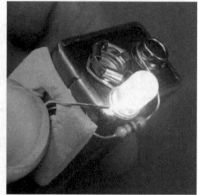

Figure 2-14

Did the LED light up? If so, congratulations! You've successfully built your first circuit!

If your LED did not light up, make sure that the resistor and LED leads make contact when you press down. If your circuit is still not working, check your connections and make sure that your LED is oriented correctly. If your LED still doesn't light up, you may need to start over again using another battery and another LED.

LED flashlight switch

Did you know that within your circuit, you've made a switch? In fact, you've made a *momentary normally open switch* using the resistor lead, the LED lead, and the foam cutout.

Your switch is a *momentary* switch because it's only on momentarily (for a short time) when you depress it. And it's a *normally open* switch because under normal conditions, you're not pressing the switch, and the switch is *open* (which, in switch-speak, means off).

Make a case for your flashlight

Your LED flashlight is a complete, working circuit, but wouldn't it be nice if it had a cover so that the circuit isn't exposed? You can make a simple case using more of your adhesive-backed foam sheet. Just follow these steps:

1. Cut out a piece of adhesive-backed foam, using the dimensions shown in Figure 2-15.

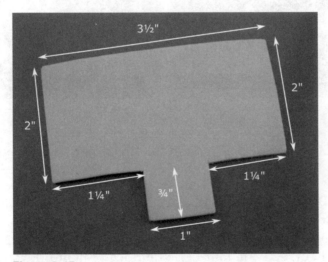

Figure 2-15

2. Remove the backing from the foam cutout.

3. Lay the foam cutout on a flat surface, sticky side up.

4. Place the LED flashlight on the foam cutout, as shown in Figure 2-16.

   Make sure that the LED sticks up from the top edge of the foam. Press the battery into the foam.

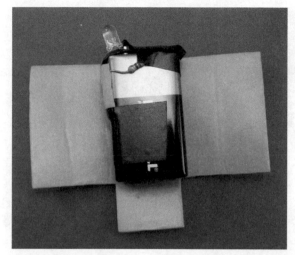

Figure 2-16

5. Wrap the foam cutout around the battery. (See Figure 2-17.)

Wrap the bottom of the battery first, then the sides, and finally the top surface.

Figure 2-17

6. Make a top for the case. (See Figure 2-18.)

Cut a piece of adhesive-backed foam roughly 1 inch by 3/4 inch. Cut a quarter circle out of one corner to make room for the LED. Remove the backing and press the foam down on top of your LED flashlight.

 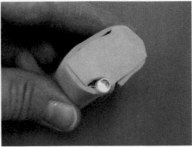

Figure 2-18

7. Use a pen, a Sharpie marker, or something else to mark the spot you need to press to turn the LED on. (See Figure 2-19.)

Figure 2-19

Turn off the lights and try out your LED flashlight in the dark. Pretty cool, isn't it?

Decorate your case. To add some sparkle, use adhesive-backed glitter foam for your case, like the flashlight shown on the first page of this project.

You may want to make some LED flashlights for your friends or for car owners in your family, so they can keep a flashlight in the glove compartment.

LED Flashlight Circuit Diagram

Have you ever played a musical instrument or sung in a chorus? If so, you may have some experience reading sheet music. Sheet music uses symbols to represent musical notes, such as middle C, D, and E. Composers use musical notation to write melodies that they create.

Something similar happens in electronics. When people design circuits, they use symbols to represent the circuit components in a diagram so that the design can be captured on paper (or on a computer).

A *schematic* (pronounced "skee-mat-ick") is a diagram of a circuit. Schematics use symbols to represent circuit components and lines to show the connections between components. What schematics don't do is tell you how to arrange your circuit (or whether or not to use foam cutouts). It's up to you to decide how to lay out your circuit.

It's difficult to build a circuit that has more than a few components if you don't have a schematic to guide you. Imagine building a large house without using a drawing, or *blueprint*, listing the materials, dimensions, and locations of all the components used to construct the house. Schematics are as essential to electronics as blueprints are to construction.

Figure 2-20 shows the schematic for the LED flashlight circuit, along with labels for the components.

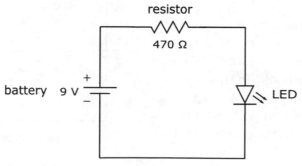

Figure 2-20

Note that the symbol for the resistor is symmetrical, meaning that you could flip it and it would still be the same, but the symbols for the battery and the LED are not symmetrical. Remember that it doesn't matter which way you insert resistors in the circuit, but it does matter with LEDs and batteries. The symbols give you a hint about whether a component must be inserted a certain way or not.

The schematic also tells you the following information:

✔ The positive terminal of the 9-volt battery is connected to one side of the 470 Ω resistor.

✔ The other side of the 470 Ω resistor is connected to the anode (positive side) of an LED. (The anode is represented by the wide side of the triangle in the LED symbol.)

✔ The cathode (negative side) of the LED is connected to the negative terminal of the 9-volt battery. (The cathode is represented by the line in the LED symbol.)

Think about your LED flashlight. Do the components and the connections you made match those shown in the schematic?

If you notice a slight difference between the circuit you built and the schematic in Figure 2-20, give yourself a pat on the back. Your LED flashlight circuit also includes a switch between the resistor and the LED. Your switch isn't a separate component that you can buy, like the switches I ask you to use in other projects in this book. But it's still a switch, and it should appear in your circuit diagram.

Figure 2-21 shows the schematic for your LED circuit with the switch added. The switch is open (meaning off) in this schematic. So this schematic represents your circuit when you're not pressing down on the foam cutout.

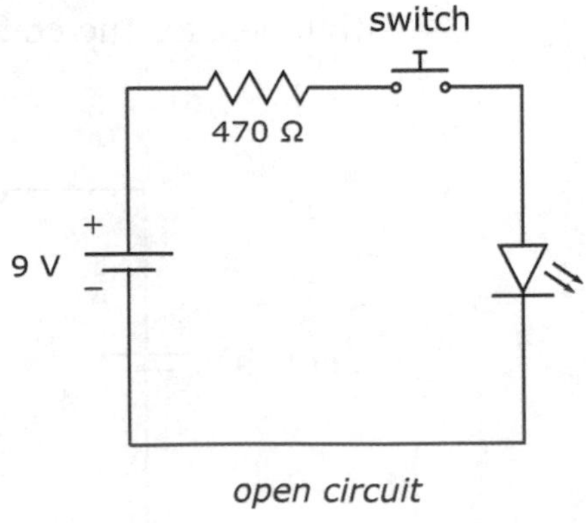

switch

470 Ω

9 V

open circuit

Figure 2-21

This type of circuit is an *open circuit*. Current can't flow through an open circuit because there's a gap in the path. The LED isn't lit when the circuit is open.

The diagram in Figure 2-22 represents your circuit when you are pressing down on the foam cutout, causing the LED and resistor leads to make contact with each other. (In case you're wondering, the hand in the diagram is *not* an official circuit symbol!) The switch in this diagram is closed (meaning on). This circuit is a *closed circuit*, and current flows around the circuit — and the LED lights — because the path is complete.

Do the schematics in Figures 2-21 and 2-22 help you visualize what's going on in your LED flashlight circuit? If you know how to read schematics, you will find it easier to understand how circuits work. And when you start building more advanced circuits, such as the ones later in this book, you'll rely on schematics to guide you as you build — and troubleshoot — your circuits.

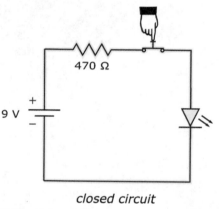

closed circuit

Figure 2-22

Solderless Breadboard

This project shows you how to use an awesome circuit-building tool called a *solderless breadboard* to test different ways to connect two LEDs in a circuit. All the projects in this book, except Project 2 (the LED flashlight), require a solderless breadboard, so the sooner you know how to use one, the better.

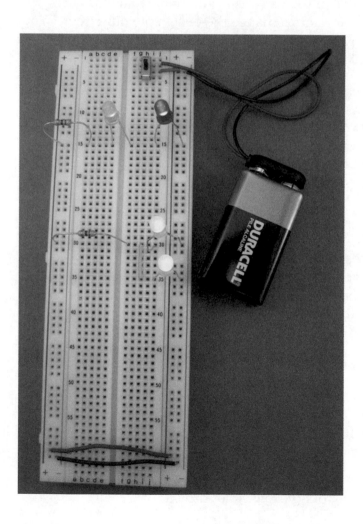

Why Use a Solderless Breadboard?

The LED flashlight circuit in Project 2 uses just three components and is probably the simplest circuit you'll ever build. It was easy to package that circuit in a case so that it looks like a finished product (well, sort of — "Foam flashlights for sale! Get 'em while they last!").

But as your circuits get more complicated, you'll discover that it's not always wise to create a permanent, packaged circuit right off the bat. What if you make a mistake and connect an LED backwards? What if you want to change the design of your circuit? You wouldn't want to tear open your handcrafted foam (or other) packaging to make changes, would you?

Not to worry. Using a *solderless breadboard*, or *breadboard* for short, allows you to build flexible circuits that you can change whenever you want — without ripping permanent connections apart. And it's actually fun — and easy — to build and play with circuits using a breadboard.

So let's gather up the necessary parts and start breadboarding!

Get Your Components Ready

The main ingredients of the test circuits for your solderless breadboard are a battery, two resistors, and four LEDs. You also need a few parts to help you connect the main components, and a switch so you can connect and disconnect your battery from the circuit.

Here's a complete list of the parts you need for this project (see Figure 3-1):

⮞ One 9-volt battery

⮞ One battery clip

⮞ Two 470 Ω resistors (yellow-violet-brown)

✔ Four LEDs (any colors, but two of the four LEDs must be the same color; any size)

✔ One single-pole, double-throw (SPDT) slide switch (intended for breadboard use)

✔ Two 2-inch (minimum) jumper wires (any color, but preferably two different colors and ideally red and either black or blue)

✔ One 1/4-inch (minimum) jumper wire (any color)

✔ One 1/2-inch (minimum) jumper wire (any color)

✔ Solderless breadboard

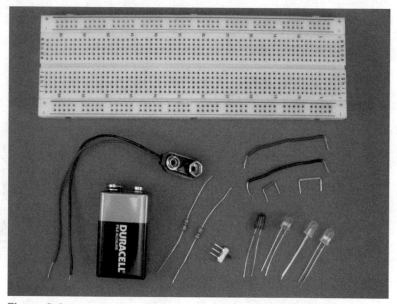

Figure 3-1

Jumper wires

A *jumper wire* is a short insulated wire with bare (meaning stripped of insulation) ends. You use jumper wires to connect two points in a breadboard circuit.

Note that the parts list calls for four jumper wires of various lengths. In each case, the length refers to the minimum length of the main section of the jumper wire, not including the bare ends that you will stick into the breadboard holes. You can use a longer jumper wire, but a shorter one won't do.

You can buy precut jumper wires (as I suggest in Project 1) or you can make your own jumper wires. A box of precut wires in assorted lengths and colors cost about $7, but they make your electronics life a lot easier. Homemade wires are cheaper, but they involve a bit more work. It's your choice: your money or your time.

If you choose to make your own jumper wires, visit www.dummies.com/extras/electronicsfk for step-by-step instructions and illustrations.

Use a battery clip

To make it easier to connect your battery to your breadboard, snap the *battery clip* (sometimes called a *snap connector*) onto the terminals. The battery clip contains two leads, which are wires that are electrically connected to the battery terminals when the clip is attached to the battery.

Figure 3-2 shows you how a 9-volt battery looks with the clip attached. The red lead is connected to the positive battery terminal and the black lead is connected to the negative battery terminal.

Figure 3-2

Explore Your Solderless Breadboard

Figure 3-3 shows you one type of solderless breadboard. This rectangular plastic board contains 830 holes nicely organized into rows and columns. (Does the board remind you of the game Battleship?) Some breadboards have more holes and some have fewer, but they all work the same way.

Contact holes

The holes in a breadboard are not just plain ordinary holes. They are *contact holes*. Inside the board are strips of metal that connect groups of neighboring contact holes together. (More on which ones are connected to which other ones in a minute.) Each metal strip contains tiny metal clips — one for each hole — designed to grab onto a wire or lead that you stick into the hole.

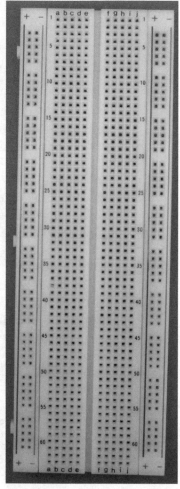

Figure 3-3

Say you poke a resistor lead into a hole and it gets grabbed by a clip on one of the metal strips inside, and then you poke an LED lead into another hole that makes contact with the same metal strip. The metal strip acts like a wire, making an electrical connection between the resistor and the LED!

Try it yourself: Take a 470 Ω resistor (yellow-violet-brown) and insert one of its leads into any contact hole in your solderless breadboard. Did you feel the metal clip grab the lead? Now, gently remove the lead from the hole. You should feel the clip release the lead as you pull the lead out.

When you insert a lead into a contact hole, make sure that the lead gets grabbed by the metal clip, but don't jam the lead in with all your might just because you can. If you push the lead in too far, it could worm its way around the inside of the board, and it may touch another one of the metal strips — and that's a big no-no.

The idea is to use the breadboard to make connections between your circuit components. By plugging components and battery leads into the breadboard in the right way, you can build an entire circuit in minutes! Best of all, if you change your mind about, say, the value of a resistor in your circuit, you can just pull out the resistor and plug in a different resistor. Pretty cool, eh?

Connections

Ready to start building your first breadboard circuit? Not so fast! You need to know which contact holes are connected to which other contact holes inside the board before you start plugging parts in randomly!

I have good news and bad news about the connections. The bad news is that you can't see the connections just by looking at the breadboard. The good news is that there's a pattern to the connections.

Take a look at your breadboard. Check out the columns and rows in the two center sections. Do you see the column labels, a through j, at the top of the breadboard? Note that there are two groupings of columns — a-b-c-d-e and f-g-h-i-j — separated by a sort of ditch in the plastic between columns e and f.

Now, look at the row labels. Not every row is labeled, but you should be able to figure out the number of each row.

Figure 3-4 shows you part of my breadboard, with yellow lines added to show you where the connections are in the center sections (ignore the outer columns for now).

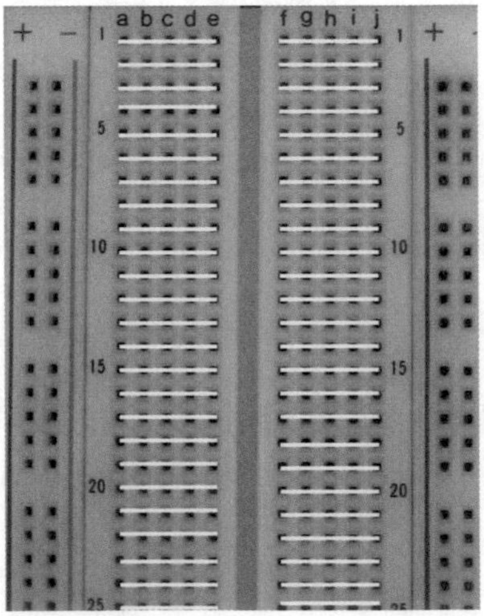

Figure 3-4

Here's what this figure is telling you:

- Within each row, there are two groupings:

  - The five contact holes in columns a, b, c, d, and e are connected to each other.

  - The five contact holes in columns f, g, h, i, and j are connected to each other.

✔ The two groupings of five holes in each row are NOT connected to each other. (Think of the ditch as separating those two groupings of holes.)

✔ There are no connections between rows.

So, for instance, hole 2a is connected to holes 2b, 2c, 2d, and 2e, but not to holes 2f, 2g, 2h, 2i, or 2j, and not to any of the holes in rows 1, 3, or any other row.

Those two center sections are where you plug in most of the components in your circuits.

Power rails

Most breadboards have two pairs of columns labeled + and – on the outer edges of the breadboard. Those four columns are known as *power rails*, and you use them to connect your battery to other parts of your circuits. Locate the four power rails on your breadboard.

The yellow lines in Figure 3-5 show you where the connections are within the power rails.

Here is what the figure is telling you:

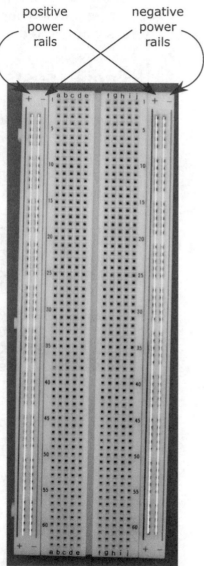

Figure 3-5

✔ Within each power rail, every contact hole is connected to every other contact hole in that same power rail.

✔ There are no connections between power rails.

The idea is to plug your positive battery lead into any hole in one of the positive power rails, and plug your negative battery lead into any hole in one of the negative power rails. Then, as you build your circuit in the center of the breadboard, you can make connections to your battery terminals using holes in the power rails you selected.

Binding posts

Some breadboards have three colored binding posts next to one side of the board. *Binding posts* connect wires together. You place the stripped end of one wire through a hole at the base of the binding post and the stripped end of another wire through the same hole. Then you screw the cap down to hold the two wires together. (See Figure 3-6.)

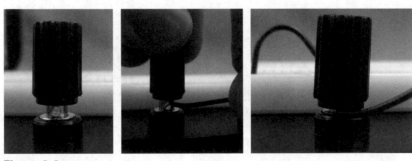

Figure 3-6

Binding posts are commonly used to connect a battery to the breadboard without having to plug the battery lead wires into contact holes. Most battery leads contain *stranded wire*, which consists of several very fine wires twisted together. Stranded wire can easily break when plugged into a contact hole multiple times, as you insert and remove your battery repeatedly. The binding post enables you to connect the battery lead wire to a piece of solid (meaning not stranded) wire, and plug the solid wire into the breadboard. (See Figure 3-7.)

TIP If your breadboard has binding posts, it's a good idea to use them. If not, no big deal, you can just plug your battery leads directly into the contact holes when you are ready to add power to your circuits. Just remember to be careful when you plug in the battery leads, so you don't damage the wires.

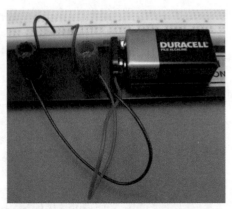

Figure 3-7

Breadboard an LED Circuit

Building a single LED circuit on a breadboard is a snap! Grab one 470 Ω resistor (yellow-violet-brown), any LED, your battery with battery clip, and needle-nose pliers. Then place your breadboard on a flat surface and follow these three steps:

1. Insert an LED into the breadboard:

    a. Using your needle-nose pliers, gently bend the leads of the LED out and down, as shown in Figure 3-8, left.

    b. Insert the longer LED lead (positive side, or anode) into hole *9j* (that is, the hole located in row *9*, column *j*).

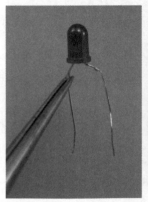 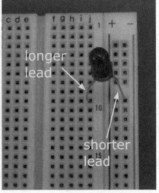

Figure 3-8

c. Insert the shorter lead (negative side, or cathode) into any hole in the nearby negative power rail (but I recommend that you use the hole closest to row **9** of your breadboard). Refer to Figure 3-8, right.

2. Insert the 470 Ω resistor into the breadboard:

a. Gently bend the leads of the resistor so that they are at 90° angles to the body of the resistor. (A 90° angle is what you find in each corner of a square.)

b. Because it doesn't matter which way you orient the resistor in a circuit, insert either lead into hole **9h** and the other lead into any hole in the column labeled +. (I used the hole in row **13**, as shown in Figure 3-9.)

Because holes **9h** and **9j** are connected, the resistor and the LED are connected.

Figure 3-9

3. Connect the 9-volt battery to the power rails of the breadboard:

a. Insert the black battery lead (negative battery terminal) into the top hole in the rightmost column, labeled –. (You could insert the black lead into any of the holes in this column, because they're all connected.) You are connecting the negative battery terminal to the negative side (cathode) of the LED.

b. Insert the red battery lead (positive battery terminal) into the top hole in the leftmost column, labeled +. (You could insert the red lead into any of the holes in this column, because they're all connected.) You are connecting the positive battery terminal to the resistor, completing the circuit.

Figure 3-10 shows how your finished circuit should look.

Did your LED turn on? If it did, congratulations! You've successfully breadboarded your first circuit!

If your LED did not turn on, go back and review the steps for building your circuit. Here are some questions to ask yourself as you *troubleshoot*, or track down the source of the problem with your circuit:

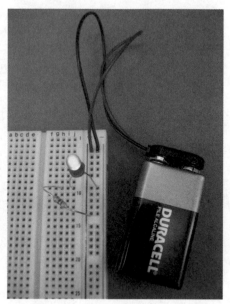

Figure 3-10

✔ Is each component inserted into the correct hole in your solderless breadboard?

✔ Are all the leads pushed firmly, but not excessively, into the breadboard?

✔ Is the battery clip snapped firmly onto the battery terminals?

✔ Are you using a fresh battery? (If you're not sure, try using another battery.)

✔ Is your LED oriented correctly?

✔ Did your LED go kaput somehow? (If you're not sure, try using another LED.)

If you notice something really wrong with your circuit — like the resistor is melting or smoke is rising — hold your needle-nose pliers by their insulated handles and pull one of the battery leads out of the breadboard. Removing the battery powers down the circuit so no further damage can occur. Then check your connections to see what's wrong and fix it right away. (You may need to replace the resistor, the LED, or both.)

If you built the LED flashlight in Project 2, you probably realize how much easier it is to build the same circuit — yes, this is the same circuit (minus the switch) — on a breadboard. No need to wrap leads around battery terminals. No electrical tape holding parts in contact with each other. And with your breadboard circuit, if one part is bad, you can simply remove it and replace it with another part. With your foam-wrapped LED flashlight circuit, it's much more difficult to replace a bad part.

Add a Power Switch

In the LED flashlight in Project 2, the combination of the foam cut-out and the resistor and LED leads forms a switch. In your breadboard LED circuit, the resistor and LED are always connected, so if you want to preserve battery power, you have to add a switch component to your circuit. After you have a power switch in place on your breadboard, you can (and should) use it for all the remaining projects in this book.

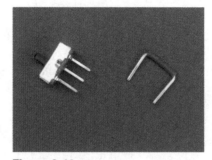

Figure 3-11 shows what you need to grab from the parts you gathered at the start of this project: a single-pole, double-throw (SPDT) slide switch designed for breadboard use and a short (1/4-inch minimum) jumper wire.

Figure 3-11

Understand how your switch works

Take a close look at your switch. Note that it has three prongs, or *terminals*, and a *slider*, which is the black knob that moves back and forth (try it and see).

The slider controls what connection is made inside the switch. Figure 3-12 shows the connection that is made for each position of the slider.

✔ With the slider positioned toward the terminal labeled 3, terminals 2 and 3 are connected inside the switch (as shown by the black line in Figure 3-12, left).

✔ With the slider positioned toward the terminal labeled 1, terminals 1 and 2 are connected inside the switch (as shown by the black line in Figure 3-12, right).

Figure 3-12

Think about your switch connection

Figure 3-13 shows how to connect your switch, the jumper wire, and the red (+) and black (–) battery leads. The photo on the left shows the switch lying on its side so you can see which holes its terminals go into. The photo on the right shows the completed switch connection. Examine Figure 3-13 before you follow the steps to connect your switch.

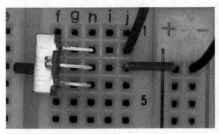

Figure 3-13

Can you predict what will happen when you install and operate the switch as shown in Figure 3-13, right? Think about it a bit before reading further.

Here's what to expect:

✔ **When the slider is in the upper position, the switch connects the five holes in row 2 to the five holes in row 3.**

The switch connects the red battery lead (positive battery terminal) to the orange jumper wire, which is connected to the positive power rail. This means that the switch connects the positive battery terminal to the positive power rail.

From your circuit's point of view (if it has a point of view), the battery is connected because its positive and negative terminals are connected to the positive and negative power rails, respectively.

✔ **When the slider is in the lower position, the switch connects the five holes in row 3 to the five holes in row 4.**

But there is nothing else connected in row 4, so the left side of the orange jumper wire isn't connected to anything! In this case, the red battery lead (and thus the positive battery terminal) is disconnected from the positive power rail, so the battery is not powering your circuit (even though the battery is always on).

 A battery is never off — even if it's disconnected from your circuit — and can be dangerous if you're not careful. Make sure that the two battery terminals are never *shorted*, meaning connected together through just a wire or other purely conductive path. A short can cause the battery to heat up and possibly explode. And never put a battery in your pocket along with, say, a penny or a metallic hair clip. The coin or clip may short the battery terminals — and you could end up with a nasty burn.

Connect your switch

Leave the LED, resistor, and black battery lead the way they were in your LED circuit (refer to Figure 3-10). Then follow these steps to add the switch to your LED circuit (refer to Figure 3-13):

1. Move the red battery lead.

   Remove the red battery lead from the positive power rail and then connect it to hole *2j*.

2. Insert the jumper wire.

   Insert one end of the jumper wire into hole *3j*. Insert the other end of the jumper wire into the hole in the positive power rail (+ column) to the right of row *3*.

3. Insert the switch.

   Plug the three leads of the switch into holes *2h*, *3h*, and *4h*. (It doesn't matter which way you orient the switch.)

Test your switch

Slide the black knob on the switch back and forth. Does the LED in your circuit turn on and off? Figure 3-14 shows the LED circuit with the switch off (left) and on (right). Here's how the circuit works with the switch in place:

✔ With the switch in the lower position (Figure 3-14, left), the battery is disconnected, so the LED is off.

✔ With the switch in the upper position (Figure 3-14, right), the battery is connected, so the LED is on.

It's a good idea to use a switch to connect and disconnect power with every circuit you build, so I recommend that you leave the switch and jumper wire in place for all the projects in this book.

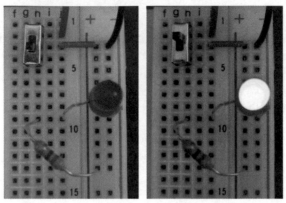

Figure 3-14

Connect the Power Rails

Several projects in this book involve ten or more components. It's much easier to breadboard such circuits when you can make connections to power on either the right or the left side of the breadboard. So let's connect the two positive power rails together and the two negative power rails together using the 2-inch jumper wires you set aside at the beginning of this project.

Follow these steps to connect the power rails (see Figure 3-15):

1. Make sure each of your jumper wires is at least two inches long (not including the bare ends).

   Using two different colors (ideally red for the positive rails and black or blue for the negative rails) is preferable but not necessary.

2. Connect one jumper wire (preferably black or blue) between the two negative power rails in row *61* of your breadboard.

3. Connect the other jumper wire (preferably red) between the two positive power rails in row *60* of your breadboard.

By making these connections at the bottom of your breadboard, you have clear space along the rest of the board to build your circuits.

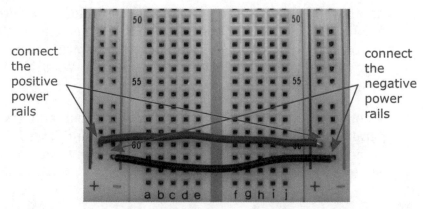

connect the positive power rails

connect the negative power rails

Figure 3-15

Now all the contact holes in the left positive power rail are connected to all the contact holes in the right positive power rail. And all the contact holes in the left negative power rail are connected to all the contact holes in the right negative power rail. These connections give you access to both the positive and negative battery terminals on both sides of the breadboard.

 Like your power switch, it's a good idea to leave your power rail connections in place all the time as you work on the projects in this book.

Now that you have your breadboard set up, it's time to experience the fun of playing with circuits on a breadboard!

Series and Parallel Circuits

In your single LED circuit, current can follow only one path. This type of circuit is known as a *series circuit*, because all components (battery, resistor, and LED) are connected in series. In a series circuit, all the current coming out of the battery flows through all the components and then back into the battery.

Another type of circuit is a *parallel circuit*, which has more than one branch, or path, for current to follow. When current flowing out of the battery reaches a junction, it splits, with some of the current flowing through each of the branches. When the branches come together again, so does the current.

In this section, you build a two-LED series circuit and a two-LED parallel circuit. Then — because it's so easy and fun to do on a breadboard — you remove one LED from each circuit and observe what happens.

Prepare your breadboard

Clear your LED circuit from your breadboard by removing the LED and the 470 Ω resistor. Leave everything else — your battery, switch circuit, and power rail connections — in place. Power down your breadboard by sliding the switch that disconnects the battery (always a good idea before you start messing around with your breadboard).

Build the two-LED series circuit

You need two LEDs and one 470 Ω resistor from the parts you gathered earlier in this project. The LEDs can be any color, but make sure that you save two matching LEDs for the parallel circuit in the next section.

Follow these three steps to build the series circuit (refer to Figure 3-16):

1. Insert the first LED into the breadboard.

   Plug the cathode (shorter lead) into the negative power rail to the right of row *15*. Plug the anode (longer lead) into hole *15j*.

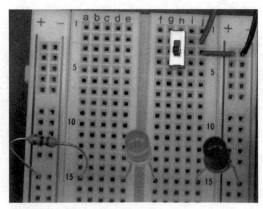

Figure 3-16

2. Insert the second LED into the breadboard.

   Plug the cathode (shorter lead) into hole *15f*. Plug the anode (longer lead) into hole *15e*.

3. Insert the 470 Ω resistor into the breadboard.

   Plug one lead into hole *15a*. Plug the other lead into the positive power rail to the left of row *15*.

Now test your circuit by turning on the power switch, as shown in Figure 3-17. Did both LEDs light up? If not, troubleshoot by checking that your LEDs are oriented correctly, the LEDs and resistor are inserted firmly into the correct contact holes, and your battery is connected to your circuit (that is, the power switch is turned on).

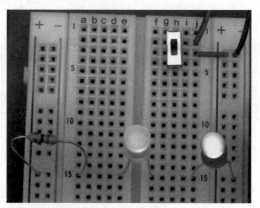

Figure 3-17

Build the two-LED parallel circuit

You need two same-color LEDs, one 470 Ω resistor, and a short (1/2-inch or longer) jumper wire from the parts you gathered at the start of this project.

Leave your two-LED series circuit connected. Slide the power switch to the off position. Then follow these steps to add the two-LED parallel circuit to your breadboard (refer to Figure 3-18):

1. Insert the first LED into the breadboard.

   Plug the cathode (shorter lead) into the negative power rail to the right of row *30*. Plug the anode (longer lead) into hole *30j*.

2. Insert the second LED into the breadboard.

   Plug the cathode (shorter lead) into the negative power rail to the right of row **35**. Plug the anode (longer lead) into hole **35j**.

3. Insert a 1/2-inch (or longer) jumper wire into the breadboard.

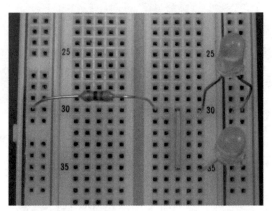

Figure 3-18

Plug one end of the jumper wire into hole **30h** and the other end into hole **35h**. This action connects the anodes of the two LEDs together.

4. Insert the 470 Ω resistor into the breadboard.

   Plug one lead into hole **30f**. Plug the other lead into the positive power rail to the left of row **30**.

Now turn on the power switch. Did the two LEDs in your parallel circuit light up, as shown in Figure 3-19, in addition to the two LEDs in your series circuit? If not, troubleshoot!

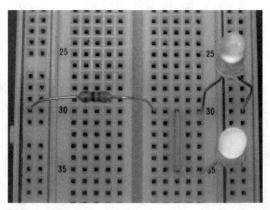

Figure 3-19

Compare circuits

With your power switch on, pull out one of the LEDs from the series circuit (row 15). Did the other LED go out? Next, pull out one of the LEDs (row 30 or 35) from the parallel circuit. Did the other LED stay lit?

Figure 3-20, left, shows what your circuits should look like with the LEDs removed. (Note that the battery, switch, and power rail connections are still in place, even though they don't appear in the photo.)

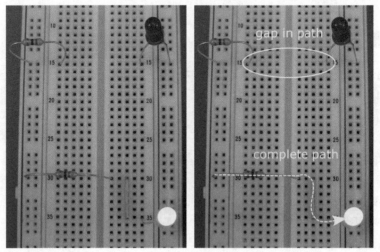

Figure 3-20

In the series circuit, removing one LED breaks the path, so current doesn't flow and the remaining LED doesn't light. In the parallel circuit, removing one LED breaks one of the parallel paths, but the other path is still complete, so the remaining LED lights.

Look at Figure 3-20, right. The gap in the path (row 15) of the series circuit prevents current from flowing through the red LED. But in the lower circuit, current flows from the positive battery terminal, through the 470 Ω resistor (row 30), through the green jumper wire, through the yellow LED, and into the negative battery terminal — so the LED lights.

Visualize the flow of current

You may find it easier to follow the path of current flow if you look at the schematics of the two-LED series and two-LED parallel circuits.

Figure 3-21 shows the schematic for the two-LED series circuit (with some color and a switch-operating hand added). It's clear that the current has only one path and both LEDs are in that path.

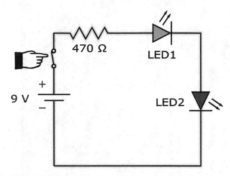

Figure 3-21

When you remove LED1, the path is broken, so LED2 doesn't light, as shown in Figure 3-22.

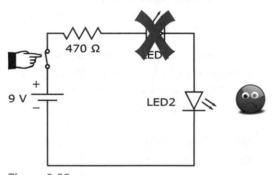

Figure 3-22

The schematic for the two-LED parallel circuit, shown in Figure 3-23, shows a split path — like a fork in the road — on one side of the resistor. Each branch contains one of the LEDs. Current flows through both branches, lighting both LEDs.

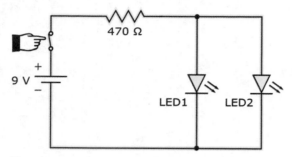

Figure 3-23

When you remove LED1, there's still a path for current to flow, and LED2 lights, as shown in Figure 3-24.

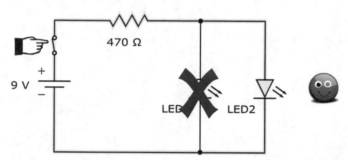

Figure 3-24

You experience parallel circuits every day in your home and school. For instance, when you plug a lamp into an outlet, you are adding another parallel branch to the many circuits in your home. Creating a gap in this branch by switching off the lamp doesn't affect the other electrical components in your house.

Think about what would happen if, say, your TV, refrigerator, and a lamp were wired in series instead of in parallel: If you turn off the lamp, you break the circuit, so your TV and fridge don't receive current — and your family is very upset with you. And who knows? You might even hear your parent say, "If I've told you once, I've told you a thousand times: When you leave the room, LEAVE THE LIGHTS ON!"

Part II
Simple Projects That Control Light

In this part, you'll build

To see a video of the stage lights dimmer in action, visit www.dummies.com/extras/electronicsfk.

Two-Way Traffic Light

Project 3 explains how to build a circuit that switches LEDs on and off. This project shows you how to use a single switch to control two LEDs, so that when one is on, the other is off, and vice versa. If you use a red and a green LED, you can use the circuit as a two-way manual traffic light.

Collect and Prepare Components

The components of your two-way traffic light circuit are a battery, a resistor, two LEDs, and a switch. You build the circuit on a solderless breadboard that is prepared with a switch for your battery and connections between power rails. (Refer to Project 3 for detailed steps on how to connect the power switch, battery leads, and power rails.) You also need a jumper wire to help you connect the main components.

Gather the parts in this list (see Figure 4-1):

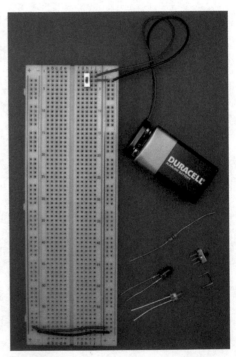

- Solderless breadboard prepared with the following:

  - One 9-volt battery with battery clip

  - Power switch and jumper wire

  - Power rail jumper-wire connections

- One 470 Ω resistor (yellow-violet-brown)

- One red LED (any size)

- One green LED (any size)

- One single-pole, double-throw (SPDT) switch

Figure 4-1

- One short (1/4-inch) jumper wire (precut or homemade)

Create Neater Circuits

As you build more complex circuits with many components, you may find that making connections on your solderless breadboard is a bit like playing Twister — right leg on red dot, left leg stretched out to blue dot, right arm wrapped around your back and on the yellow dot. The arrangement, or *layout,* of your circuit can get complex quickly.

What do you think would happen if a lead from one component in a complicated circuit touched a lead from another component, and they weren't supposed to be touching? If you think that your circuit might not work as expected, you're right!

To prevent you from getting your wires crossed, I recommend that you get into the habit of building neat circuits with trimmed leads. Neatness counts — for your homework and in electronics! In this project, I show you simple ways to build a neater circuit.

Construct the Two-Way Traffic Light Circuit

Follow these steps to put together the two-way traffic light circuit:

1. Double-check your solderless breadboard (see Figure 4-2):

   a. Make sure that the two positive power rails are connected, and the two negative power rails are connected.

   b. Check that your power switch and jumper-wire connections are properly installed and that the switch is in the off position.

   c. Verify that the leads from your battery clip are snugly plugged into the correct contact holes in your breadboard.

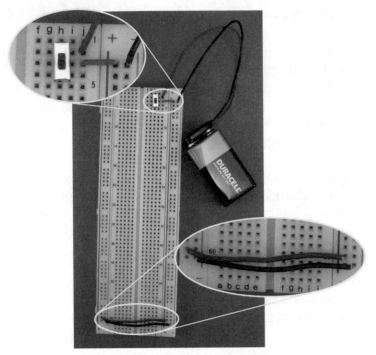

Figure 4-2

2. Clip the 470 Ω resistor (yellow-violet-brown) leads so that about 1/4 inch of the lead is sticking down below the bend.

   Figure 4-3, left, shows you how to clip the resistor leads using the sharp scissorlike part of your wire cutters. Remember to wear your safety glasses to avoid harm from fast-flying clipped leads. Figure 4-3, right, shows you what the resistor looks like after clipping its leads when held up against the edge of the breadboard. Note that each resistor lead is just long enough to reach from the top surface of the breadboard to the bottom.

3. Insert the 470 Ω resistor into the breadboard, as shown in Figure 4-4.

   Insert one resistor lead into hole **11a** (that is, the hole in row 11, column a). Insert the other resistor lead into the positive power rail to the left of row **11**.

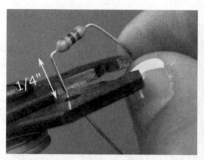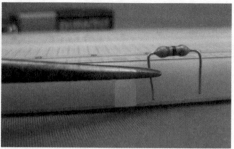

Figure 4-3

4. Insert the 1/4-inch (or longer) jumper into the breadboard.

Plug one end of the jumper wire into hole **11e** and the other end into hole **11f,** as shown in Figure 4-5.

The jumper wire connects the two sides of row 11, so now all ten contact holes in row 11 (holes 11a–11j) are electrically connected.

The purpose of this jumper wire is to connect the resistor to a switch that you place in hole 11h in Step 8. Instead of using the jumper wire, you could just leave your resistor leads long and connect one side of the resistor to hole 11f, but then you would have a long exposed lead stretching across your bread-board. Using the jumper wire allows you to keep your resistor leads short so that only a tiny bit of each lead is exposed on the top of the breadboard. Trimming leads and using insulated jumper wires help reduce the risk of problems.

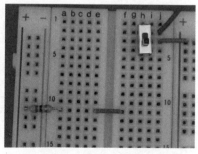

Figure 4-4   Figure 4-5

5. Bend and clip the leads of each LED.

   Use your needle-nose pliers to bend the LED leads out and down, bending the positive (longer) lead, or anode, out a bit more than the negative (shorter) lead, or cathode. Then use your wire cutters to clip the LED leads so that the length of the lead below the bend is about 1/4 inch. (See Figure 4-6.)

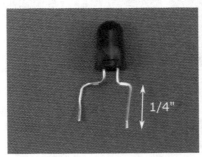 

Figure 4-6

6. Insert the trimmed red LED into the breadboard.

   You must orient the LED properly or it won't work. If you can't tell which lead was longer before you clipped the leads, remember that you can always peek inside the case to see the larger piece of metal, which is the negative lead (cathode) and the smaller piece of metal, which is the positive lead (anode). Or you can identify the cathode by finding the flat edge of the LED case. (See Figure 4-7, left.)

   Insert the positive side (anode) into hole **10j**. Insert the negative side (cathode) into the hole in the negative power rail to the right of row **10** on your breadboard. (See Figure 4-7, right).

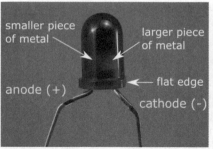

Figure 4-7

7. Insert the trimmed green LED into the breadboard.

   Insert the positive side (anode) into hole **12j**. Insert the negative side (cathode) into the hole in the negative power rail to
   the right of row **12** on your breadboard. (See Figure 4-8).

8. Insert the switch into the breadboard.

   Insert the three terminals of the SPDT switch into holes **10h**,
   11h, and **12h**, as shown in Figure 4-9.

   This switch connects either the red LED or the green LED to
   the 470 Ω resistor in row 11, through the jumper wire inserted
   in Step 4. Let's call this the *LED selector switch* for this circuit.

Figure 4-8   Figure 4-9

Figure 4-10 shows how the complete finished circuit looks.

Turn on the power switch. Does one of the LEDs light, as in Figure 4-11? If not, troubleshoot by making sure that all leads (including the battery clip leads and the switch terminals) are inserted firmly, but not excessively, into the correct contact holes, and that both LEDs are oriented correctly. If you still don't see the light, try replacing the LEDs or using a fresh battery.

Now move the slider on the LED selector switch. Does the other LED light, as in Figure 4-12?

With the LED selector switch slider in the up position (toward row 1 of the breadboard), you connect the five holes in row 11, columns f–j (where the central switch terminal is plugged in) to the five holes in row 10, columns f–j (where the upper switch terminal is plugged in). By moving the slider down (toward row 60), you connect the five holes in row 11, columns f–j (central switch terminal) to the five holes in row 12, columns f–j (lower switch terminal).

Figure 4-10

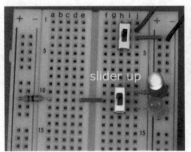 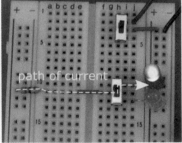

Figure 4-11

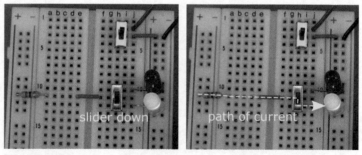

Figure 4-12

One side of the red LED is in row 10, and one side of the green LED is in row 12. So the switch is alternately connecting the red LED and the green LED to whatever is in row 11, columns f–j.

The only connection in row 11, columns f–j (other than the central switch terminal) is the jumper wire, which connects the two sides of row 11. Because one side of the 470 Ω resistor is plugged into hole 11a and the central terminal of the switch is plugged into hole 11h, the resistor is connected to the central terminal of the switch.

The bottom line is this: By moving the LED selector switch slider up and down, you connect the resistor to either the red LED (slider up) or the green LED (slider down). You've built a two-way traffic light circuit.

Two-Way Traffic Light Schematic

The schematic, or circuit diagram, for the two-way traffic light is shown in Figure 4-13. Note the symbol for the LED selector switch: The input (left) side of the switch is connected to the 470 Ω resistor, and the output (right) side of the switch alternates between being connected to LED1 (green) and LED2 (red). This sort of connection is sometimes called an *on/on switch*, because the switch is always on — it just switches between two circuit paths. (In this schematic, both LEDs are off because the power switch is off.)

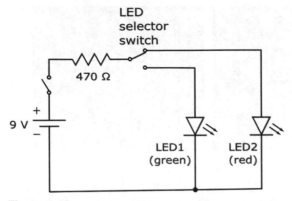

Figure 4-13

Figure 4-14 shows what the circuit looks like when the battery is connected. The upper schematic shows the LED selector switch directing current through the red LED. The lower schematic shows the LED selector switch directing current through the green LED.

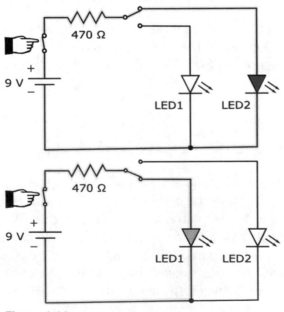

Figure 4-14

Don't Underestimate Your Switch

Your LED selector switch plays an important role in your circuit. The switch directs current to different paths in the circuit. The function of a switch may seem simple to you, but you should know that switching is one of the most important functions in the field of electronics.

Switching is what enables you to access any one of millions of websites from your smartphone, tablet, computer, or TV — just by typing in or clicking a web address. Switching allows you to direct text messages or phone calls to specific people (well, really to specific devices that, you hope, specific people are using).

The type of switching that controls the telephone network and the Internet is sophisticated. The switches in those networks are electronically controlled switches, not manual (hand-operated)

switches like the one in your two-way traffic light. Many years ago, however, telephone switching was controlled by operators making connections between circuits manually. See Figure 4-15, a photo of an international switchboard in 1943, courtesy of U.S. National Archives.

Figure 4-15

In Project 13, you build a three-way traffic light using electronic components to automate the sequence and timing of the lights. You also use electronically controlled switching in other projects in this book, to switch a speaker or a light on or off when certain actions take place in your circuit.

Light Timer

In the LED flashlight (Project 2) and two-way traffic light (Project 4) circuits, each LED is either on or off, and the only way to turn any of them on or off is to flip a switch that is part of the circuit. In this project, you use a resistor and a new (to you) component called a *capacitor* to make an LED grow dimmer and dimmer until it finally goes out.

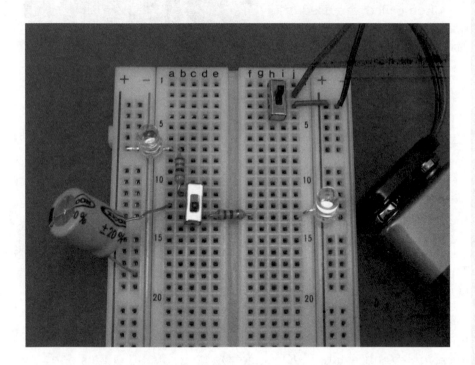

What Is a Capacitor?

A capacitor is a pretty simple device. It consists of two electrical conductors (known as *plates*) that are separated by a special type of insulator (that is, a nonconductor) known as a *dielectric* (pronounced "die ih LECK trick"). Leads are attached to each plate and a coating or other case is placed around the capacitor. The plates and the dielectric can be made from a variety of different materials, so different kinds of capacitors have different qualities and uses. Figure 5-1 shows an assortment of capacitors.

Capacitors, or *caps* as they are often called, are used in many ways in circuits. In this project, you use caps to

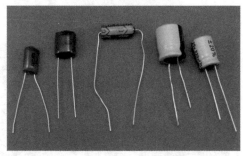

✔ **Store electrical energy:** A capacitor can act like a temporary battery, providing energy to other components in a circuit even

Figure 5-1

when there is no battery or other voltage source.

✔ **Create a timer:** Working with a resistor, a capacitor can control the amount of time it takes for an event, such as the sounding of a buzzer or the lighting of an LED, to occur in a circuit.

The value of a capacitor is known as its capacitance. *Capacitance* is a measure of how much energy a capacitor can store.

Capacitance is measured in units called *farads* (abbreviated *F*), but most capacitors used in electronics have capacitances in the *microfarad* (abbreviated *μF*) range. One microfarad equals one millionth (or 10^{-6}) of a farad.

In this project, you store energy in a capacitor, release that energy to light an LED, and control how long the LED stays lit by using a resistor along with the capacitor.

Check Out Your Capacitor

You need a 470 microfarad (μF) *electrolytic capacitor*, like the one shown in Figure 5-2, for this project. Electrolytic capacitors are *polarized*, which means the way that they are connected in a circuit matters. To tell which side is which, look for a large stripe or a minus sign (or both) on one side of the capacitor. The lead closest to that stripe or minus sign is the negative lead, and the other lead (which is unlabeled) is the positive lead. Another way to tell the sides apart is to look at the length of the leads. The shorter lead is the negative lead and the longer lead is the positive lead. If you clip the leads, you can still look for the stripe or minus sign.

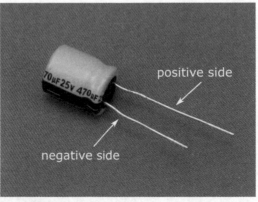

positive side

negative side

Figure 5-2

The value of most electrolytic capacitors is marked on the case. Other types of capacitors are so small that there's not enough room for the value, so manufacturers use a code. Don't worry: You don't need to know the capacitor code for the projects in this book because I tell you what to look for on the capacitors you use.

Note the value "470 μF 25V" marked (and repeated) on the capacitor in Figure 5-2. This marking means that the capacitance is 470 μF and the maximum voltage that this capacitor should be exposed to is 25 V. This project uses a 9 V battery, so the 25 V rating is fine (and a capacitor rated for 16 V works fine, too). You should know that if you use a capacitor rated for a lower voltage than the power supply in your circuit, you risk damaging your capacitor.

Gather Components and Tools

In addition to your capacitor, you need a battery, a few resistors, two LEDs, and a switch for this project. You build the circuit on a solderless breadboard that is prepared with a switch for your battery and connections between power rails. (Refer to Project 3 for detailed steps on how to connect the power switch, battery leads, and power rails.)

Gather all the parts in this list (see Figure 5-3):

- Solderless breadboard, prepared with

    - 9-volt battery with battery clip

    - Power switch and jumper wire

    - Power rail jumper-wire connections

- One 470 µF electrolytic (polarized) capacitor

- One 47 Ω resistor (yellow-violet-black)

- One 330 Ω resistor (orange-orange-brown)

- One 1 kΩ resistor (brown-black-red)

- One 5.1 kΩ resistor (green-brown-red)

- Two LEDs (any size, any color; I used clear pink and blue)

- One single-pole, double-throw (SPDT) switch

- (Optional) One or more additional resistors in your choice of values that are greater than 330 Ω

- (Optional) One 220 µF electrolytic (polarized) capacitor

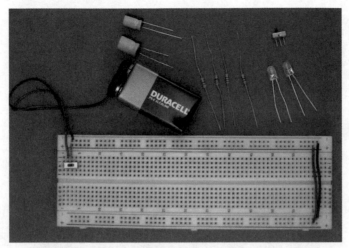

Figure 5-3

I recommend that you keep your wire cutters nearby so you can clip the leads of the resistors, the LEDs, and (optionally) the capacitor to avoid having leads touch when they're not supposed to. Needle-nose pliers come in handy for inserting and removing resistors, but they're not absolutely necessary.

Build the Capacitor Circuit

Follow these steps to build the circuit:

1. Double-check your solderless breadboard (see Figure 5-4).

   a. Make sure that the two positive power rails are connected and the two negative power rails are connected.

   b. Check that your power switch and jumper-wire connections are properly installed and that the switch is in the off position.

   c. Verify that the leads from your battery clip are snugly plugged into the correct contact holes in your breadboard.

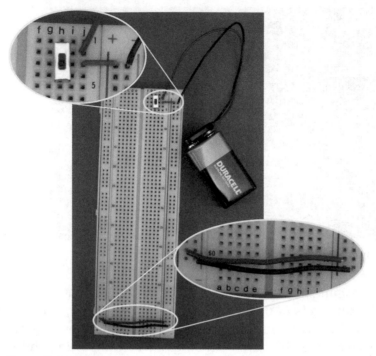

Figure 5-4

2. Insert the 47 Ω resistor (yellow-violet-black) into the breadboard, as shown in Figure 5-5.

   a. Trim the resistor leads, leaving them long enough to insert
      the resistor between column a and the positive power rail to
      the left of row 11.

   b. Plug one lead into hole *11a* (that is, row *11*, column *a*)
      and the other lead into the positive power rail to the left
      of row *11*.

3. Insert the 470 µF electrolytic capacitor into the breadboard, as
   shown in Figure 5-6.

   a. If you want, trim the capacitor leads so that each lead is
      about 1/2-inch long. (My capacitor leads are untrimmed so
      that you can see how they are connected in the photos.)

b. Plug the positive lead (unlabeled) into hole **12a**. Plug the negative lead (stripe or negative sign) into the negative power rail on the left side of the breadboard. (Any hole in the negative power rail will do. I used the hole next to row 18.)

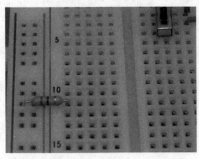

Figure 5-5   Figure 5-6

4. Insert the SPDT switch into the breadboard, as shown in Figure 5-7.

   Plug the three switch terminals into holes **11c**, **12c**, and **13c**. (It doesn't matter which end is which for the switch.)

5. Insert one of the LEDs into the breadboard, as shown in Figure 5-8.

   a. Bend and trim the LED leads so that each lead is about 1/4-inch long below the bend (I show you how to do this in Project 3).

   b. Insert the cathode (negative side, flat edge, larger piece of metal inside the case) into the negative power rail to the right of row **13**. Insert the anode (positive side) into hole **13j**.

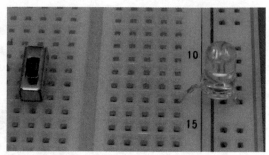

Figure 5-7   Figure 5-8

6. Insert the 1 kΩ resistor (brown-black-red) into the breadboard, as shown in Figure 5-9.

Trim the resistor leads so that each lead is about 1/4-inch long. Plug one lead into hole **13e** and the other lead into hole **13f**.

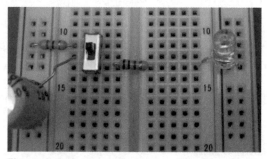

Figure 5-9

The completed circuit is shown in Figure 5-10 (except that you can't see the battery or the power rail connections at the bottom of the breadboard).

Note that when the capacitor switch is in the up position (that is, the slider is closer to row 1), the positive side of the capacitor is connected to the 47 Ω resistor (in row 11) through the switch. When the capacitor switch is in the down position (that is, the slider is closer to row 60), the positive side of the capacitor is connected to the 1 kΩ resistor (in row 13).

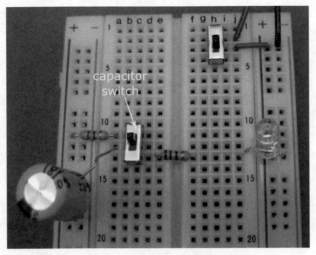

Figure 5-10

Figure 5-11 shows the schematic for your circuit. The capacitor is shown in the middle of the schematic, with the plus sign indicating which way the cap is oriented in the circuit.

Now it's time to see what your capacitor can do!

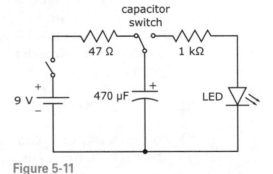

Figure 5-11

Operate the Capacitor Circuit

Turn on the power switch (up position). Move the slider on the capacitor switch up (toward row 1). Does the LED light? (It shouldn't.)

Next, turn off the power switch (down position). Your battery is no longer powering the circuit. Move the slider on the capacitor switch down (toward row 60). Does the LED light? (It should.)

Does the LED stay lit? (It should grow dimmer until it eventually goes out, after a few seconds.)

The capacitor is powering the LED! (If you think that the battery is somehow still connected, try repeating the process of operating the circuit. But this time, instead of just turning off the power switch as instructed in the paragraph before this one, remove the battery leads from the breadboard so that you know the battery is not connected. Once you move the slider on the capacitor switch down, you'll see the LED light.)

To understand what is happening in your circuit, let's explore the schematic.

Charge your capacitor

Figure 5-12 shows that when you turn on the power switch and move the capacitor switch slider up, you connect the capacitor to the battery through the 47 Ω resistor.

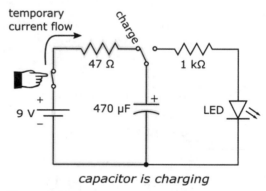

Figure 5-12

When the capacitor is connected to the battery, current flows as electrons coming out of one side of the battery pile up on one of the capacitor plates. Because an insulator (the dielectric) is between the capacitor plates, electrons cannot flow from one plate to the other. But electrons are pulled off the other capacitor plate by the other side of the battery, so current makes its way around the circuit. This process is known as *charging the capacitor*.

Once the capacitor is fully charged (meaning, it is stashing all the electrons it can handle), it stops grabbing electrons from the battery, so current stops flowing.

Store electrical energy

When you remove the battery (by turning the power switch off) after charging the capacitor, the capacitor remains charged because there is no conductive path for the electrons to flow through. (See Figure 5-13.) The capacitor is storing electrical energy, and there is a voltage (you may remember that voltage is a form of potential energy) between the capacitor plates. When the capacitor is fully charged, it has a voltage of 9 V — the same voltage as the battery — across its plates.

Does "storing electrical energy" sound to you like something a battery does? If so, you're right. A capacitor is like a rechargeable battery. It stores the energy it gets from a battery or other voltage source. So what does the capacitor do with the energy it stores?

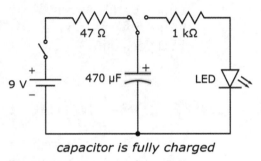

capacitor is fully charged

Figure 5-13

It holds on to it until you give it a way to release the energy, by connecting it to components in a complete path.

Discharge your capacitor

Figure 5-14 shows what happens when you move the slider on the capacitor switch down (that is, toward row 60). This action connects the capacitor — which is charged — to the 1 kΩ resistor and the LED. (My LED emits pink light.)

The three components — the capacitor, the LED, and the resistor — form a complete path, so now the capacitor can unload the electrons it picked up from the battery. This process is called *discharging the capacitor.*

Even though there is no battery in the discharge path, current flows while the capacitor discharges through the circuit. As the current flows through the circuit, it energizes the LED, lighting it. Once the capacitor is discharged, the current stops flowing and the LED goes out.

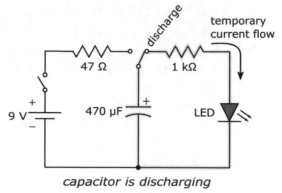

capacitor is discharging

Figure 5-14

Change the Timing of the Light

Here's what makes using a capacitor to light an LED in a circuit special: You can change the time it takes to discharge the capacitor, which means that you can change the time the LED stays lit.

Meet the RC time constant

It turns out that the discharge time depends on the values of the resistor in the discharge path and the capacitor. If you multiply the resistance by the capacitance, you get something called the *RC time constant*. And after five time constants, the capacitor is almost completely (actually, 99 percent) discharged.

In your circuit, the value of the resistor in the discharge path is 1 kΩ (or 1,000 Ω), and the capacitance is 470 μF (or 0.000470 F). You multiply these numbers together to get the RC time constant:

$$RC \text{ time constant} = 1 \text{ k}\Omega \times 470 \text{ μF}$$
$$= 1,000 \times 0.000470$$
$$= 0.47 \text{ second}$$

The RC time constant is a little less than half a second, so five times the RC time constant is a little less than 2.5 seconds (2.35 seconds, to be exact). So the math predicts that it takes about 2.5 seconds for the LED to go out.

Test the math by operating your circuit again. First, turn on the power switch and move the capacitor switch to the charge position (up) so that the capacitor charges. Then move the capacitor switch to the discharge position (down) so that the capacitor discharges, and try counting "one Mississippi, two Mississippi, three Mississippi" to see if the LED goes out before you get to three.

Note that the power switch can be on or off during the discharge cycle. It won't make a difference either way because the battery isn't connected to the capacitor when the capacitor switch is in the discharge position.

Increase the capacitor discharge time

Now let's see what happens when you change the RC time constant by swapping out the 1 kΩ resistor for a larger value of resistance. Grab the 5.1 kΩ resistor (green-brown-red) from the parts you gathered at the start of this project, and follow these steps:

1. Turn off the power switch.

   It's always a good idea to switch off power before you start fiddling with a circuit.

2. Remove the 1 kΩ resistor from holes *13e* and *13f*.

   Your needle-nose pliers may make this removal easier.

3. Insert the 5.1 kΩ resistor into holes *13e* and *13f*.

   You may want to trim the resistor leads before inserting the resistor. Using your needle-nose pliers may make it easier to insert the resistor.

4. Figure out the new RC time constant by calculating or estimating.

   The calculation is

   $$\text{RC time constant} = 5.1 \text{ k}\Omega \times 470 \text{ }\mu\text{F}$$
   $$= 5,100 \times 0.000470$$
   $$= 2.397 \text{ seconds}$$

   The new RC time constant is about 2.4 seconds.

   Note that instead of doing this calculation, you can just estimate the RC time constant. The new resistance (5.1 kΩ) is about five times the original resistance (1 kΩ), so you should expect the new RC time constant to be about five times the original RC time constant (0.47 seconds), or a little less than 2.5 seconds.

5. Figure out the new capacitor discharge time.

   The new discharge time is five times the new RC time constant (2.4 seconds, as found in the preceding step), or $5 \times 2.4 = 12$ seconds. So it should take about 12 seconds for the LED to go out.

Now test the math. Turn the power switch on and move the capacitor switch up so that the capacitor charges. Then move the slider on the capacitor switch down to discharge the capacitor, and observe the LED as you recite your Mississippis. Did the LED stay lit for about 12 seconds?

Did you notice that the LED doesn't glow as brightly as it did when you had the 1 kΩ resistor in the circuit? The 5.1 kΩ resistor limits current more than the 1 kΩ resistor does, and less current means that the LED doesn't glow as brightly.

Decrease the capacitor discharge time

Try replacing the 5.1 kΩ resistor with the 330 Ω resistor (orange-orange-brown) from your parts list. This new resistance is about one-third the resistance of the original 1 kΩ resistor. Then charge and discharge the capacitor. You should see the LED light for less than one second, because $5 \times 330 \times 0.000470 = 0.7755$, which is about 0.8 second (or "one Missi").

You can try other values of resistance if you like, but please don't try anything less than 330 Ω, or you won't provide enough protection for your LED and it might go bye-bye.

Can you think of another way to change the timing of the LED lighting? If you think that changing the capacitance can alter the timing, you're right!

Before you replace a capacitor, make sure that it's discharged. If you touch a charged capacitor, you can get a shock because the capacitor will discharge through you! The cap thinks your body is a giant resistor (which it is, in an electronics way). Although there's not much danger at the low voltages you use in the projects in this book, charged capacitors can be very dangerous at higher voltage levels. It's a good idea to get into the habit of discharging capacitors before you handle them.

If you have the optional 220 µF electrolytic cap from the parts list on hand, try substituting it for the 470 µF cap (being careful to observe polarity). The new capacitance is about half the original capacitance, so you should expect the discharge times to be about half what they are for the 470 µF cap for a given resistance.

Control the Timing of Two LEDS

The LED in your circuit lights temporarily because current flows temporarily as your capacitor discharges. But doesn't current flow temporarily while the capacitor is charging, too? (Refer to Figure 5-12.) What do you think would happen if you put an LED in the charging circuit (meaning, the highlighted part of the circuit shown in Figure 5-12)? Let's find out!

Add an LED to the charging circuit

Before you add an LED to the charging circuit, restore your capacitor circuit to the original values you used when you first built the circuit (that is, a 1 kΩ resistor in the discharge path and a 470 μF capacitor). Then follow these steps to add an LED to the charging circuit:

1. Turn off the power switch.

2. Remove the 47 Ω resistor from the breadboard.

   One of the resistor leads is in hole **11a**, and the other lead is in the positive power rail to the left of row **11.** You should not use this resistor in the charging circuit once you put in the LED. Do you know why not? (Hint: LEDs have current limits.)

3. Insert the 330 Ω resistor (orange-orange-brown) into the breadboard, as shown in Figure 5-15.

   Plug one lead into hole **7b** and the other lead into hole **11b**. This 330 Ω resistance is large enough to protect an LED.

4. Insert an LED into the breadboard, as shown in Figure 5-16.

   a. Bend and trim the LED leads so that each lead is about 1/4-inch long below the bend.

   b. Insert the cathode (negative side, flat edge, larger piece of metal inside the case) into hole **7a**. Insert the anode (positive side) into the positive power rail to the left of row **7**.

   c. Double-check to make sure you have the LED oriented correctly.

Figure 5-15

Figure 5-16

Test the two-LED circuit

Figure 5-17 shows the two-LED circuit and its schematic. Turn the power switch on (up). Now move the capacitor switch slider up (toward row 1) and observe the newly installed LED (labeled LED2 in the schematic). Did you see it go on briefly?

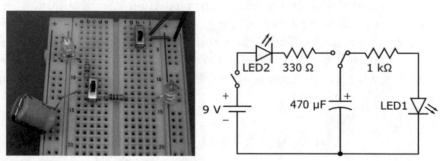

Figure 5-17

Figure 5-18 shows what happens when you charge the capacitor. LED2 lights for as long as it takes the capacitor to charge, which is five times the RC time constant. (Yes, the RC time constant works for charging, as well as discharging, a capacitor.) But now the *R* in the RC time constant is the resistance in the charging path, which is 330 Ω. So five times the RC time constant is $5 \times 330 \times 0.000470 = 0.7755$, or roughly 0.8 second.

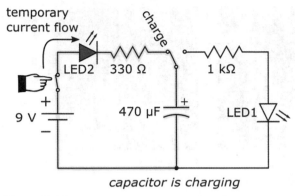

capacitor is charging

Figure 5-18

Now move the capacitor switch slider down (toward row 60) and observe the original LED (labeled LED1). Did LED1 go on and stay on for a few seconds?

Figure 5-19 shows what happens when you discharge the capacitor. LED1 lights for as long as it takes the capacitor to discharge. The R in the discharge circuit is 1 kΩ, so five times the RC time constant is $5 \times 1,000 \times 0.000470 = 2.35$, or roughly 2.4 seconds (which is that same value as for the first circuit you set up earlier in this project).

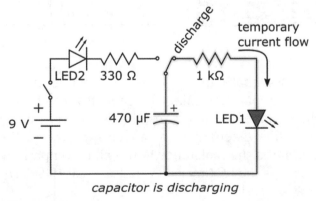

capacitor is discharging

Figure 5-19

To verify that LED1 uses the energy from the capacitor — not the battery — to light, try operating your circuit again, but disconnect the battery after you charge the capacitor. (In other words, move the capacitor switch slider up to light LED2 while charging the capacitor, and then turn off the power switch before moving the capacitor switch slider down to light LED1 while discharging the capacitor.)

Next, after turning off the power switch, swap out the 330 Ω resistor for a 5.1 kΩ resistor (green-brown-red), and try operating your circuit. The capacitor charge time is about 12 seconds, so LED2 should remain lit for about 12 seconds. You haven't changed the discharge resistor, so LED1 should still light for about 2.4 seconds.

Now try something new: Begin charging the capacitor by moving the capacitor switch slider up, but then move the capacitor switch slider down after just a few seconds — before the capacitor has completely charged. What do you notice about the discharge time (meaning, how long LED1 stays lit) and the brightness of LED1? The discharge time remains the same, although LED1 is not quite as bright as it was when the capacitor was fully charged. Because the capacitor did not charge all the way, its voltage is less than 9 V and it doesn't store as much energy as a fully charged capacitor, so LED1 doesn't glow as brightly.

You can try different values of resistance in both the charge and discharge circuit paths to vary the timing of the two LEDs. As always, make sure you choose resistors that are at least 330 Ω to protect your LEDs.

Why Use Capacitors?

Capacitors are extremely useful in electronics and, chances are, you've used them many times without realizing it. Here are some places where you may have met up with capacitors:

- **Alarm clocks:** Many alarm clocks keep charged capacitors on hand in case there's a power failure. When the power goes out, the capacitor discharges — sending current through the clock circuit to keep the circuit running.

✔ **Smartphone screens:** Your body has a certain amount of capacitance, meaning that it can (and does) store some electric charge. If you touch the screen of nearly any smartphone (except really old ones), tiny electronic circuits inside the phone sense the stored charges in your finger. The circuits figure out what part of the screen you're touching and use that information to determine what you want the smartphone to do. This type of screen is known as a *capacitive touchscreen*.

✔ **Power converters:** Capacitors are also used in circuits that convert *alternating current (AC)* — which alternates between flowing forward and backward — to *direct current (DC)* — which flows in only one direction. The wall sockets in your home and school provide AC power, but your TV, stereo, computers, tablets, phones, and many other electronic devices need DC power to operate. Circuitry in the device itself or in an external *power converter* that plugs into the device (for instance, a smartphone charger) transforms the AC power into DC power, and capacitors are an important part of that circuitry.

✔ **Stereo systems:** If you've ever adjusted the treble (high-pitched) or bass (low-pitched) sounds in your family's car or home stereo system, you've used capacitors to change the sound of your music. Capacitors are used in special circuits called *filters* to boost or lower certain sounds in the music. So if you like to emphasize, say, the drums in the music you listen to, you turn up the bass and turn down the treble. Capacitors and other components inside the stereo are what make it possible for you to do this.

Stage Lights Dimmer

Have you ever been at a play or other show where the stage lights start out bright (usually while a host or other announcer addresses the audience before the start of the show) and then are gradually dimmed as the curtain opens to reveal the set? Well, in this project, you use a new (to you) component called a *transistor* along with a capacitor, several resistors, and some LEDs in a circuit to create the same effect as dimming a series of bright stage lights.

The Amazing Transistor

Transistors are tiny semiconductor devices (as are LEDs and other diodes) that have three leads and can do some incredible things. Transistors can act like tiny automatic switches, redirecting current within a circuit, and can *amplify*, or boost, current.

Figure 6-1 shows an assortment of transistors. They may not look very exciting (in fact, they look pretty boring), but the drab, uninteresting packaging of the average transistor is just a cover for its exciting, game-changing interior.

Figure 6-1

You may not realize it, but you use transistors every day. Transistors are located in your phone, your TV, your computer, and nearly every other electronic product in the world — helping each product do what it's supposed to do. Many products contain millions — or even billions — of transistors. For instance, the Apple iPhone 6 contains over 2 billion transistors!

Transistors and faucets

Have you ever thought about what happens when you turn on a faucet? (I know, it's a really exciting thing to think about!) By turning the handle, you switch the water on or off. By adjusting how much you turn the handle, you control how much water flows.

A transistor acts, in a way, like a faucet for electric current. One part of the transistor — the *base* — controls the flow of current between the other two parts of the transistor — the *collector* and the *emitter*. (See Figure 6-2.)

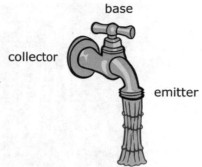

Figure 6-2

By applying a high enough voltage to the base (like exerting pressure on a faucet handle), you switch the transistor on, and current flows from the collector to the emitter (like the water flows through the pipe part of the faucet). If the voltage at the base is too low, you switch off the transistor, and no current flows from the collector to the emitter.

When the transistor is switched on, you control the amount of current that flows from the collector to the emitter by controlling how much current flows into the base of the transistor. And the nice part about this fact is that small currents in the base control large currents flowing from the collector to the emitter.

You don't have to worry about the details of exactly how you apply voltage to the base and control the base current. The circuit you build in this project will take care of the details for you. Just know that what happens at the base controls what happens at the collector and emitter.

Explore a transistor

Figure 6-3 shows the front and back views of a certain type of transistor, known as an NPN bipolar transistor. (Don't worry about the cryptic name. Call it "Ralph," if you like.) This particular NPN bipolar transistor has the model identifier 2N3904 (along with some other characters) stamped on one side of its case. Each transistor model is associated with a long list of features, such as how much current the transistor can handle, but I won't get into all those details here. Just know that there are many models of NPN bipolar transistors, of which the 2N3904 is one.

Figure 6-3

Note that the 2N3094 transistor has three leads, or terminals, which are often called *pins*. These pins connect to the base, collector, and emitter inside the transistor case (that black plastic blob on top of the leads is the case). You tell which pin is which by looking at a *pin diagram*, such as the one shown in Figure 6-4, left. (This pin diagram is on the back of the RadioShack package that my 2N3904 transistor came in.)

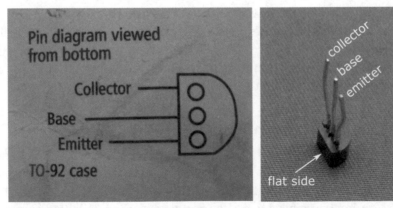

Figure 6-4

Transistors sold by RadioShack come in packages that show the pin diagram (which is sometimes called the *pinout*), but not all vendors provide the pin diagram in their packaging. To figure out which pin is which, you can always search the Internet for a particular transistor model's pinout (for instance, search for "2N3904 pinout"), or search for the datasheet for that model of transistor. The *datasheet* is a technical document (meaning, not very enjoyable nonfiction) that lists all the features of the transistor and includes a pin diagram. The datasheet is like a biography — with photos! — of the transistor.

Depending on where you get your transistors, the pin assignments may or may not be the same as the standard pin assignments used by most manufacturers (refer to Figure 6-4). Be sure to check the packaging or documentation that comes with your transistor to determine which pin is which.

Pick up your 2N3904 transistor. Hold it so you are looking directly at its underside (the side with the leads sticking out). Now compare your transistor to its pin diagram and note which pin is which.

When you plug your transistor into the solderless breadboard as you build the circuit in this project, you'll need to make sure you orient the transistor correctly. It matters — very much — how you connect the base, collector, and emitter of a transistor.

Why Use a Transistor?

You don't have to read this section to do Project 6. This section is only for readers who are curious about why a transistor makes a difference in a circuit. If you just want to go ahead and build the project, feel free to skip this section and get right to the parts list and circuit building in the next couple of sections.

The problem with the RC time constant

To get an idea of how important a transistor is in a circuit, let's think about the circuit from Project 5, which changes the dimming time of an LED.

In Project 5, you set up a circuit with a resistor and a capacitor to dim the light from an LED over a predictable time interval.

But the longer the time interval, the less brightly the LED glows — even before it dims as the capacitor discharges!

Do you know why the LED glows less brightly when the dimming time is extended? The answer is in the RC time constant.

The RC time constant determines how long it takes the capacitor to discharge, which, in turn, determines how long it takes to dim the LED. To extend the dimming time, you increase either the resistance (the *R*) or the capacitance (the *C*), so that the RC time constant is larger. But huge capacitors are hard to find (and very impractical), so increasing the resistance is the better way to greatly extend the dimming time.

Increasing the resistance successfully increases the RC time constant — but it also weakens the current flowing through the LED. (Remember, more resistance means less current.) A very large resistance restricts the current so much that the LED doesn't glow brightly when it's first turned on.

What if you wanted to, say, turn on the lights over a stage and then bring down the lights slowly as the curtain opens? Or turn on the dome light in your family's car when you open the car door, and dim the light slowly when you close the car door? The fact that the large resistance produces a weak current can be a problem: The lights won't ever glow brightly — even when they first turn on!

The solution to the problem

Using a transistor to boost the weak current solves the problem. By placing a transistor between the resistor-capacitor combination and the LED-resistor combination, you essentially jack up the current so that the lights glow brightly when they first turn on!

The way it works is this: You feed the weak current coming from the resistor-capacitor part of the circuit into the base of the transistor. You use that weak base current to control a stronger current flowing from the collector to the emitter, and you use that stronger current to power the LEDs so that they shine brightly (that is, before they dim).

Figure 6-5 lays out your plan of attack for this project. It's useful to visualize what's happening with a *block diagram* like this because you can easily lose track of the big picture when you start plugging components into the breadboard.

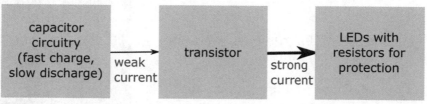

Figure 6-5

Ready to charge ahead and build the new circuit?

Gather Components and Tools

Gather all the parts on this list (see Figure 6-6):

✔ Solderless breadboard, prepared with

- 9-volt battery with battery clip

- Power switch and jumper wire

- Power rail jumper-wire connections

✔ One 2N3904 NPN bipolar transistor

✔ One 470 µF electrolytic (polarized) capacitor

✔ One 47 Ω resistor (yellow-violet-black)

✔ Four 100 Ω resistors (brown-black-brown)

✔ One 220 Ω resistor (red-red-brown)

✔ One 1 kΩ resistor (brown-black-red)

✔ One 10 kΩ resistor (brown-black-orange)

✔ Eight clear 5 mm LEDs (any size, any color; I used white LEDs)

✔ One single-pole, double-throw (SPDT) switch

✔ Three 1/2-inch (minimum) jumper wires (precut or homemade)

✔ One 5/16-inch (minimum) jumper wire

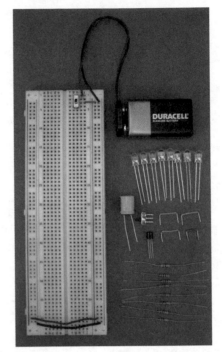

Figure 6-6

✔ Optional components: assorted resistors of any value (suggested values: 100 Ω, 1 kΩ, 100 kΩ, and 1 MΩ)

Clipping leads is an absolute must for this project. Otherwise, it's highly likely that leads will touch each other when they're not supposed to. So please have your wire cutters on hand. Grab your needle-nose pliers, too. They make it much easier to insert and remove components and jumper wires.

Build the Basic Stage Lights Dimmer Circuit

In this project, you strategically position a transistor between the capacitor charging/discharging part of a circuit and an LED-with-protective-resistor part of a circuit. The transistor amplifies the weak current, so that a much larger current flows through the LED.

Just for fun, for the first part of this project, you use two LEDs instead of just one (as you use in Project 5). Later in this project, for more fun, you add another six LEDs, for a total of eight LEDs. And all eight glow like crazy (that is, until they dim and go out) because your transistor provides enough current to drive them all!

Follow these steps to build your circuit:

1. Double-check your solderless breadboard (see Figure 6-7).

   a. Make sure that the two positive power rails are connected and the two negative power rails are connected.

   b. Check that your power switch and jumper-wire connections are properly installed and that the switch is in the off position.

   c. Verify that the leads from your battery clip are snugly plugged into the correct contact holes in your breadboard.

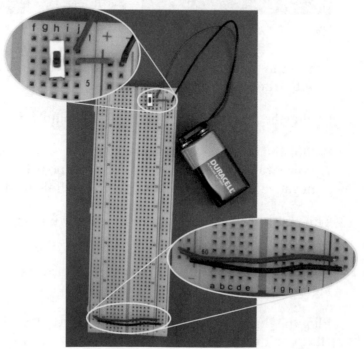

Figure 6-7

2. Insert the 47 Ω resistor (yellow-violet-black) into the breadboard, as shown in Figure 6-8.

 a. Bend and trim the resistor leads so that each lead is about 3/8-inch long below the bend.

 b. Plug one lead into hole **30a** and the other lead into the positive power rail to the left of row **30**.

3. Insert the 470 μF electrolytic capacitor into the breadboard, as shown in Figure 6-9.

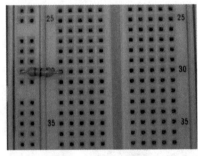

Figure 6-8   Figure 6-9

 a. You can use the same capacitor from Project 5, if you like, with trimmed or untrimmed leads.

 b. Plug the positive lead (unlabeled) into hole **31a**.

 c. Plug the negative lead (stripe or minus sign) into the negative power rail on the left side of the breadboard. (Any hole in the negative power rail will do. I used the hole next to row 35.)

The resistor-capacitor combination shown in Figure 6-9 is the capacitor charging part of your circuit.

4. Insert the SPDT switch into the breadboard, as shown in Figure 6-10.

Plug the three switch terminals into holes **30c, 31c,** and **32c.** (It doesn't matter which end is which for the switch.)

5. Insert the 5/16-inch (minimum) jumper wire into the breadboard.

   Plug one end of the jumper wire into hole **31e** and the other end of the jumper wire into hole **31f**. (See the orange jumper wire in Figure 6-11.)

Figure 6-10    Figure 6-11

6. Insert the 1 kΩ resistor (brown-black-red) into the breadboard, as shown in Figure 6-12.

   a. Bend and trim the resistor leads so that each lead is about 1/4-inch long below the bend.

   b. Plug one end of the resistor into hole **28g** and the other end of the resistor into hole **31g**.

Figure 6-12

7. Insert the 10 kΩ resistor (brown-black-orange) into the breadboard, as shown in Figure 6-13.

   a. Bend and trim the resistor leads so that each lead is about 3/8-inch long below the bend.

Figure 6-13

b. Plug one end of the resistor into hole **28j** and the other end of the resistor into the negative power rail to the right of row **28**.

Together, the 1 kΩ and 10 kΩ resistors you insert in Steps 6 and 7 make up the resistance in the discharge path. These two resistors and the capacitor you insert in Step 3 make up the discharge part of your circuit.

8. Insert the 220 Ω resistor (red-red-brown) into the breadboard, as shown in Figure 6-14.

   a. Bend and trim the resistor leads so that each lead is about 3/8-inch long below the bend.

   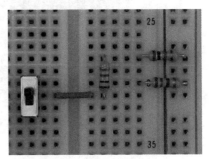

   Figure 6-14

   b. Plug one end of the resistor into hole **30j** and the other end of the resistor into the negative power rail to the right of row **30**.

9. Prepare your 2N3904 transistor for inserting into the breadboard.

   a. Use your needle-nose pliers to gently bend the transistor pins out and down, so the transistor looks like a walking robot with a flat face and its tail (the base, or middle pin) hanging back between its legs. (See Figure 6-15.)

   b. Hold the transistor so that its pins are facing down and the flat part of the transistor case is facing right. (See Figure 6-16.)

10. Insert the transistor into the breadboard.

    a. The easiest way to plug transistor pins into a breadboard is to position the pins over the correct breadboard holes and then plug all three pins in at the same time.

Figure 6-15

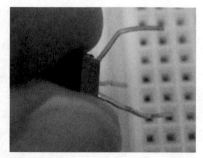

Figure 6-16

b. Using your fingers or needle-nose pliers to gently move the pins, position the collector (top) pin into the opening to hole **26i**, the base (middle) pin into the opening to hole **28h**, and the emitter (bottom) pin into the opening to hole **30i**. (See Figure 6-17, left.) (Note that if your transistor uses a different pin assignment than mine, you may need to orient the transistor differently to get the right pins positioned over the right holes.)

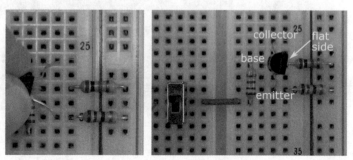

Figure 6-17

c. Holding the transistor by its case, gently push down on the transistor, rocking it back and forth as you push down, until each pin is plugged in firmly, but not excessively. (See Figure 6-17, right.)

11. Prepare the eight LEDs for inserting in the breadboard.

    a. For each LED, bend one lead slightly out and then down.

    b. Trim both leads so that they are about 1/2-inch long from end to end. (See Figure 6-18.)

    You use two of the trimmed LEDs in this part of the project, and you add the other six LEDs during the second part of the project.

12. Insert one of the trimmed LEDs (let's call it LED1) into the breadboard.

    Insert the cathode (negative side, flat edge, larger piece of metal inside the case) into hole **26j,** and insert the anode (positive side) into hole **24j**. (See Figure 6-19.)

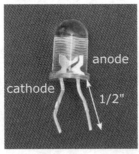
Figure 6-18

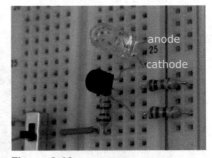
Figure 6-19

13. Insert another trimmed LED (let's call it LED2) into the breadboard, as shown in Figure 6-20.

    Insert the cathode (negative side, flat edge, larger piece of metal inside the case) into hole **24h**, and insert the anode (positive side) into hole **22h**.

14. Insert a 100 Ω resistor (brown-black-brown) into the breadboard, as shown in Figure 6-21.

Figure 6-20   Figure 6-21

a. Trim the resistor leads so that each lead is about 1/4-inch long.

b. Plug one end of the resistor into hole **22j** and the other end of the resistor into the positive power rail to the right of row **22**.

This 100 Ω resistor protects LED1 and LED2. Because you use the two LEDs in series, this protective resistor can be smaller than the 330 Ω protective resistor you need in Project 5, which uses only one LED.

Figure 6-22 shows the complete circuit (except that you can't see the battery, the power switch, or the power rail connections at the bottom of the breadboard).

Note that when the capacitor switch is in the up position (that is, the slider is closer to row 1), the capacitor is charging,

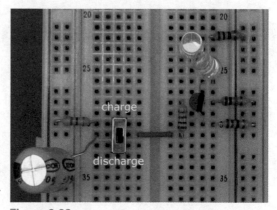

Figure 6-22

because the positive side of the capacitor is connected to the battery through the 47 Ω resistor. This is the same charging circuit as in Project 5. But the rest of this circuit is very different from the circuit in Project 5, as you discover when you operate the circuit.

Figure 6-23 shows the schematic for your circuit. The transistor is represented by the symbol that has a circle around it. Note the labels for the base, collector, and emitter.

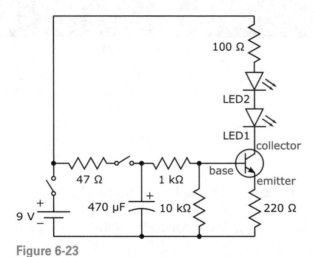

Figure 6-23

Operate the Stage Lights Dimming Circuit

Turn on the power switch (up position). Move the slider on the capacitor switch up (toward row 1). Do the two LEDs light? (They should.) Are they shining nice and brightly? (They should be.)

Next, move the slider on the capacitor switch down (toward row 60) but leave the power switch on. Keep your eye on the two LEDs. They should gradually dim and eventually go out after several seconds.

Do you want to change the dimming time interval? If so, substitute a different value of resistance (using the optional extra resistors from the parts list) for the 10 kΩ resistor (located between hole 28j and the negative power rail). For resistances lower than 10 kΩ, the LED dimming time decreases. For resistances higher than 10 kΩ, the LED dimming time increases. When you finish trying different resistances, please put the 10 kΩ resistor back in the circuit.

Explore the Schematic

If you want to understand how your circuit operates, check out what is happening by looking at the schematic when the capacitor is charging and discharging. If you don't want to dive into the schematic, feel free to skip this section and move on to the next section, "Add More Lights." There won't be a quiz on this material!

Capacitor charging

Figure 6-24 shows that when you turn on the power switch and move up the slider on the capacitor switch, the capacitor charges quickly. The reason why the capacitor charges quickly is that the 47 Ω resistor is relatively small, so five times the RC time constant is a small number. Project 5 explains how a capacitor charges and how to figure out how long it takes to charge.

But the capacitor is also connected to the base of the transistor through the 1 kΩ resistor. Because the capacitor charges quickly, the voltage at the base quickly becomes high enough to turn the transistor fully on (like turning a faucet fully on), and lots of current flows from the collector to the emitter. That same current flows through the two LEDs, lighting them up — brightly.

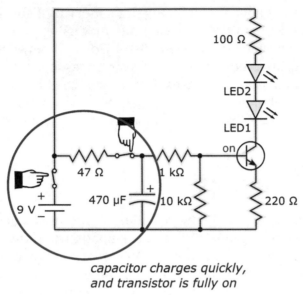

capacitor charges quickly,
and transistor is fully on

Figure 6-24

Capacitor discharging

Figure 6-25 shows what happens when you move the slider on the capacitor switch down (toward row 60). This action disconnects the battery from the capacitor. (But note that the battery is still connected to the 100 Ω resistor that protects LED1 and LED2.)

The capacitor discharges through two resistors: the 1 kΩ resistor and the 10 kΩ resistor. Because these resistors are relatively large, the capacitor discharges relatively slowly (compared to how quickly it charges using the 47 Ω resistance in the charging path).

As the capacitor discharges, the current flowing into the base of the transistor decreases, causing the current that flows from the collector to the emitter to decrease.

Think about adjusting the flow of water from a faucet that started out fully turned on: As you turn the handle, you decrease the flow of water. The small base current is like the faucet handle: It is controlling the larger collector and emitter currents, just as the faucet handle controls the flow of water.

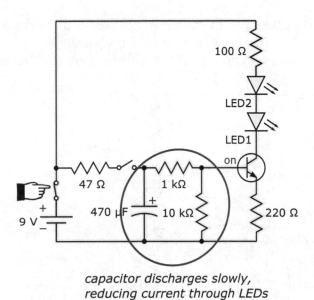

capacitor discharges slowly,
reducing current through LEDs

Figure 6-25

The transistor is still on (as is the faucet), because there is still enough voltage at its base to keep it on — for a while, anyway. Because the current flowing through the LEDs is decreasing, the LEDs begin to shine less brightly.

Just as in Project 5, as the capacitor discharges, the LEDs dim. The difference between the Project 5 circuit and this circuit is that in this circuit, the LEDs start off shining very brightly, even for a long dimming time. In Project 5, when the dimming time was extended, the LED didn't start off shining brightly because the resistance in the discharge path limited the current passing through the LED.

Transistor shutting off

Figure 6-26 shows what happens after the capacitor discharges for a while. Eventually, the voltage across the capacitor gets pretty low, so the voltage at the base of the transistor drops below the level needed to keep the transistor switched on. At that point, the transistor switches off and no current flows from the collector to the emitter, so the LEDs go out.

Think (again) of turning the faucet handle as you decrease the flow of water. Eventually, you position the handle so that it no longer allows water to flow at all, so you turn off the faucet.

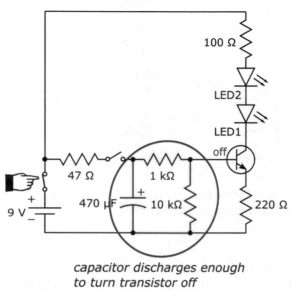

capacitor discharges enough to turn transistor off

Figure 6-26

Add More Lights

Now the fun part of this project begins! Because your tiny transistor can control a pretty large current, you can add more LEDs to your circuit — and they will all shine brightly when you first turn them on!

So, gather up the remaining components from your parts list, and extend your stage light dimming circuit by following these steps:

1. Turn off the power switch before making changes to your circuit.

2. Insert the three 1/2-inch (minimum) jumper wires into the breadboard, as shown in Figure 6-27:

   a. Plug one end of the first jumper wire into hole **11f** and the other end of this jumper wire into hole **16f**.

b. Plug one end of the second jumper wire into hole **16g** and the other end of this jumper wire into hole **21g**.

c. Plug one end of the third jumper wire into hole **21f** and the other end of this jumper wire into hole **26f**.

These jumper wires give you the space you need to add six more LEDs and three more resistors.

3. Insert the three 100 Ω resistors (brown-black-brown) into the breadboard, as shown in Figure 6-28:

a. For each resistor, bend and trim the leads so that each lead is about 1/4-inch long below the bend.

b. Plug one end of the first resistor into hole **7j** and the other end of this resistor into the positive power rail to the right of row **7**.

c. Plug one end of the second resistor into hole **12j** and the other end of this resistor into the positive power rail to the right of row **12**.

d. Plug one end of the third resistor into hole **17j** and the other end of this resistor into the positive power rail to the right of row **17**.

 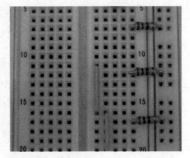

Figure 6-27   Figure 6-28

4. Insert two trimmed LEDs (let's call them LED3 and LED4) into the breadboard, as shown in Figure 6-29:

    a. Insert the cathode (negative side, flat edge, larger piece of metal inside the case) of LED3 into hole *21j*, and insert the anode (positive side) into hole *19j*.

    b. Insert the cathode of LED4 into hole *19h*, and insert the anode into hole *17h*.

5. Insert two more trimmed LEDs (LED5 and LED6) into the breadboard, as shown in Figure 6-30:

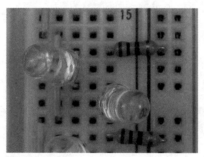 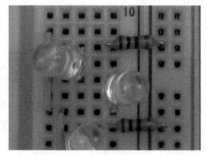

Figure 6-29   Figure 6-30

    a. Insert the cathode of LED5 into hole *16j*, and insert the anode into hole *14j*.

    b. Insert the cathode of LED6 into hole *14h*, and insert the anode into hole *12h*.

6. Insert the final two trimmed LEDs (LED7 and LED8) into the breadboard, as shown in Figure 6-31.

Figure 6-31

a. Insert the cathode of LED7 into hole *11j,* and insert the anode into hole *9j.*

b. Insert the cathode of LED8 into hole *9h,* and insert the anode into hole *7h*.

The complete eight-LED circuit (except for the battery, power switch, and power rail connections) is shown in Figure 6-32.

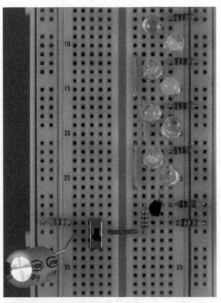

Figure 6-32

Operate the Eight-Light Dimming Circuit

Before you operate this circuit, I strongly recommend that you double-check (and even triple-check) all your connections. Make sure that all the leads are plugged into the correct breadboard holes and that your LEDs are oriented correctly.

When you're ready, turn on the power switch. Then charge the capacitor by moving the slider on the capacitor switch up (toward row 1). Do all eight LEDs light up brightly, as shown in Figure 6-33? If they don't, turn off the power switch and check all your connections again.

Figure 6-33

Now discharge your capacitor by moving the slider on the capacitor switch down (toward row 60). Watch the LEDs slowly grow dimmer and then eventually go out.

If your circuit works properly, give yourself a pat on the back! This circuit is much more involved that the circuits in Projects 2 through 5, so it's a real accomplishment to get it right!

If you want to change the dimming time interval, swap out the 10 kΩ resistor (in hole 28j and the negative power rail) for other values of resistance. Smaller resistances decrease the dimming time. Larger resistances increase the dimming time.

Check Out the Schematic

Figure 6-34 shows the schematic for the complete eight-LED circuit. This schematic is not very different from the one for the two-LED circuit (refer to Figure 6-23), and the two circuits operate in the same way.

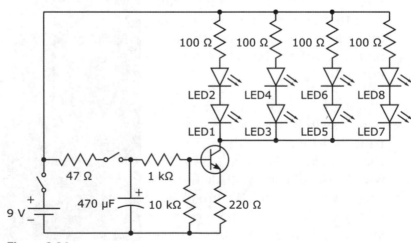

Figure 6-34

This schematic shows that there are four identical parallel branches, each with two LEDs and a protective resistor, connected to the collector of the transistor. Current flows through each of the four branches, lighting all eight LEDs. The transistor provides enough current to drive all those LEDs. The transistor also doubles as a switch, turning the LEDs on and (eventually) off.

I hope you agree that transistors are truly amazing!

Smart Nightlight

Have you ever heard of a sensor? A *sensor* is a device that detects changes in light, motion, heat, humidity, or another physical quantity, and responds by producing changes in voltage, capacitance, or another electrical quantity. Because sensors convert physical quantities into electrical quantities, you can use sensors to control what happens in a circuit based on what's happening in the environment around the circuit.

In this project, you use a type of sensor called a *photoresistor* to detect changes in light. Your circuit — which consists of just seven components and a battery — uses the photoresistor to control whether an LED is on or off. In this way, your circuit operates as a smart nightlight — turning the LED on only when it's dark in the room.

Make Sense of Your Photoresistor

A *photoresistor*, which is also called a light-dependent resistor (LDR) or *photocell*, consists of a piece of semiconductor material that exhibits an interesting characteristic: It acts like a resistor except that the value of resistance depends on how much light is shining on it.

You can see an assortment of photoresistors in Figure 7-1, left, and a close-up of one photoresistor in Figure 7-1, right. Note that these little devices have no identifying marks, such as a model number, which makes working with them a bit sketchy, er, I mean, loads of fun!

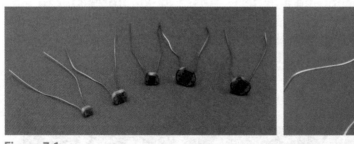

Figure 7-1

Pinning down the exact resistance of a photoresistor is like trying to catch a feather as it floats down through the air. Part of the problem is that you never really know exactly how much light is shining — that is, unless you happen to own a special device called a light meter, which measures light energy. (Add it to your holiday wish list or borrow one from a photographer friend!)

In general, a photoresistor works like this:

- ✓ In bright light, its resistance is relatively low (usually less than 10 kΩ).

- ✓ In darkness, its resistance is relatively high (usually more than 1 MΩ).

If your photoresistor doesn't behave the same as mine, not to worry! You find out in this project how to make adjustments to your circuit, if needed, to get it to work the way you want it to — even in the face of hardship, uncertainty, and mysterious photoresistors. (This *will* be fun, I promise!)

Check Out a PNP Transistor

Another new (to you) component that you will use in this project is a PNP transistor. Look at the two 2N3906 PNP transistors shown in Figure 7-2. Do they look like the 2N3904 NPN transistor you use in Project 6? Yup. Are these transistors the same as the one you use in Project 6? Nope. Does it matter if you get the 2N3904 and 2N3906 transistors mixed up? Yessirree, Bob!

Figure 7-2

In this project, you use *both* a 2N3904 NPN transistor *and* a 2N3906 PNP transistor, so you really need to keep track of which is which. The good thing about these types of transistors (especially compared to those troublesome photoresistors) is that their model numbers are stamped on their cases, so you can always tell at a glance which one is which.

Like the 2N3904 transistor, the 2N3906 transistor has three leads, also called terminals or pins. These pins connect to the base, collector, and emitter inside the transistor case, as shown in Figure 7-3 and indicated in the pin diagram on the product packaging or datasheet (check the Internet). The pin diagram for the 2N3906 transistor is the same as that of the 2N3904 transistor.

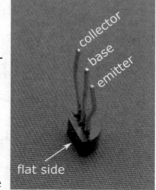

collector
base
emitter

flat side

Figure 7-3

Depending on where you get your transistors, the pin assignments may or may not be the same as the pin assignments shown in Figure 7-3. Check the packaging or documentation that comes with your transistor to determine which pin is which.

When you plug your transistors into the solderless breadboard as you build the circuit in this project, you need to make sure that you use the correct transistor (that is, 2N3904 or 2N3906) as instructed and that you orient the transistor leads correctly. (I know I am repeating myself, but these points are really important.)

Round Up Components and Tools

Gather all the parts on this list (see Figure 7-4):

- Solderless breadboard, prepared with a

  - 9-volt battery with a battery clip

  - Power switch and jumper wire

  - Power rail jumper-wire connections

- One photoresistor

- One 2N3904 NPN bipolar transistor

- One 2N3906 PNP bipolar transistor

- One 330 Ω resistor (orange-orange-brown)

- One 10 kΩ resistor (brown-black-orange)

- One 1 MΩ resistor (brown-black-green)

- One 5 mm clear white LED

- Two 5/16-inch (minimum) jumper wires

✔ Additional resistors may be required to make adjustments to the circuit:

- One 100 kΩ resistor (brown-black-yellow)

- One 470 kΩ resistor (yellow-violet-yellow)

- One 4.7 MΩ resistor (yellow-violet-green)

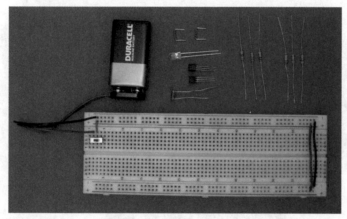

Figure 7-4

The circuit in this project consists of just seven components (not including the three "adjustment" resistors), so it's fairly easy to keep all the leads from touching each other and not absolutely necessary to clip any leads. But keep your wire cutters nearby in case you want your circuit to look a bit neater. And you may find your needle-nose pliers useful for inserting and removing components.

Build the Smart Nightlight Circuit

In this project, you use your photoresistor to sense how much light is in the room and to control whether the two transistors are switched on or off. When the transistors are switched on, they allow current to flow through an LED. The transistors also amplify the current so that it is strong enough to light the LED brightly.

Follow these steps to build your nightlight circuit:

1. Double-check your solderless breadboard (see Figure 7-5).

   a. Make sure that the two positive power rails are connected and the two negative power rails are connected.

   b. Check that your power switch and jumper-wire connections are properly installed and that the switch is in the off position.

   c. Verify that the leads from your battery clip are snugly plugged into the correct contact holes in your breadboard.

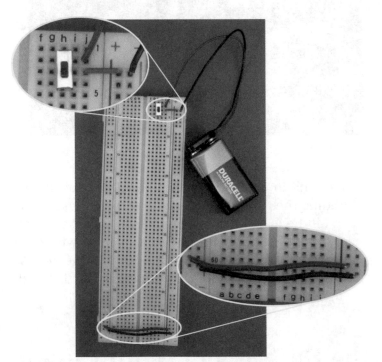

Figure 7-5

2. Insert the 1 MΩ resistor (brown-black-green) into the breadboard, as shown in Figure 7-6.

   If you'd like to make your circuit neater, bend and trim the resistor leads so that each lead is about 3/8-inch long below the bend. Plug one lead into hole **19a** and the other lead into the positive power rail to the left of row **19**.

3. Insert a 5/16-inch (minimum) jumper wire into the breadboard.

   Plug one end of the jumper wire into hole **21a** and the other end of the jumper wire into the negative power rail to the **left** of row **21**. (See the orange jumper wire in Figure 7-7.)

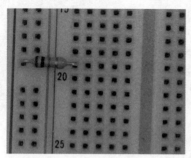
Figure 7-6

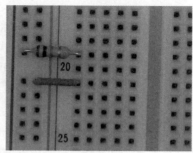
Figure 7-7

4. Insert the 2N3904 NPN transistor into the breadboard.

   a. Double-check that you have selected a 2N3904 transistor. (If you mix up the transistors, your circuit won't work.)

   b. Use your needle-nose pliers to gently bend the transistor pins out and down, as shown in Figure 7-8.

   c. Hold the transistor so that its pins are facing down and the flat part of the transistor case is facing right. (See Figure 7-9.)

Figure 7-8

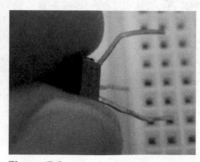
Figure 7-9

d. Using your fingers or needle-nose pliers to gently move the pins, position the collector (top) pin into the opening to hole **17d**, the base (middle) pin into the opening to hole **19c**, and the emitter (bottom) pin into the opening to hole **21d**. (Note that if your transistor uses a different pin assignment than mine, you may need to orient the transistor differently to get the right pins positioned over the right holes.)

e. Then, holding the transistor by its case, gently push down on the transistor, rocking it back and forth as you push down, until each pin is plugged in firmly but not excessively. (See Figure 7-10.)

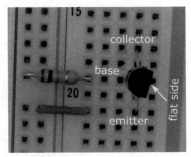

Figure 7-10

5. Insert the photoresistor into the breadboard, as shown in Figure 7-11.

Plug one lead (either one) into hole **19b** and the other lead into any hole in the negative power rail on the left side of the board. (I used the hole to the left of row 25.)

6. Insert the 10 kΩ resistor (brown-black-orange) into the breadboard, as shown in Figure 7-12.

Figure 7-11

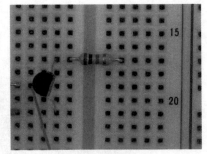

Figure 7-12

Bend and trim the resistor leads if you'd like. Then plug one lead into hole **17e** and the other lead into hole **17g**.

7. Insert the 2N3906 PNP transistor into the breadboard.

   a. Double-check that you have selected a 2N3906 transistor.

   b. Use your needle-nose pliers to gently bend the transistor pins out and down (refer to Figure 7-8).

   c. Hold the transistor so that its pins are facing down and the flat part of the transistor case is facing left. (See Figure 7-13.)

   d. Plug the emitter (top) pin into the opening to hole **15h**, the base (middle) pin into the opening to hole **17j**, and the collector (bottom) pin into the opening to hole **19h**. (See Figure 7-14.) (Note that if your transistor uses a different pin assignment than mine, you may need to orient the transistor differently to get the right pins positioned over the right holes.)

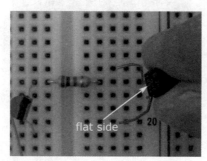

Figure 7-13

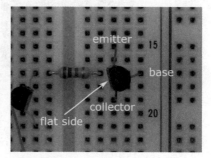

Figure 7-14

8. Insert a 5/16-inch (minimum) jumper wire into the breadboard.

Plug one end of the jumper wire into hole **15j** and the other end of the jumper wire into the positive power rail to the right of row **15**. (See the orange jumper wire in Figure 7-15.)

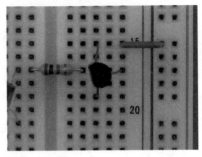

9. Insert the LED into the breadboard.

Figure 7-15

If you'd like, trim the LED leads so that they are at least 1/2-inch long from end to end. (See Figure 7-16.)

Plug the cathode (negative side, flat edge, larger piece of metal inside the case) into hole **21f** and the anode (positive side) into hole **19f**. (See Figure 7-17.)

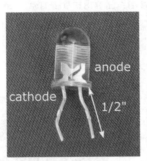

Figure 7-16

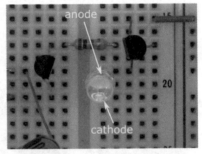

Figure 7-17

10. Insert the 330 Ω resistor (orange-orange-brown) into the breadboard, as shown in Figure 7-18.

Bend and trim the resistor leads if you'd like. Then plug one lead into hole **21j** and the other lead into the negative power rail to the right of row **21**.

Figure 7-19 shows the completed circuit (except that you can't see the battery, the power switch, or the power rail connections at the bottom of the breadboard).

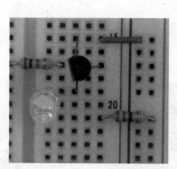

Figure 7-18

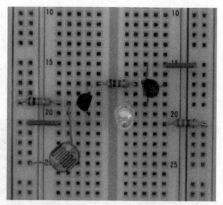

Figure 7-19

Double-check all your connections and the orientation of your LED. Make sure you have the 2N3904 NPN transistor on the left side of your breadboard and the 2N3906 PNP transistor on the right side of your breadboard. Once you are sure that your circuit is set up correctly, it's time to try it out!

Test Your Nightlight Circuit

The best place to test out your circuit is in a room that has shades, blinds, or other window coverings. (But don't worry if you have no way to darken the room. You can still test your circuit.)

With the room lights on (or sunlight shining into the room), turn on the power switch. Did the LED light up? It shouldn't. If it does, you can make adjustments to the circuit, as described in the next section.

If the LED did not light up, that's good!

Now turn off the lights (or block the sunlight from coming in the windows). Did the LED light up? It should! (See Figure 7-20.)

Figure 7-20

If the LED does not light up when the lights are off, use your fingers to cover the top or the top and sides of the photoresistor, as shown in Figure 7-21, so that little or no light gets in. If the LED still doesn't light up, you may need to make an adjustment to your circuit, as described in the next section.

Figure 7-21

Make Adjustments

If your nightlight circuit doesn't work (the LED doesn't turn on when it's relatively dark in the room, or the LED turns on when the light in the room is bright or fairly bright), you can make an adjustment to your circuit. Making a change is common in a circuit like this because the level of light in a room can vary and each photoresistor is a bit different in terms of sensitivity to light.

Before you make any changes, turn off the power switch. Then make an adjustment based on which of the following problem conditions you are experiencing:

> ✔ **Your LED turns on even when there's still quite a bit of light in the room.**
>
> You need to make your circuit more sensitive to lighting conditions. Swap out the 1 MΩ resistor (row 19 on the left side of the board) for a larger value, such as the 4.7 MΩ resistor (yellow-violet-green) on the parts list. This action increases the light sensitivity of the circuit so that your room must be

darker to turn on the LED. Once you swap out the 1 MΩ resistor, turn on the power switch and test the circuit again.

⌐ **Your LED doesn't turn on when the room is fairly dark but does turn on when you cover the photoresistor with your fingers.**

Try replacing the 1 MΩ resistor (row 19) with a smaller resistance, like, say, 470 kΩ (yellow-violet-yellow) or 100 kΩ (brown-black-yellow). This action decreases the light sensitivity of the circuit so that your room doesn't have to be quite so dark to turn on the LED. After swapping out the 1 MΩ resistor, turn on the power switch and test the circuit again.

⌐ **Your LED doesn't turn on at all — even when you cover the photoresistor.**

It's time to troubleshoot your circuit to figure out what's wrong. Here's what to look for:

- Is your power switch on? (Don't laugh; I neglected to turn on the power switch while testing my circuit for this project, and scratched my head for a few minutes before I figured out what was wrong!)

- Is your LED oriented correctly (as specified in Step 9 earlier in this project)?

- Is the transistor on the left side of the board a 2N3904 NPN transistor? Is the flat side of this transistor case facing right (assuming your transistor uses a standard pin assignment)? Are the collector, base, and emitter leads firmly plugged into the correct breadboard holes (as specified in Step 4)?

- Is the transistor on the right side of the board a 2N3906 PNP transistor? Is the flat side of this transistor case facing left (assuming your transistor uses a standard pin assignment)? Are the collector, base, and emitter leads firmly plugged into the correct breadboard holes (as specified in Step 7)?

- Are all components and jumper wires inserted firmly, but not excessively, into the correct breadboard holes?

If your circuit is still not working after you've tried everything in the preceding checklist, try using a fresh 9-volt battery. Still not working? Try replacing the photoresistor in your circuit, if you have another. If you replace the photoresistor, you may have to try different values of resistance in place of the 1 MΩ resistor to adjust the light sensitivity of the circuit.

If you still don't see the light, try replacing one or both transistors. Transistors are sensitive little devices that are easily damaged and don't give off smoke or other evidence of their injuries, so it's hard to tell whether or not they're okay. If you discover that you have a bad transistor, toss it in the trash right away so you don't inadvertently use it in another circuit.

Explore the Schematic

 If you're interested in understanding how your smart nightlight circuit works, read this section. However, you don't need to explore the schematic and follow the explanation of how the circuit works if you don't want to.

Figure 7-22 shows the schematic for the smart nightlight circuit. The circuit symbol for the photoresistor is labeled. Note that the circuit symbol for the PNP transistor (model 2N3906 in this circuit) is slightly different from the symbol for the NPN transistor (model 2N3904 in this circuit).

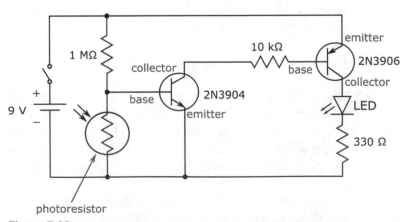

Figure 7-22

The direction of the arrow in each transistor symbol indicates the direction of current flow when the transistor is on. In an NPN transistor, current flows from the collector to the emitter. In a PNP transistor, current flows from the emitter to the collector.

This circuit consists of three parts, or _circuit stages_.

Stage 1

The first stage (circled in Figure 7-23) is a _voltage divider_. When two resistors are placed across a voltage source, the voltage from the voltage source is distributed proportionally to each resistor. So, for instance, if one of the two resistors has twice the resistance of the other resistor and the total battery voltage is 9 volts, the voltage across the larger resistor is 6 volts and the voltage across the smaller resistor is 3 volts.

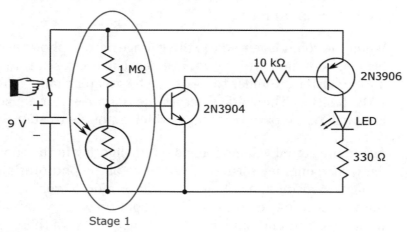

Stage 1

Figure 7-23

In your nightlight circuit, the photoresistor has a variable resistance: Its resistance changes depending on lighting conditions. The exact amount of resistance is difficult to determine because it's hard to know the exact amount of light shining on the photoresistor. However, when the room is fairly bright, the resistance is relatively low (less than 10 kΩ), and when the room is fairly dark, the resistance is relatively high (greater than 1 MΩ). You use these resistance estimates to figure out how the photoresistor affects the operation of the circuit.

When the room is very brightly lit, the voltage across the photoresistor is very small because the resistance of the photoresistor is so much smaller than that of the 1 MΩ resistor, so most of the battery's voltage is across the 1 MΩ resistor. The voltage across the photoresistor is likely less than 1/100 of the battery voltage (9 volts), or less than 0.09 volts.

Note that the actual value of the photoresistor voltage depends on the amount of light shining on the photoresistor, which you can't determine without a light meter. The variation in lighting is the reason why you may need to try different resistances in place of the 1 MΩ resistor. By changing the 1 MΩ resistor, you change the voltage divider, so more or less of the battery's voltage is distributed to the photoresistor.

When the room is very dark, the voltage across photoresistor is a big chunk of the battery's voltage because the resistance of the photoresistor is similar to — or maybe greater than — that of the 1 MΩ resistor. The voltage across the photoresistor is likely at least half of the battery voltage, which amounts to about 4.5 volts.

Again, the actual value depends on the lighting in the room. A dimly lit room may raise the resistance of the photoresistor enough to result in a voltage of 1 volt or more across the photoresistor, which may cause the LED to light up when you really don't want it to. You find out why by reading the rest of this section.

Here's the key part of stage 1: The voltage across the photoresistor is also the voltage applied to the base of the 2N3904 NPN transistor. But that's part of the second stage.

Stage 2

The second stage (circled in Figure 7-24) is simply an NPN transistor that acts as both a switch and a current amplifier.

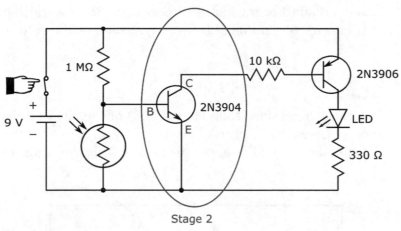

Stage 2

Figure 7-24

The voltage at the base of the 2N3904 NPN transistor determines whether the transistor is switched on or off. In Project 6, you find out that if the base voltage of an NPN transistor is above a certain voltage (about 0.7 V), the transistor is on; otherwise, the transistor is off.

In your smart nightlight circuit, the voltage at the base of the 2N3904 NPN transistor is the same as the voltage across the photoresistor in stage 1. So, when the room is brightly lit, the photoresistor voltage — and, therefore, the base voltage — is low, and the transistor is off. When the room is dark, the photoresistor voltage (and the base voltage) is high enough to turn on the transistor.

When the 2N3904 NPN transistor is off, no current flows from its collector to its emitter. When the 2N3904 NPN transistor is on, current flows from its collector to its emitter. That collector current is a larger version of the current flowing into the base, due to the current boost provided by the transistor. However, the base current is really tiny because of the very large resistances in stage 1 of the circuit (that is, the 1 MΩ resistor and the greater-than-1-MΩ resistance of the photoresistor in darkness). The amplified current flowing from the collector to the emitter is larger than the base current — but it's still too small to light an LED brightly.

You need another transistor to boost the 2N3904 transistor current enough to light an LED brightly, which leads us to the third stage.

Stage 3

The third stage (circled in Figure 7-25) of the circuit consists of a second transistor, a current-limiting 10 kΩ resistor at the base of the transistor, an LED, and a protective 330 Ω resistor for the LED.

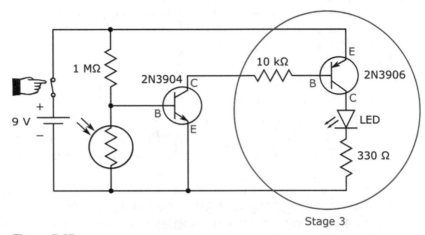

Stage 3

Figure 7-25

The current flowing out of stage 2 (that is, the collector current of the 2N3904 NPN transistor) flows through the 10 kΩ resistor and into the base of the 2N3906 PNP transistor in stage 3. The job of the 10 kΩ resistor is to ensure that the base current never gets so big that it damages the 2N3906 transistor. The job of the 2N3906 transistor is to amplify the small current coming from stage 2 so that it is large enough to light the LED brightly. But to amplify the current, the 2N3906 transistor has to be switched on.

The control of the switching action of a PNP transistor (such as the 2N3906) works differently from that of an NPN transistor (such as the 2N3904). The voltage at the base of a PNP transistor has to be *below* a certain voltage (0.7 V) to turn on the transistor (whereas the voltage at the base of an NPN transistor has to be *above* a certain voltage to turn on the transistor).

When the 2N3904 NPN transistor from stage 2 is off, the voltage at the base of the 2N3906 PNP transistor is relatively high (trust me on this!) and the 2N3906 PNP transistor is off. When the 2N3904 NPN transistor from stage 2 is on, the voltage at the base of the 2N3906 PNP transistor is brought down low enough to turn on the 2N3906 PNP transistor.

When the 2N3906 PNP transistor is on, it amplifies the current flowing into its base. So the current flowing from the 2N3906 transistor's emitter to its collector is large enough to light the LED brightly!

The 330 Ω resistor in stage 3 is there to protect the LED. The resistor limits the current, but the current is still enough to light the LED brightly.

Put it all together

You can see the big picture by looking at the schematics for the circuit operating in a brightly lit room and in a dark room.

Figure 7-26 shows that when the room is brightly lit, the photoresistor's resistance is low, so the voltage at the base of the first transistor is too low to turn the transistor on. Neither transistor is on, so no current flows in most of the circuit — including through the LED. The LED is off.

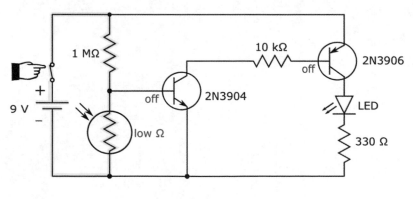

brightly lit room

Figure 7-26

Figure 7-27 shows that when the room is dark, the photoresistor's resistance is high, so the voltage at the base of the first transistor is high enough to turn on that transistor. Because the first transistor is on, it switches the second transistor on. Current flows through both transistors and is amplified each time. The current that flows through the LED is strong enough to light it brightly.

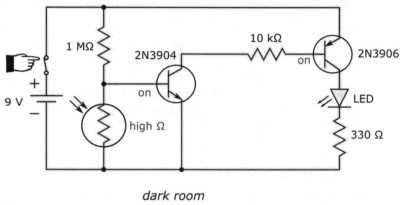

dark room

Figure 7-27

Congratulations on building a three-stage circuit and using your first sensor to control your circuit!

Part III
Do More with Less: Integrated Circuits

In this part, you'll build

Check out the video of the light-controlled sounds effects project at www.dummies.com/extras/ electronicsfk.

Blinking LED

Would you believe it if I told you that with just 11 components, you can build a circuit that sounds an alarm when a light goes on? Or that you can build a keyboard for the C-major scale using just 23 components — 8 of which are the "keys" for your keyboard?

You build those circuits in Projects 9 and 11, respectively — as well as several other seemingly complex circuits in other projects — and each one may take you just an hour or two! The secret to the simplicity of these circuits is a marvelous innovation known as the integrated circuit (IC).

In this project, one of the most popular ICs in the world — the 555 timer — does the majority of the work in a seven-component circuit that makes an LED blink automatically. Then, you use another new (to you) component, called a *potentiometer*, to vary the blink rate simply by turning a knob.

What's an Integrated Circuit?

All the circuits in Projects 2 through 7 involve *discrete components* — that is, individual electronic devices, such as resistors, capacitors, LEDs, and transistors. You connect the components as you build your circuit. An *integrated circuit (IC)* contains anywhere from a few dozen to many billions (yes — billions!) of circuit components packaged in a single device that can fit into the palm of your hand.

The components in an IC aren't just randomly thrown together in the package. They are connected to form a miniature circuit that performs one or more functions, such as counting or adding two numbers. Among the most complex ICs are the *microprocessors* that do most of the work involved in running your laptop, tablet, smartphone, and other devices. Microprocessors — which contain millions (or billions) of tiny transistors and other components — perform many functions and are often called the brains of computing.

Check out some chips

Figure 8-1 shows a variety of ICs, which are often called *chips*. Hidden from view inside each black plastic case is the tiny circuit. The *pins* sticking out from each case are leads that you use to connect parts of the tiny circuit to the world outside the IC. ICs commonly used in basic electronics typically have 8, 14, or 16 pins, while advanced microprocessors have hundreds of pins!

Figure 8-1

Because an IC does not have a power source, at least two pins on every IC are used to connect a battery or other power source to the circuit inside the chip. In a way, the chip is like one stage of a multistage circuit: By connecting the leads of discrete components to the chip's pins, you connect the stages of a larger circuit.

Every chip has a model number (among other things) stamped on its case. The model number tells you the chip's function (well, not in so many words — you may have to look up the model number to find out what the chip does). Thousands of different ICs are available today, and each one has a datasheet that tells you exactly what it does, how much power it needs, and what each of its pins is used for. For the projects in this book, you won't need the datasheet because I tell you exactly how to use each chip in your circuit.

Pay attention to the pinout!

Never — *never!* — make random connections to IC pins thinking you can simply "explore" different ways to get the chip to work. You can't even count on the power connections being the same for two different types of ICs that have the same number of pins.

Because every IC model is different, each pin diagram, or *pinout*, is different, too. The pinout tells you the *pin assignment*, or how each pin is used inside the chip. Even though the pin assignments are not the same for different ICs, the way you determine which pin is pin 1, which is pin 2, and so on is the same for every common IC.

Here's how you figure out which pin is which for common ICs (see Figure 8-2):

✔ Look for the *clocking mark*, which may be a small notch in the case, a little dimple in the case, or a white or colored stripe (they couldn't make it easy for you, could they?).

✔ Set the IC down so it looks like it's standing on its legs (pins), and orient it so that the clocking mark is on the north (12 o'clock) or northwest (11 o'clock) part of the chip.

✔ The upper-left pin (closest to the clocking mark) is pin 1.

✔ The pins are numbered *counterclockwise* (that is, in the reverse direction to the way in which a clock's hands move).

✔ The last pin (pin 8, 14, 16, or whatever) is the upper-right pin.

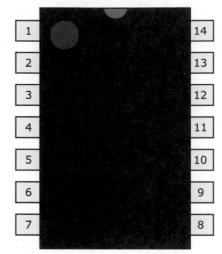

Figure 8-2

Meet the 555 Timer

The 555 timer IC (shown in Figure 8-3, with pin labels added) is a time machine in a tiny package. This 8-pin chip can perform several timing functions, depending on how you connect it in a circuit.

The details of how the 555 timer works are fairly technical, and I'm not going to explain them in this book (hope you're not too disappointed). This is all you need to know about the 555 timer IC for the projects in this book:

Figure 8-3

✔ **Pins 1 and 8 are used for power connections.**

You connect the positive terminal of a battery to pin 8 and the negative terminal of a battery to pin 1.

✔ **Pins 2, 4, 5, 6, and 7 are used to control what goes on inside the chip.**

You connect circuit components (most often resistors or capacitors) or power levels (meaning, the positive or negative side of a battery) to these pins in a certain arrangement so as to make the circuit inside the 555 timer IC operate in a particular way.

✔ **Pin 3 is the *output pin*.**

Depending on what's going on inside the chip, the output pin is, in a sense, either on or off. In reality, it either has a voltage equal to the battery voltage applied to it (on) or it has no voltage applied to it (off). In electronics, the on state is known as *high* and the off state is known as *low*.

The idea is to connect something you want the chip to control, such as an LED (with a protective resistor), to the output pin. When the output pin goes high, the LED is on. When the output pin goes low, the LED is off.

Your mission in this project is to use the 555 timer to make an LED blink and then to vary the blink rate. The steps in the section titled "Build the Blinking LED Circuit" walk you through connecting your battery to pins 1 and 8, your LED (with a protective resistor) to pin 3, and a few resistors and capacitors to the other pins. The specific arrangement and values of the resistors and capacitors determine exactly when — and for how long — the output pin goes high or low. By changing just one of the resistors, you change the LED blink rate.

Round Up Components and Tools

Gather all the parts on this list (see Figure 8-4):

✔ Solderless breadboard, prepared with

- 9-volt battery with battery clip

- Power switch and jumper wire

- Power rail jumper-wire connections

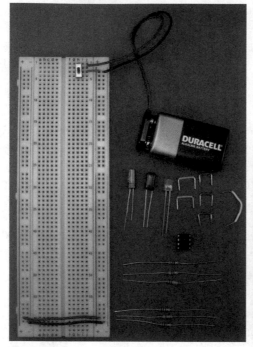
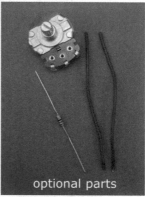

optional parts

Figure 8-4

✔ One LM555 timer IC

✔ One 0.01 µF film (nonpolarized) capacitor

✔ One 4.7 µF electrolytic (polarized) capacitor

✔ Resistors for the main circuit:

- One 330 Ω resistor (orange-orange-brown)

- One 47 kΩ resistor (yellow-violet-orange)

- One 100 kΩ resistor (brown-black-yellow)

✔ Resistors for modifying the circuit:

- One 1 kΩ resistor (brown-black-red)

- One 470 kΩ resistor (yellow-violet-yellow)

- One 1 MΩ resistor (brown-black-green)

✓ One LED (any size, any color; I used a 5 mm green diffused LED)

✓ Three 5/16-inch (minimum) jumper wires

✓ Two 3/8-inch (minimum) jumper wires

✓ One 1-inch (minimum) jumper wire

✓ Optional: One 500 kΩ or 1 MΩ potentiometer (preferably linear taper), along with two 3-inch wires (22-gauge) and one 100 Ω resistor (brown-black-brown)

The Optional Potentiometer

Pot is the shortened name for a potentiometer. (The nickname saves a lot of typing.) A *potentiometer* (pronounced "poe-ten-shee-AH-meh-ter") is a variable resistor.

The use of a potentiometer in this project is optional but recommended. The pot enables you to vary the blink rate of the LED without changing any components in your circuit. If you choose not to use a pot, you don't have to read this section. Feel free to skip ahead to the section titled "Build the Blinking LED Circuit."

Examine a pot

Pots come in various shapes, sizes, and values, but they all have the following things in common:

✓ They have three terminals (or connection points).

✓ They have a knob, screw, or slider that can be moved to vary the resistance between the middle terminal and either one of the outer terminals.

✓ The resistance between the two outer terminals is a fixed (constant) resistance, and it is the maximum resistance of the pot. This resistance doesn't vary even when the knob, screw, or slider is moved.

✔ The resistance between the middle terminal and either one of the outer terminals varies from 0 Ω to the maximum resistance of the pot as the knob, screw, or slider is moved.

Figure 8-5 shows the front and back of a potentiometer, along with some added labels. Does it look very different from the electronic components you have used up till now?

Figure 8-5

The maximum resistance (between terminals 1 and 3) of the pot — 10 kΩ — is stamped on the back of its case. If the control knob is positioned at the midpoint of its full range, the resistance between terminals 1 and 2 will be 5 kΩ and the resistance between terminals 2 and 3 will be 5 kΩ. As you turn the knob, the two variable resistances — that is, the resistance between terminals 1 and 2 and the resistance between terminals 2 and 3 — change, but their sum is always the maximum resistance of the pot.

For instance, say you turn the knob so that the resistance between terminals 1 and 2 is 2 kΩ. In this case, the resistance between terminals 2 and 3 is 8 kΩ. As you vary the resistance between terminals 1 and 2 from 0 Ω to 10 kΩ, the resistance between terminals 2 and 3 varies the opposite way — that is, from 10 kΩ to 0 Ω.

For this project, all you need to know are the maximum value of the pot and the fact that you insert a variable resistance into your circuit by connecting the middle terminal and *either one* of the end terminals in your circuit. The value of the variable resistance ranges from 0 Ω to the maximum resistance of the pot as you turn the knob.

Prepare your pot

To use your potentiometer with your solderless breadboard, you need to attach leads to the middle terminal and one of the outer terminals (either one will do). You use the two 3-inch wires from your parts list to make leads.

Soldering (pronounced "SAHD-er-ing") is the best way to attach leads to a pot. *Soldering* involves applying heat to a joint (in this case, the stripped end of a wire and the metal pot terminal) and holding a special type of metal (solder) up against the joint until the solder melts. When the solder cools, it solidifies, holding the joint together in a conductive bond.

If you have experience with soldering or know someone who does, you (or your knowledgeable friend) can solder the leads onto the pot terminals. However, for this project, you can get by without soldering by following these steps to attach leads to your pot:

1. Strip roughly 3/8 inch of insulation off each end of a wire, as shown in Figure 8-6.

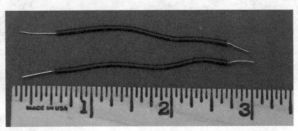

Figure 8-6

2. Use your needle-nose pliers to make a loop in one end of the wire, as shown in Figure 8-7.

3. Hook the loop around the end of the middle terminal of the pot, as shown in Figure 8-8.

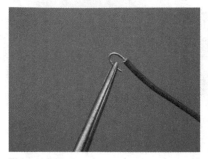

Figure 8-7

Figure 8-8

4. Use your needle-nose pliers to compress the loop and twist it a bit until it is somewhat snug against the terminal, as shown in Figure 8-9.

   If the loop is a little loose, that's okay. But if it's very loose, compress the loop some more.

Figure 8-9

5. Repeat Steps 1 through 4 for the other wire, attaching it to either one of the outer terminals.

Figure 8-10 shows how your pot should look with the leads attached. If you attach leads this way (without soldering), you should check the leads periodically to make sure they are snug against the pot terminals and give 'em a squeeze with your needle-nose pliers if they become loose.

Figure 8-10

Pot leads attached without soldering tend to break easily, so handle your pot with care and be on the lookout for broken leads. If a lead breaks, you'll need to restrip and reattach the lead wire — or invest a little time (and money) in soldering (preferably with help from a parent or other adult).

Build the Blinking LED Circuit

In this project, you use a 555 timer chip to make an LED turn on and off. You control the timing of the 555 timer chip's output using two resistors and a capacitor. By swapping out one of the two resistors for different values of resistance, you change the timing of the LED's blink. And if you use a potentiometer in place of that resistor, you can change the blink rate simply by turning the pot's control knob, which varies the resistance.

As you build the circuit, note that you begin by inserting the IC into the center section of the breadboard. Then you work your way around the IC, inserting components that are connected to pin 1, then pin 2, and so on, until you complete the circuit. You don't have to build a circuit in this organized fashion, but I highly recommend that you do because you are less likely to forget a component.

Follow these steps to build your blinking LED circuit:

1. Double-check your solderless breadboard (see Figure 8-11).

   a. Make sure that the two positive power rails are connected and that the two negative power rails are connected.

   b. Check that your power switch and jumper-wire connections are properly installed and that the switch is in the off position.

   c. Verify that the leads from your battery clip are snugly plugged into the correct contact holes in your breadboard.

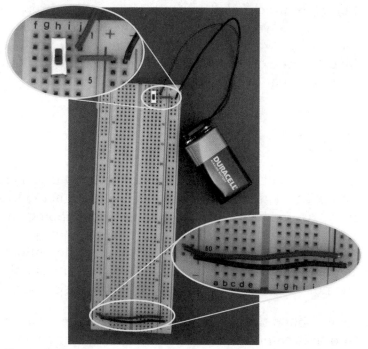

Figure 8-11

2. Insert the 555 timer chip into the breadboard.

The eight pins on this chip are pretty sturdy, but you still have to be careful not to bend them when you insert them into the contact holes in your breadboard. The best way to insert an IC in a breadboard is to place the IC on top of the contact holes, gently direct its pins into the openings of the contact holes, and then press down slowly on the top of the chip to ease the pins into the holes.

a. Orient the 555 timer IC with the dimple (clocking mark) in the upper-left corner, as shown in Figure 8-12. (I added corner pin labels to the figure.)

b. Place the chip on top of holes *21–24e* (left side of chip) and *21–24f* (right side of chip), so that you are lining up the corner pins like this: pin 1 into hole *21e*, pin 4 into hole *24e*, pin 5 into hole *24f*, and pin 8 into hole *21f*.

c. Press down slowly on the body of the chip, applying even pressure across the top of the chip, to insert the pins into the contact holes. As you press down, look at all the pins to make sure they are going into the holes. If any pin is not going in, stop pressing down, gently guide the pin into the hole, and then press down on the chip again until the pins are snugly inserted. (See Figure 8-13.)

Figure 8-12   Figure 8-13

The underside of the chip should be laying right on the bread-board, and the chip should be level (see Figure 8-14, left) — not tilted right or left. If one side of the chip is tilted up (see Figure 8-14, right), chances are the pins on that side are not properly inserted into the breadboard.

Figure 8-14

3. Insert a 5/16-inch (minimum) jumper wire into the breadboard.

Plug one end of the jumper wire into hole **21a** and the other end of the jumper wire into the negative power rail to the left of row **21.** (See the orange jumper wire in Figure 8-15.)

4. Insert the 47 kΩ resistor (yellow-violet-orange) into the breadboard.

   If you'd like to make your circuit neater, bend and trim the resistor leads so that each lead is about 1/4-inch long below the bend. Plug one lead into hole **18c** and the other lead into hole **22c**, as shown in Figure 8-16.

Figure 8-15   Figure 8-16

5. Insert a 5/16-inch (minimum) jumper wire into the breadboard.

   Plug one end of the jumper wire into hole **18e** and the other end of the jumper wire into hole **18f**. (See the orange jumper wire above the chip in Figure 8-17.)

6. Insert a 3/8-inch (minimum) jumper wire into the breadboard.

   Plug one end of the jumper wire into hole **18g** and the other end of the jumper wire into hole **22g**. (See the yellow jumper wire in Figure 8-18.)

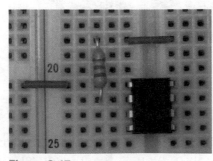

Figure 8-17   Figure 8-18

7. Insert the 4.7 μF electrolytic capacitor into the breadboard, as shown in Figure 8-19.

If you like, trim the capacitor leads so that each lead is about 1/2-inch long below the body of the capacitor. Plug the negative side

Figure 8-19

(identified by a minus sign or black stripe) into the negative power rail on the left (I used the hole next to row 23). Plug the positive (unlabeled) side into hole **22a**.

8. Insert the 1-inch (minimum) jumper wire into the breadboard.

This jumper wire connects pins 2 and 6 on the 555 timer IC. Plug one end of the jumper wire into hole **22d** and the other end of the jumper wire into hole **23g**. You can leave the jumper wire straddling the chip or you can bend the wire down. (See Figure 8-20.)

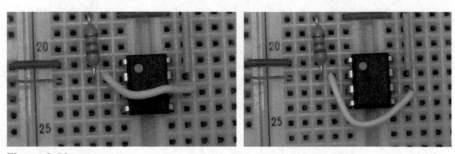

Figure 8-20

9. Insert the 330 Ω resistor (orange-orange-brown) into the breadboard, as shown in Figure 8-21.

If you'd like, bend and trim the resistor leads so that each lead is about 1/4-inch long below the bend. Plug one lead into hole **23b** and the other lead into hole **27b**.

10. Insert the LED into the breadboard.

    If you'd like, trim the LED leads so that they are at least 1/2-inch long from end to end. (See Figure 8-22.) Plug the cathode (negative side, flat edge, larger piece of metal inside the case)

Figure 8-21

into the negative power rail to the left of row **27**, and the anode (positive side) into hole **27a**. (See Figure 8-23.)

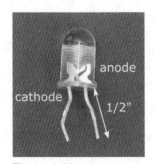

Figure 8-22

Figure 8-23

11. Insert a 3/8-inch (minimum) jumper wire into the breadboard.

    Plug one end of the jumper wire into hole **24a** and the other end of the jumper wire into the positive power rail to the left of row **24**. (See the yellow jumper wire in Figure 8-24.)

12. Insert the 0.01 μF capacitor into the breadboard, as shown in Figure 8-25.

    This film capacitor is nonpolarized, meaning it doesn't care which way it is oriented in a circuit. Plug one lead into hole **24j** and the other lead into the negative power rail to the right of row **24**.

Figure 8-24   Figure 8-25

13. Insert the 100 kΩ resistor (brown-black-yellow) into the breadboard.

   If you'd like, bend and trim the resistor leads so that each lead is about 1/4-inch long below the bend. Plug one lead into hole **22j** and the other lead into the positive power rail to the right of row **22**, as shown in Figure 8-26.

14. Insert a 5/16-inch (minimum) jumper wire into the breadboard.

   Plug one end of the jumper wire into hole **21j** and the other end of the jumper wire into the positive power rail to the right of row **21**, (See the orange jumper wire to the right of the chip in Figure 8-27.)

Figure 8-26   Figure 8-27

Figure 8-28 shows the completed circuit (except that you can't see the battery, the power switch, or the power rail connections at the bottom of the breadboard).

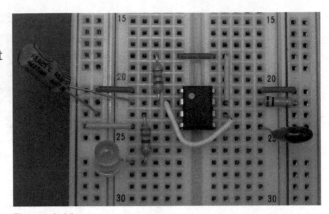

Figure 8-28

Double-check all your connections and the orientation of the LED and the 4.7 µF electrolytic capacitor. Once you've checked your circuit, you'll be ready to make the LED blink.

Operate the Blinking LED Circuit

Turn on the power switch. Look at your LED. Is it turning on and off in a regular pattern? (It should. If the LED is not blinking, check your connections again and check the orientation of the LED and the electrolytic capacitor. If it's still not working, use a different LED or a fresh battery.)

Try to estimate how long the LED is on. It should be roughly half a second. The LED should be off for just a split second before it turns on again.

Change the timing

You can change how long the LED stays lit by replacing the 100 kΩ resistor (row 22) with a different resistance. For a longer "on" time, you use a larger resistance. For a shorter "on" time, you use a smaller resistance.

Turn off the power switch. Then remove the 100 kΩ resistor (row 22) and replace it with the 470 kΩ resistor (yellow-violet-yellow). Turn on the power switch and watch the LED blink. Is the LED on for a longer time than when you used the 100 kΩ resistor? (It should be on for a little more than 1.5 seconds.)

Next, turn off the power switch and replace the 470 kΩ resistor with the 1 MΩ resistor (brown-black-green). Turn on the power switch and watch the LED blink. Is the LED on for an even longer time compared to when you used the 470 kΩ resistor? (Expect the LED to be on for nearly 3.5 seconds.)

Finally, turn off the power switch and replace the 1 MΩ resistor with a 1 kΩ resistor (brown-black-red). Turn on the power switch and observe the LED. Is it blinking faster than ever before? (The LED should be on for just a split second.)

Use a potentiometer (optional)

Swapping out resistors isn't that hard to do, but there's an easier way to vary the resistance so you can change the timing of the LED blink action: You can use a potentiometer to vary the resistance.

To use a potentiometer, follow these steps:

1. Turn off the power switch.

2. Remove the resistor (whatever value is currently there) in row 22.

3. Insert the 100 Ω resistor (brown-black-brown) into the breadboard, as shown in Figure 8-29.

   Plug one resistor lead into hole *19i* and the other resistor lead into hole *22i*.

Figure 8-29

4. Plug the potentiometer leads into the breadboard.

   Plug one lead into hole **19j** and the other lead into the positive power rail on the right (I used the hole to the right of row 19), as shown in Figure 8-30.

5. Turn on the power switch.

6. Slowly turn the potentiometer knob as you observe the LED, as shown in Figure 8-31.

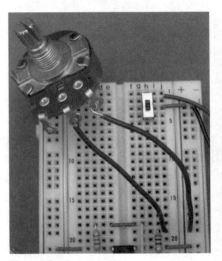 

Figure 8-30   Figure 8-31

Does the LED blink rate change? The blink rate should change noticeably as you rotate the pot knob through its entire range.

Take a Look at the Schematic

Figure 8-32 shows the schematic for your circuit. The 555 timer IC is represented by a rectangle with pin numbers around the perimeter.

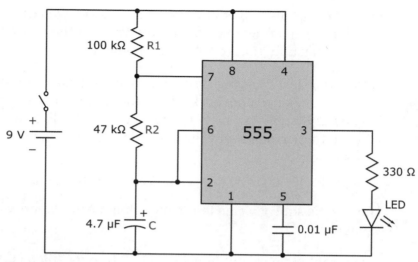

Figure 8-32

All ICs look basically the same in schematics — and you can't tell what function they perform in the circuit just by looking at them in a schematic. You usually have to look up the datasheet for the IC to figure out how it works. In this book, I tell you how each IC works in your circuits, so you don't have to look up any data-sheets (but you can if you want!).

The particular arrangement of resistors and capacitors around the 555 timer shown in Figure 8-32 makes the chip output an alternating up-and-down voltage on pin 3. This kind of circuit is known as an *oscillator* (pronounced "AH-sill-ay-ter"), because the output oscil-lates, or swings back and forth, between two voltages repeatedly.

The amazing thing about this 555 timer circuit is that you can calculate how long pin 3 is high or low during each back-and-forth voltage swing by using just the values of two resistors and one capacitor in the circuit. In Figure 8-32, these values are labeled R1, R2, and C. R1 is the 100 kΩ resistor, R2 is the 47 kΩ resistor, and C is the 4.7 µF capacitor.

If you're not afraid of a little math, and you want to figure out how long pin 3 is high (which is the same as how long the LED is on), do the following calculation:

$$0.693 \times (R1 + R2) \times C$$

This formula tells you to add the values of the two resistors (R1 and R2), multiply that sum by the value of the capacitance, and then multiply that result by the number 0.693.

Before you start plugging the values of R1, R2, and C in the formula, remember to convert kΩ to Ω and μF to F. R1 is 100 kΩ, or 100,000 Ω, R2 is 47 kΩ, or 47,000 Ω, and C is 4.7 μF, or 0.0000047 F. You use these converted values to calculate how long the LED is on, as follows:

$$0.693 \times (100,000 + 47,000) \times 0.0000047 \approx 0.48 \text{ second}$$

The double squiggly sign in the equation means "approximately equal to."

If you want to figure out how long pin 3 is low (which is the same as how long the LED is off), do the following calculation:

$$0.693 \times R2 \times C$$

Using the values of 47,000 for R2 and 0.0000047 for C, you get:

$$0.693 \times 47,000 \times 0.0000047 \approx 0.15 \text{ second}$$

When you modify your circuit, you swap out the 100 kΩ resistor (R1) for other values. You can calculate how long the LED is on in your modified circuit by substituting the new value of R1 in the first formula. For instance, when R1 is 1 MΩ, the new LED-on time is $0.693 \times (1,000,000 + 47,000) \times 0.0000047 \approx 3.4$ seconds. Note that because the formula for how long pin 3 is low (or the LED is off) doesn't depend on R1, this time remains the same (roughly 0.15 second).

Try it yourself! Figure out how long the LED is on when you use a 1 kΩ resistor for R1 in your circuit. Then use the 1 kΩ resistor in the circuit, and see if your estimated LED-on time seems accurate.

If you really want a challenge, estimate how long the LED is on — and off — when you use a 1 MΩ resistor for R2. Then insert the 1 MΩ in place of the 47 kΩ resistor (holes 18c and 22c), and see if your math predictions come true.

Light-Sensing Alarm

Do you suspect someone has been snooping around in your dresser drawers? Is a family member taking your favorite cookies from the kitchen pantry before you get a chance to have any? Has one of the hundreds of pieces of junk in your closet gone missing? If so, sound the alarm!

In this project, you use just 11 components and a battery to build a light-sensing alarm. If you place the alarm at the crime scene, er, in a dark place (such as a drawer, a closet, or even a refrigerator), and someone lets light into that dark place (by opening the door or drawer), a *speaker* alerts you by letting out a fairly loud and definitely annoying tone. Then you can identify the culprit — and restore law and order to your home.

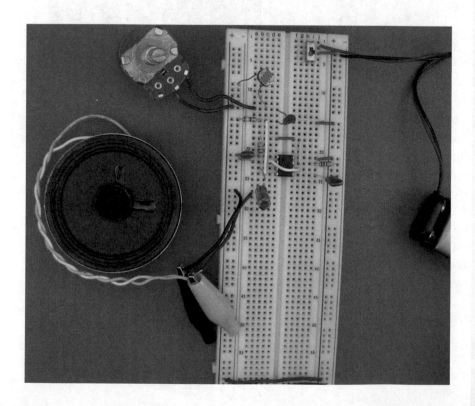

How a Speaker Works

This project uses a mini-speaker to play a loud tone, which is like a single note on a musical instrument, when a light is shining on the circuit. Figure 9-1 shows the front and back of one type of mini-speaker. Speakers (unlike potentiometers) usually come with leads attached. The leads are twisted together to keep things neat and tidy. You attach the leads to components in your circuit so that electrical current passes from your circuit into the speaker. The speaker then converts the current into sound.

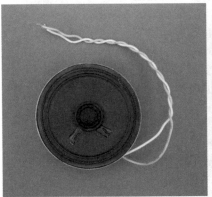

Figure 9-1

A typical speaker contains two magnets and a cone made of paper or plastic (see Figure 9-2). The black material you see in the mini-speaker shown in Figure 9-1 is the paper cone. One of the speaker's magnets is a permanent magnet (meaning that it is always magnetized) and the other is an electromagnet. An *electromagnet* is just a coil of wire wrapped around a hunk of iron. If no

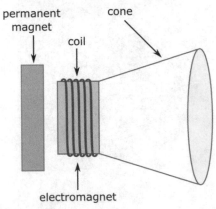

Figure 9-2

current passes through the coil of wire, the electromagnet is not magnetized. When current passes through the coil of wire, the electromagnet becomes magnetized and gets pulled and then pushed away from the permanent magnet. The cone is attached to the electromagnet, so when the electromagnet moves, the cone vibrates, creating sound (which is just moving air).

If you look closely at the back of the speaker in Figure 9-1, right, you might be able to see that one side of each lead wire is sticking through the back of the black cone. Those wires are connected to the coil inside the speaker. By connecting the other side of the lead wires to your circuit, you control the flow of current through the coil. Depending on what your circuit is doing, current may or may not flow through the coil, and you may or may not hear sound coming from the speaker.

For this project, you set up a circuit that sends current through the speaker only when a substantial amount of light is shining on your circuit. If the light level is low, the circuit does not send any current into the speaker.

Gather Components and Tools

Gather all the parts on this list (see Figure 9-3):

✔ Solderless breadboard, prepared with

- 9-volt battery with battery clip

- Power switch and jumper wire

- Power rail jumper-wire connections

✔ One 8 Ω speaker

✔ One LM555 timer IC

✔ One 2N3906 PNP bipolar transistor

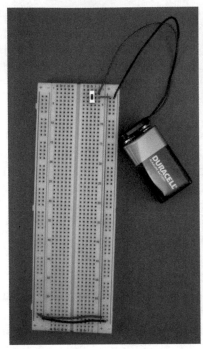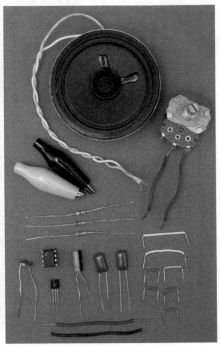

Figure 9-3

✔ One photoresistor

✔ One 100 kΩ potentiometer (preferably linear taper) with attached leads

✔ Two 0.01 μF film (nonpolarized) capacitors

✔ One 4.7 μF electrolytic (polarized) capacitor

✔ Resistors:

- One 3.9 kΩ resistor (orange-white-red)

- One 10 kΩ resistor (brown-black-orange)

- One 47 kΩ resistor (yellow-violet-orange)

- (Optional) One 100 kΩ resistor (brown-black-yellow)

  ✔ Four 5/16-inch (minimum) jumper wires

  ✔ One 3/8-inch (minimum) jumper wire

  ✔ Two 1-inch (minimum) jumper wires

  ✔ Two 2-inch (or so) 22-gauge solid wires with stripped ends (like jumper wires, only the ends don't need to be bent down)

  ✔ Two insulated mini alligator clips

In Project 8, I explain how to attach leads to your potentiometer.

Have your wire cutters (for trimming leads) and your needle-nose pliers (for inserting components into your breadboard) handy.

Prepare Your Speaker

Each lead wire on most speakers is made from *stranded wire*, which is a bunch of very fine wires twisted together. Stranded wire doesn't easily plug into the contact holes in a breadboard, so you need to attach solid wires to the speaker wires to use the speaker in your circuit.

If you (or a friend) know how to solder, you may want to solder solid wires to the speaker's lead wires. If not, simply read on for another way to attach solid wires.

It's easy to attach solid lead wires to the speaker wires without soldering. You need two jumper wires (at least two inches long each) and two mini alligator clips from your parts list. An *alligator clip* is a metal fastener that resembles the jaws of an alligator. The gripping part of the alligator clip contains metal teeth designed to hold wires or leads together. Figure 9-4 shows an insulated mini alligator clip and a clip with its insulation removed.

Figure 9-4

For each speaker wire, use a mini alligator clip to connect the end of the speaker wire to one end of the jumper wire, as follows (see Figure 9-5):

1. Press the separated sides of the clip together to open the jaws.

2. Place the end of the speaker wire and one end of the jumper wire in the jaws.

3. Release the side of the clip that you are pressing on.

4. Gently tug on each wire to make sure it's secure in the jaws of the clip.

   If either or both wires come loose, repeat Steps 1–3.

Figure 9-5

Figure 9-6 shows how the mini-speaker looks with solid wire leads attached.

You use a mini-speaker in Projects 10, 11, 12, and 14, as well as in this project, so I recommend that you leave the solid wire leads attached after you finish this project.

Now that your speaker is breadboard-eligible, are you ready to make some noise?

Figure 9-6

Build the Light-Sensing Alarm Circuit

In Project 8, you meet the 555 timer integrated circuit (IC) and use it to make an LED blink repeatedly at a rate determined by your choice of two resistors and a capacitor. The 555 timer applies an alternating high/low (or on/off) voltage to its output pin (pin 3), and that on/off voltage controls the on/off action of the LED.

In this project, you use a 555 timer chip in a similar way to that of Project 8. You send an alternating voltage to your speaker by way of the 555 timer output (pin 3) — but only if a light is shining on a photoresistor in your circuit. If there's not enough light on the photoresistor, the 555 timer shuts down, in a way, and no current flows through your speaker. Your speaker sounds the alarm only when there's enough light to trigger the 555 timer chip to function.

Follow these steps to build your light-sensing alarm circuit:

1. Double-check your solderless breadboard (see Figure 9-7).

    a. Make sure that the two positive power rails are connected and the two negative power rails are connected.

    b. Check that your power switch and jumper-wire connections are properly installed and that the switch is in the off position.

    c. Verify that the leads from your battery clip are snugly plugged into the correct contact holes in your breadboard.

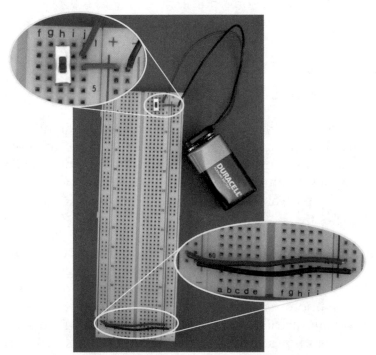

Figure 9-7

2. Insert the 555 timer chip into the breadboard.

a. Orient the 555 timer IC with the dimple (clocking mark) in the upper-left corner, as shown in Figure 9-8. (I added corner pin labels to the figure.)

Figure 9-8

b. Place the chip on top of holes **21–24e** (left side of chip) and **21–24f** (right side of chip), so that you are lining up the corner pins like this: pin 1 into hole **21e,** pin 4 into hole **24e,** pin 5 into hole **24f,** and pin 8 into hole **21f.**

c. Press down slowly on the body of the chip until the pins are snugly inserted into the contact holes. (See Figure 9-9.)

d. Make sure that the underside of the chip is laying flat on the breadboard surface.

3. Insert a 5/16-inch (minimum) jumper wire into the breadboard.

Plug one end of the jumper wire into hole **21a** and the other end of the jumper wire into the negative power rail to the left of row **21**. (See the orange jumper wire in Figure 9-10.)

Figure 9-9

Figure 9-10

4. Insert the 47 kΩ resistor (yellow-violet-orange) into the breadboard.

If you'd like to make your circuit neater, bend and trim the resistor leads so that each lead is about 1/4-inch long below the bend. Plug one lead into hole **18b** and the other lead into hole **22b**, as shown in Figure 9-11.

Figure 9-11

5. Insert a 5/16-inch (minimum) jumper wire into the breadboard.

Plug one end of the jumper wire into hole **18e** and the other end of the jumper wire into hole **18f**. (See the orange jumper wire above the chip in Figure 9-12.)

6. Insert a 3/8-inch (minimum) jumper wire into the breadboard.

Plug one end of the jumper wire into hole **18g** and the other end of the jumper wire into hole **22g**. (See the yellow jumper wire in Figure 9-13.)

Figure 9-12

Figure 9-13

7. Insert a 0.01 µF film capacitor into the breadboard.

If you'd like to make your circuit neater, bend and trim the capacitor leads so that each lead is about 3/8-inch long below the bend. This capacitor is nonpolarized, meaning it doesn't matter which way you orient it in a circuit. Plug one lead into hole **22a** and the other lead into the negative power rail to the left of row **22**. (See Figure 9-14.)

Figure 9-14

8. Insert a 1-inch (minimum) jumper wire into the breadboard.

This jumper wire connects pins 2 and 6 on the 555 timer IC. Plug one end of the jumper wire into hole **22d** and the other end of the jumper wire into hole **23g**. You can leave the jumper wire straddling the chip or you can bend the wire down. (See Figure 9-15.)

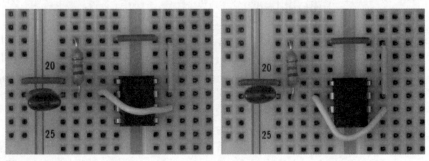

Figure 9-15

9. Insert the 4.7 µF electrolytic capacitor into the breadboard, as shown in Figure 9-16.

Plug the negative side (identified by a minus sign or black stripe) into the hole **27b**. Plug the positive (unlabeled) side into hole **23b**.

10. Insert a 1-inch (minimum) jumper wire into the breadboard.

Plug one end of the jumper wire into hole **24c** and the other end of the jumper wire into hole **15c**. (See the white jumper wire to the left of the chip in Figure 9-17.)

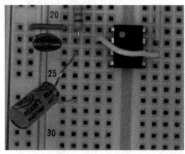

Figure 9-16   Figure 9-17

11. Insert the 3.9 kΩ resistor (orange-white-red) into the breadboard.

If you'd like to make your circuit neater, bend and trim the resistor leads so that each lead is about 1/4-inch long below the bend. Plug one lead into hole **15b** and the other lead into the negative power rail to the left of row **15,** as shown in Figure 9-18.

12. Insert the 2N3906 PNP transistor into the breadboard.

a. Double-check that you have selected a 2N3906 transistor.

b. Use your needle-nose pliers to gently bend the transistor pins out and down. Hold the transistor so that its pins are facing down and the flat part of the transistor case is facing the bottom of the breadboard (row 60). (See Figure 9-19.)

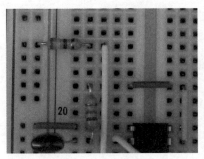

Figure 9-18

Figure 9-19

c. Plug the collector (left) pin into hole *15e,* the base (middle) pin into hole *13e,* and the emitter (right) pin into hole *15f.* (See Figure 9-20.) (Note that if your transistor uses a different pin assignment than mine, you may need to orient the transistor differently to plug the right pins into the right holes. Be sure to check the packaging or documentation that comes with your transistor to determine which pin is which.)

13. Insert the photoresistor into the breadboard, as shown in Figure 9-21.

    Plug one lead (either one) into hole *13c* and the other lead into any hole in the negative power rail on the left side of the board. (I used the hole to the left of row 9.)

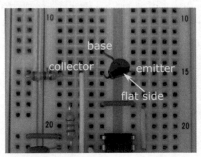

Figure 9-20

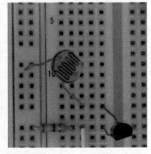

Figure 9-21

14. Insert the potentiometer into the breadboard, as shown in Figure 9-22.

    Plug one lead (either one) into hole **13a** and the other lead into any hole in the positive power rail on the left side of the board. (I used the hole to the left of row 13.)

15. Insert a 5/16-inch (minimum) jumper wire into the breadboard.

    Plug one end of the jumper wire into hole **15j** and the other end of the jumper wire into the positive power rail to the right of row **15**. (See the orange jumper wire to the right of the transistor in Figure 9-23.)

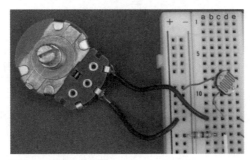

Figure 9-22   Figure 9-23

16. Insert the other 0.01 µF film capacitor into the breadboard.

    If you'd like to make your circuit neater, bend and trim the capacitor leads so that each lead is about 3/8-inch long below the bend. Plug one lead of this nonpolarized capacitor into hole **24j** and the other lead into the negative power rail to the right of row **24**. (See Figure 9-24.)

17. Insert the 10 kΩ resistor (brown-black-orange) into the breadboard.

    If you'd like to make your circuit neater, bend and trim the resistor leads so that each lead is about 1/4-inch long below the bend. Plug one lead into hole **22j** and the other lead into the positive power rail to the right of row **22,** as shown in Figure 9-25.

Figure 9-24

Figure 9-25

18. Insert a 5/16-inch (minimum) jumper wire into the breadboard.

Plug one end of the jumper wire into hole **21j** and the other end of the jumper wire into the positive power rail to the right of row **21**. (See the orange jumper wire to the right of the chip in Figure 9-26.)

19. Insert the speaker into the breadboard, as shown in Figure 9-27.

Plug one of the leads (either one) into hole **27a** and the other lead into any hole in the negative power rail on the left. (I used the hole to the left of row 27.)

Figure 9-26

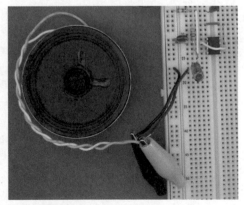

Figure 9-27

Figure 9-28 shows the completed circuit (except that you can't see the battery or the power rail connections at the bottom of the breadboard).

Double-check all your connections and the orientation of the 555 timer IC, the 2N3906 transistor, and the 4.7 μF electrolytic capacitor. Once you've checked your circuit, you'll be ready to test your light-sensing alarm.

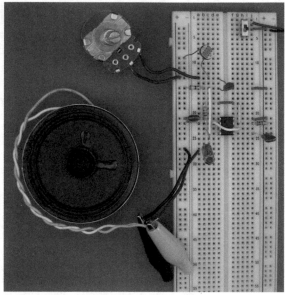

Figure 9-28

Test Your Light-Sensing Alarm

Just like the smart nightlight circuit in Project 7, the best place to test your light-sensing alarm circuit is in a room that has shades, blinds, or other window coverings. (But if you have no way to darken the room, you can still test your circuit.)

With the room lights off (or the sun blocked from shining into the room, or your fingers covering the photoresistor), turn on the power switch. Does the speaker sound? You don't want it to in darkness, but it might. If it does, slowly turn the knob on the potentiometer one way or the other until the speaker stops blaring. Try not to turn the knob past the point at which the speaker goes quiet.

Now turn on the lights (or let the sun shine through the windows, or remove your fingers from the photoresistor). Does the speaker start squawking? It should! If it doesn't, turn the pot knob until the speaker makes a sound. If it still doesn't make a sound, go back and check all your connections.

You can adjust the light sensitivity of your alarm circuit at any time simply by turning the pot knob. Exactly how much light should set off the alarm is up to you and depends on how you want to use the alarm.

For instance, if you intend to place the alarm in your refrigerator, the circuit doesn't have to be sensitive to light levels, because when the fridge door is closed, it's really dark inside, and when the fridge door is open, the fridge light brightens the interior. But if you want the alarm to sound when someone opens your closet door and your lamp is on the other side of your room, you may need to adjust the pot so that the alarm goes off in lower lighting conditions.

If you like to wake up at the crack of dawn, you can use your light-sensing alarm as a sunrise alarm clock. Just place the circuit near a window in your room and adjust the pot so that the alarm goes off when sunlight begins to stream into the room. Remember to turn on the alarm (meaning, turn on the power switch) only when it's very dark in your room, before you hit the sack. When it's dark and you're sleeping, the alarm is nice and quiet, but as soon as sunlight starts streaming in your window, the alarm goes off and wakes you — and probably your entire family!

Check Out the Schematic

Figure 9-29 shows the schematic for the light-sensing alarm circuit. If you want, you can explore the schematic and the information in this section to get a good understanding of how the alarm works. Or you can just skip this section and move on to another project.

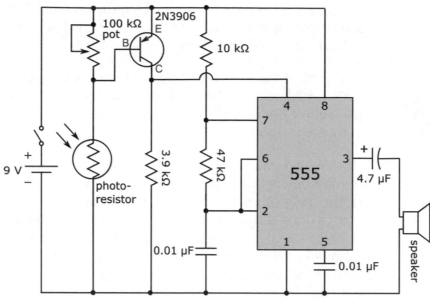

Figure 9-29

To understand how the light-sensing alarm works, let's start by looking at the end of the circuit (that is, the speaker at the output), and then work our way back to the beginning of the circuit (that is, the photoresistor at the input).

How the tone is generated

If you look at the right half of the schematic (see the highlighted section of Figure 9-30), you may realize that it is similar to the blinking LED circuit in Project 8. However, instead of a resistor and an LED at the output of the 555 timer, this circuit has a capacitor and a speaker at the output. The arrangement of the other resistors and capacitors is the same (although the values of those components are not the same) as in the blinking LED circuit.

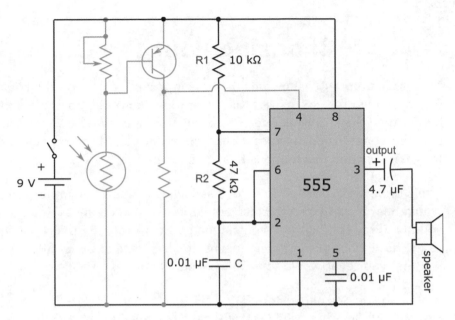

555 timer outputs voltage → alarm sounds

Figure 9-30

As in Project 8, the 555 timer IC in this circuit is used as an *oscillator*, applying an alternating high/low voltage to output pin 3. The job of the 4.7 μF capacitor is to change the shape of the current that flows out of the 555 timer chip before it reaches the speaker. The current flowing through the speaker swings up and down (due to the oscillations of the pin 3 voltage), causing the electromagnet inside the speaker to move back and forth. As a result, the cone inside the speaker vibrates at the oscillation rate, which is the rate of the up-and-down voltage and current swings, and you hear a tone.

If you want to know more about the tone that is produced by the speaker, read the sidebar "Choosing your tones."

Choosing your tones

The oscillation rate that creates the tone in this project is like the blink rate of the LED in Project 8, except the tone-producing oscillation rate is much higher than the LED blink rate. This oscillation rate is faster so that the electromagnet inside the speaker can move back and forth quickly enough to create a sound that humans hear as a tone.

If this project's oscillation rate were as low as the LED blink rate, you would hear a clicking sound instead of a tone. (You create such a clicking sound in Project 12.) And if you set the LED blink rate in Project 8 as high as the oscillation rate in the light-sensing alarm, the LED would blink so fast that your eyes would think it is constantly on.

Just as the values of resistors R1 and R2 and capacitor C (refer to Figure 9-30) determine the LED blink rate, these values also determine the oscillation rate in this circuit. The oscillation rate is also known as the *frequency,* which is measured in units called *hertz (Hz).* The higher the frequency of a tone, the higher the tone sounds. (You may know this quality of a sound as *pitch.*)

You can figure out the frequency of the tone produced by your light-sensing alarm by plugging the values of R1, R2, and C into the following scary-looking formula:

$$\text{frequency} = \frac{1.44}{(R1 + 2R2) \times C}$$

For your circuit, R1 is 10 kΩ (or 10,000 Ω), R2 is 47 kΩ (or 47,000 Ω), and C is 0.01 µF (or 0.00000001 F). You plug those values into the equation as follows:

$$\text{frequency} = \frac{1.44}{(10,000 + (2 \times 47,000)) \times 0.00000001}$$

$$= \frac{1.44}{(10,000 + 94,000) \times 0.00000001}$$

$$= \frac{1.44}{104,000 \times 0.00000001}$$

$$= \frac{1.44}{0.00104}$$

$$\approx 1385\,\text{Hz}$$

So the frequency produced by your circuit is about 1385 Hz. The frequency tells you how many times the 555 timer output voltage swings up and down each second — which is also how many times the speaker cone vibrates back and forth each second. (The frequency also tells you how many times the LED in Project 8 blinks each second.) By changing any of the values of R1, R2, and C, you change the frequency, creating a different tone.

Try it yourself! Replace the 10 kΩ resistor (R1) with a 100 kΩ resistor (brown-black-yellow). The frequency of the tone your circuit produces with this new resistance is about 742 Hz, so it should sound lower than the original tone.

How the 555 timer is switched on and off

Here's something that may surprise you about the 555 timer IC: You can *disable* the chip (shut it down, in a way) so that it doesn't output any voltage on pin 3.

Pin 4 of the 555 timer is the *reset* pin. If the voltage on pin 4 is low (such as 0 volts), the 555 timer chip is disabled and doesn't apply a voltage to output pin 3. No voltage, no oscillation — and no tone. If pin 4 is high (such as 9 volts), the 555 timer chip is *enabled* and functions in its usual way, applying an oscillating voltage to pin 3.

In the blinking LED project (Project 8), you connect pin 4 directly to the positive power rail. Because the voltage on pin 4 is always high, the 555 timer is constantly applying an oscillating voltage to its output pin, so the LED is constantly blinking. But that is not the case in this project.

Figure 9-31 highlights the section of your light-sensing alarm circuit that controls whether the 555 timer chip is enabled or disabled. Note that pin 4 is connected to the collector of the 2N3906 PNP transistor. The voltage on pin 4 differs depending on whether the transistor is on or off, as follows:

✔ When the transistor is off, no current flows through it, so the voltage on pin 4 is low and the 555 timer is disabled. No sound comes out of the speaker.

✔ When the transistor is on, current flows through the transistor, causing the voltage on pin 4 to go high and enabling the 555 timer. The timer operates normally and sound comes out of the speaker.

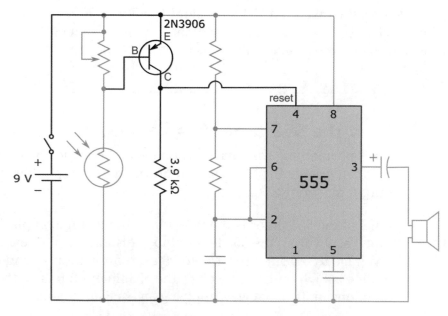

transistor on → 555 timer enabled → alarm sounds
transistor off → 555 timer disabled → no sound

Figure 9-31

Now all you need to find out is what controls the transistor switching action. (Can you guess?)

How the transistor is switched on and off

In Project 6, you find out that the voltage at the base of a transistor controls whether or not the transistor is on. For a PNP transistor, the transistor is off if the base voltage is relatively low, and the transistor is on if the base voltage is relatively high.

Figure 9-32 highlights the part of your circuit that determines the base voltage of the 2N3906 PNP transistor.

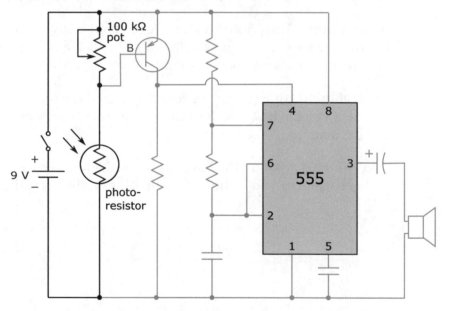

light → transistor on → 555 timer enabled → alarm sounds
dark → transistor off → 555 timer disabled → no sound
Figure 9-32

The base voltage is the same as the voltage between the photoresistor and the potentiometer (which is really the voltage across the photoresistor). You find out in Project 7 that the photoresistor and the pot split up the voltage supplied by the battery, and that the amount of voltage the battery distributes to each of those components depends on the resistance of each component.

When the resistance of the photoresistor is very high, most of the battery's voltage is across the photoresistor, and the voltage at the base of the PNP transistor is relatively high. Putting a high voltage at the base of the PNP transistor shuts off the transistor.

When the resistance of the photoresistor is very low, most of the battery's voltage is across the pot, and the voltage at the base of the PNP transistor is low. Putting a low voltage at the base of the PNP transistor turns on the transistor.

In Project 7, you find out that the resistance of a photoresistor is high in darkness and low when light is shining on it. So your circuit operates differently in darkness and in light, as follows:

✔ **Darkness:** The photoresistor's resistance is high, which makes the base voltage high, which shuts off the transistor, which means the alarm doesn't sound.

✔ **Light:** The photoresistor's resistance is low, which makes the base voltage low, which turns on the transistor, which sounds the alarm.

Give yourself a pat on the back for understanding — or at least, trying to understand — how this complex circuit works!

Light-Controlled Sound Effects

In this project, you use just seven components, a battery, and a flashlight (yes! a flashlight!) to generate some interesting sound effects. You can use this circuit to re-create the revving of a race car engine, a creaking door, a drum roll, the siren on a police car or firetruck, and much more.

Does this project sound interesting to you? If so, let's rock and roll and make some noise!

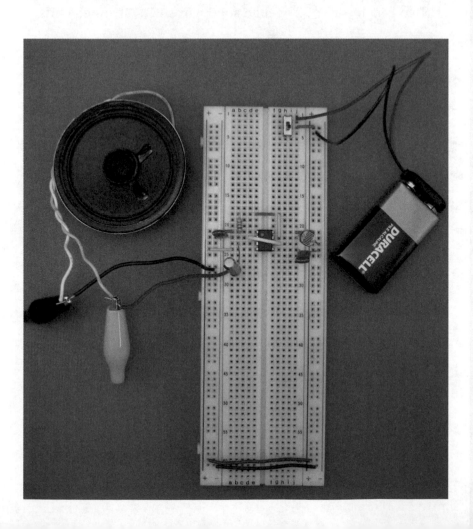

Collect the Parts You Need

Gather all the parts on this list (see Figure 10-1):

- Solderless breadboard, prepared with

  - 9-volt battery with battery clip

  - Power switch and jumper wire

  - Power rail jumper-wire connections

- One 8 Ω speaker, along with the following items:

  - Two 2-inch (or so) 22-gauge solid wires with stripped ends

  - Two insulated mini alligator clips

- One LM555 timer IC

- One photoresistor

- Two 0.01 μF film (nonpolarized) capacitors

- One 4.7 μF electrolytic (polarized) capacitor

- One 47 kΩ resistor (yellow-violet-orange)

- Three 5/16-inch (minimum) jumper wires

- Two 3/8-inch (minimum) jumper wire

- One 1-inch (minimum) jumper wires

- Optional (and not shown in Figure 10-1): one 2.2 kΩ resistor (red-red-red) and one 0.1 μF film (nonpolarized) capacitor

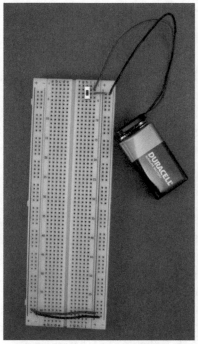
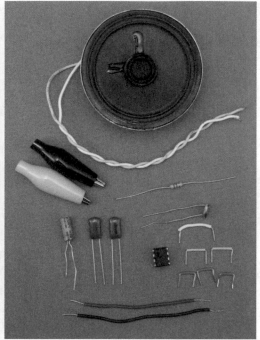

Figure 10-1

Use the mini alligator clips to connect the 2-inch (or so) solid wires to your speaker's leads. (Refer to Project 9 for details.) Figure 10-2 shows how your speaker looks with the solid wire leads attached.

Have your wire cutters handy for trimming leads, and your needle-nose pliers handy for inserting components into your breadboard. And grab a flashlight (any kind) or LED camping lantern for when you operate your circuit.

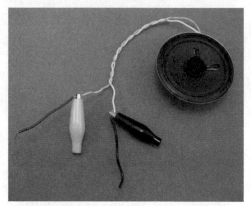

Figure 10-2

Build the Light-Controlled Sound Effects Circuit

In Project 9, you use a 555 timer chip to send an alternating voltage to a speaker by way of the 555 timer output (pin 3) — but only if a light is shining on a photoresistor in your circuit. If there's not enough light shining on the photoresistor, a transistor in the circuit shuts off, disabling the 555 timer, and no current flows through your speaker.

In this project, you use a 555 timer chip in a similar way to that of Project 9. This time, however, there is no transistor to disable the 555 timer, so the 555 timer always sends an alternating voltage to your speaker — and your speaker constantly emits sound. But instead of using two resistors and a capacitor to control the timing of the 555 output voltage, as you do in Project 9, you use one resistor, a photoresistor, and a capacitor. The pitch of the tone (that is, how high or low the tone sounds) emitted from the speaker depends on how much light is shining on the photoresistor.

Ready to get started?

Follow these steps to build your light-controlled sound effects circuit:

1. Double-check your solderless breadboard (see Figure 10-3).

    a. Make sure that the two positive power rails are connected and the two negative power rails are connected.

    b. Check that your power switch and jumper-wire connections are properly installed and that the switch is in the off position.

    c. Verify that the leads from your battery clip are snugly plugged into the correct contact holes in your breadboard.

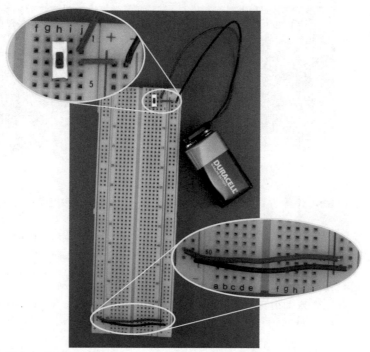

Figure 10-3

2. Insert the 555 timer chip into the breadboard.

   a. Orient the 555 timer IC with the dimple (clocking mark) in the upper-left corner, as shown in Figure 10-4. (I added corner pin labels to the figure.)

   b. Place the chip on top of holes **21–24e** (left side of chip) and **21–24f** (right side of chip), so that you are lining up the corner pins like this: pin 1 into hole **21e,** pin 4 into hole **24e,** pin 5 into hole **24f,** and pin 8 into hole **21f.**

   c. Press down slowly on the body of the chip until the pins are snugly inserted into the contact holes. (See Figure 10-5.)

   d. Make sure that the underside of the chip is laying flat on the breadboard surface.

Figure 10-4

Figure 10-5

3. Insert a 5/16-inch (minimum) jumper wire into the breadboard.

Plug one end of the jumper wire into hole **21a** and the other end of the jumper wire into the negative power rail to the left of row **21**. (See the orange jumper wire in Figure 10-6.)

4. Insert the 47 kΩ resistor (yellow-violet-orange) into the breadboard.

If you'd like to make your circuit neater, bend and trim the resistor leads so that each lead is about 1/4-inch long below the bend. Plug one lead into hole **18b** and the other lead into hole **22b**, as shown in Figure 10-7.

Figure 10-6

Figure 10-7

5. Insert a 5/16-inch (minimum) jumper wire into the breadboard.

   Plug one end of the jumper wire into hole **18e** and the other end of the jumper wire into hole **18f**. (See the orange jumper wire above the chip in Figure 10-8.)

6. Insert a 3/8-inch (minimum) jumper wire into the breadboard.

   Plug one end of the jumper wire into hole **18g** and the other end of the jumper wire into hole **22g**. (See the yellow jumper wire in Figure 10-9.)

Figure 10-8   Figure 10-9

7. Insert a 0.01 μF film capacitor into the breadboard.

   If you'd like to make your circuit neater, bend and trim the capacitor leads so that each lead is about 3/8-inch long below the bend. This capacitor is nonpolarized, meaning it doesn't matter which way you orient it in a circuit. Plug one lead into hole **22a** and the other lead into the negative power rail to the left of row **22**. (See Figure 10-10.)

Figure 10-10

8. Insert a 1-inch (minimum) jumper wire into the breadboard.

   This jumper wire connects pins 2 and 6 on the 555 timer IC. Plug one end of the jumper wire into hole **22d** and the other end of the jumper wire into hole **23g**. You can leave the jumper wire straddling the chip, or you can bend the wire down. (See Figure 10-11.)

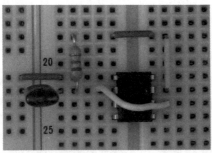

Figure 10-11

9. Insert the 4.7 µF electrolytic capacitor into the breadboard, as shown in Figure 10-12.

   Plug the negative side (identified by a minus sign or black stripe) into the hole **27b**. Plug the positive (unlabeled) side into hole **23b.**

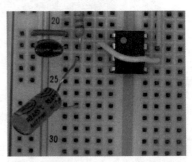

Figure 10-12

10. Insert a 3/8-inch (minimum) jumper wire into the breadboard.

    Plug one end of the jumper wire into hole **24a** and the other end of the jumper wire into the positive power rail to the left of row **24**. (See the yellow jumper wire to the left of the chip in Figure 10-13.)

Figure 10-13

11. Insert the other 0.01 μF film capacitor into the breadboard.

    If you'd like to make your circuit neater, bend and trim the capacitor leads so that each lead is about 3/8-inch long below the bend. Plug one lead of this nonpolarized capacitor into hole **24j** and the other lead into the negative power rail to the right of row **24**. (See Figure 10-14.)

12. Insert the photoresistor into the breadboard, as shown in Figure 10-15.

    Plug one lead into hole **22j** and the other lead into the positive power rail to the right of row **22**, as shown in Figure 10-15.

Figure 10-14

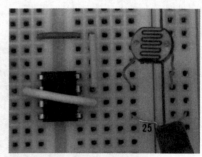

Figure 10-15

13. Insert a 5/16-inch (minimum) jumper wire into the breadboard.

    Plug one end of the jumper wire into hole **21j** and the other end of the jumper wire into the positive power rail to the right of row **21**. (See the orange jumper wire to the right of the chip in Figure 10-16.)

Figure 10-16

14. Insert the speaker into the breadboard, as shown in Figure 10-17.

   Plug one of the leads (either one) into hole **27a** and the other lead into any hole in the negative power rail on the left. (I used the hole to the left of row 27.)

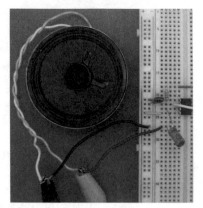

Figure 10-17

Figure 10-18 shows the completed circuit (except that you can't see the battery or the power rail connections at the bottom of the breadboard).

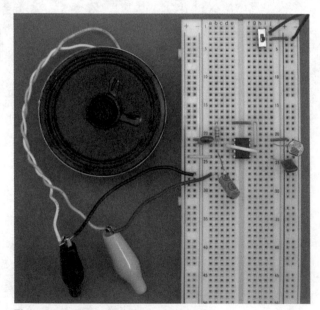

Figure 10-18

Double-check all your connections and the orientation of the 555 timer IC and the 4.7 µF electrolytic capacitor.

Once you have checked your circuit, get ready to make some light-controlled sound effects!

Create Some Sound Effects

Once you turn on your power switch, your circuit should make noise — no matter what the lighting. I recommend that you start testing your circuit in partial or complete darkness, and then add light.

Turn off the room lights, close the shades, and try to make to make the room dark. Then turn on the power switch. Do you hear a low-pitched tone or clicking from your speaker (which might remind you of a drum roll)? If not, turn off the power switch, go back through the steps to build the circuit, and make any necessary corrections. Replace the battery, if necessary.

Once your circuit is working, grab your flashlight! Holding it behind your back, turn it on. Then, very slowly, move the flashlight from behind your back to the front of your body, closer to your circuit. Do you hear the pitch of the sound increase as you move the flashlight? Does your circuit sound a bit like a creaky door?

Now hold the flashlight behind your back again. Move the flashlight from behind your back to the front of your body, closer to your circuit, but this time move it a little bit faster than before. Does the sound remind you of the revving of a racecar engine?

Next, shine the flashlight directly on the photoresistor. Is the pitch of the sound noticeably higher than when the flashlight wasn't shining directly on the photoresistor?

Hold your flashlight face down about six inches above your circuit, and then rotate your wrist to move the flashlight in a circular motion above your circuit. Is your circuit making a sound like a police siren?

Now turn on the room lights and listen to the sound from your speaker. Use your fingers to cover up the photoresistor, and then tap one or more fingers on the photoresistor (that is, move your finger on and off the photoresistor) repeatedly to create a warbling sound. To get a higher pitched sound, shine your flashlight on your circuit with the room lights still on.

Experiment with different indoor light levels. Then bring your circuit outside and try it in direct sunlight, in shadowy areas, and in other places. See how many different sound effects (buzz saw, anyone?) you can make using a combination of different room lighting, flashlight positioning, and hand movements.

Check Out the Schematic

The schematic for your light-controlled sound effects circuit is shown in Figure 10-19. Note that this schematic is similar to the one for the blinking LED circuit in Project 8. Read this section if you want to understand how your circuit makes such a variety of sound effects.

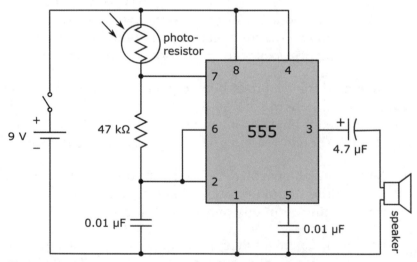

Figure 10-19

How the sound effects are created

Where Project 8 has an LED and a protective resistor at the 555 output pin (pin 3), this circuit has a speaker and a capacitor. And where Project 8 has two resistors and a capacitor controlling the timing of the alternating up-and-down voltage on pin 3, this circuit has a resistor, a photoresistor, and a capacitor controlling the timing. In Figure 10-20, the components that determine the timing, or *oscillation rate*, are labeled R1, R2, and C.

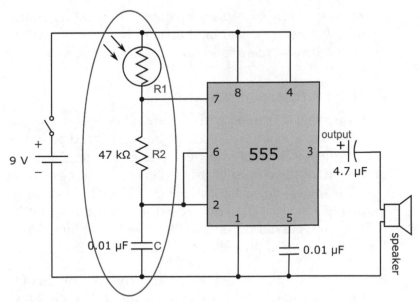

Figure 10-20

The oscillation rate is also known as the *frequency,* which is measured in units called *hertz (Hz)*. The higher the frequency of a tone, the higher the pitch.

You can calculate the frequency of the tone produced by your light-controlled sound effects circuit by plugging the values of R1, R2, and C into the following formula:

$$\text{frequency} = \frac{1.44}{(R1+2R2)\times C}$$

Don't worry. This is not math class, so you won't have to solve that equation. Besides, you don't know what R1 is, because it is the resistance of the photoresistor — and that resistance varies depending on the level of light.

The resistance R1 is the key to the sound effects. Because that resistance changes depending on the lighting conditions, the frequency (or pitch) of the sound coming from the speaker changes with the light. As you vary the amount of light that shines on the photoresistor, you are varying the frequency of the sound coming from the speaker. By rapidly changing the lighting conditions (say, by quickly moving a flashlight around in a circle near the photoresistor), you can create interesting sounds that vary in pitch.

A range of frequencies

As I was playing around with the sound effects, I was curious about the range of frequencies my circuit could produce, so I did the frequency calculation twice — once for the circuit in darkness and once for the circuit in bright light. In each case, R2 is 47 kΩ (or 47,000 Ω) and C is 0.01 µF (or 0.00000001 F). As for R1, which is the resistance of the photoresistor, I estimated that R1 is 6 MΩ (6,000,000 Ω) in darkness, and 300 Ω in bright light. Those values for R1 are in the right ballpark for my photoresistor.

So what did I come up with? The approximate range of frequencies this circuit can produce is from about 24 Hz to about 1530 Hz.

To test my assumptions and calculations, I searched the Internet for videos that would play tones at (or close to) those frequencies. I searched for *play 24 Hz tone* and *play 1500 Hz tone,* and found YouTube videos for both. (You can find just about anything on the Internet!) The 24 Hz tone sounded like a series of clicks, and the 1500 Hz tone sounded like a clear musical note. Then I played each video on my laptop while operating my circuit and used my expert hearing (lol) to compare the sounds. The sounds from the videos seemed pretty close in pitch to the sounds from my circuit!

 If you want to change the range of frequencies your circuit can produce, try replacing two components. Replace R2 (the 47 kΩ resistor in holes 18b and 22b) with a 2.2 kΩ resistor (red-red-red) and replace C (the 0.01 µF capacitor in hole 22a and the negative power rail) with a 0.1 µF film (nonpolarized) capacitor. The frequency range should be roughly 2 Hz (a slow clicking sound) to about 3000 Hz (an ear-splitting, annoying sound).

One-Octave Keyboard

Quiz time! What do the songs "Twinkle, Twinkle, Little Star," "Amazing Grace," and "Another One Bites the Dust" have in common?

And the answer is . . .

Each of those songs (and several more) can be played using just eight notes in the C-major scale. Those eight notes are known as an *octave*.

In this project, you build a simple keyboard consisting of the eight notes in an octave of the C-major scale. Your circuit uses just 22 components, including 8 pushbutton switches — which act as the keys on your keyboard — and a battery.

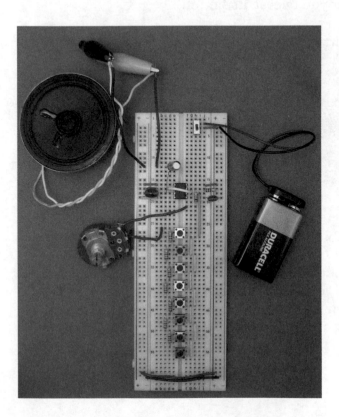

Probe a Pushbutton Switch

A *pushbutton switch* is a type of *tactile* (meaning touch) *switch*, which is an on/off switch that is activated when pressure is applied to it (usually by a finger).

Figure 11-1 shows the type of pushbutton switch you use in this project. Each of the eight switches is a normally open, momentary single-pole, single-throw (SPST) pushbutton switch. That's a lot of words just to tell you that this type of switch

✔ Makes or breaks a connection between two points

✔ Is normally open, or off (that is, the connection is broken)

✔ Is temporarily closed, or on (making the connection), when you press its button

✔ Is off again after you release its button

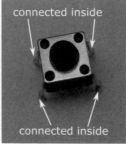

Figure 11-1

Note that the pushbutton switch shown in Figure 11-1 has four pins. Inside the switch, the top-left pin is connected to the top-right pin, and the bottom-left pin is connected to the bottom-right pin (see Figure 11-1, center). These pin pairings just give you two ways to access each side of the switch connection; you are still making or breaking a single connection.

The single make-or-break connection that the pushbutton switch controls is between the top pins and the bottom pins (see Figure 11-1, right). You can use either one of the top pins for one side of the connection in your circuit and either one of the bottom pins for the other side of the connection in your circuit.

If all this connection information sounds confusing, don't worry about it. I tell you exactly how to connect each switch in your circuit.

Collect the Parts You Need

Gather all the parts on this list (see Figure 11-2):

✔ Solderless breadboard, prepared with

- 9-volt battery with battery clip

- Power switch and jumper wire

- Power rail jumper-wire connections

✔ One 8 Ω speaker, along with the following items:

- Two 2-inch (or so) 22-gauge solid wires with stripped ends

- Two insulated mini-alligator clips

✔ One LM555 timer IC

✔ Eight 4-pin pushbutton switches (momentary on, normally open)

✔ One 10 kΩ potentiometer (preferably linear taper) with attached leads

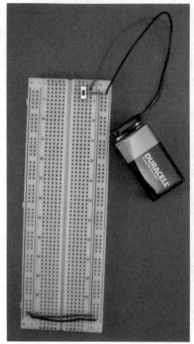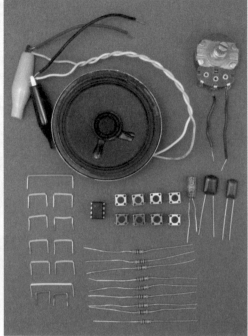

Figure 11-2

✔ Capacitors:

 • One 0.01 μF film (nonpolarized) capacitor

 • One 0.1 μF film (nonpolarized) capacitor

 • One 4.7 μF electrolytic (polarized) capacitor

✔ Resistors:

 • One 820 Ω resistor (grey-red-brown)

 • One 1.2 kΩ resistor (brown-red-red)

 • Two 1.8 kΩ resistors (brown-grey-red)

 • Two 2.2 kΩ resistors (red-red-red)

 • One 2.7 kΩ resistor (red-violet-red)

- One 3 kΩ resistor (orange-black-red)

- One 10 kΩ resistor (brown-black-orange)

✔ Jumper wires:

- Two 5/16-inch (minimum) jumper wires

- Eight 3/8-inch (minimum) jumper wires

- Two 1-inch (minimum) jumper wires

In Project 8, I explain how to attach leads to your potentiometer.

Use the mini alligator clips to connect the 2-inch (or so) solid wires to your speaker's leads (refer to Project 9 for details). Figure 11-3 shows how your speaker looks with the solid wire leads attached.

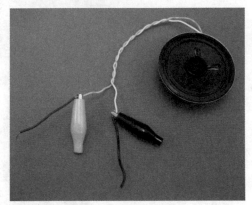

Figure 11-3

Have your wire cutters handy for trimming leads and your needle-nose pliers handy for inserting components into your breadboard (and restoring bent switch pins back to normal, if necessary).

Build Your Keyboard

Follow these steps to build your one-octave keyboard circuit:

1. Double-check your solderless breadboard (see Figure 11-4).

    a. Make sure that the two positive power rails are connected and that the two negative power rails are connected.

b. Check that your power switch and jumper-wire connections are properly installed and that the switch is in the off position.

c. Verify that the leads from your battery clip are snugly plugged into the correct contact holes in your breadboard.

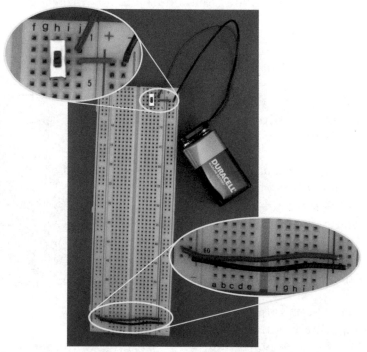

Figure 11-4

2. Insert the 555 timer chip into the breadboard.

a. Orient the 555 timer IC with the dimple (clocking mark) in the upper-left corner, as shown in Figure 11-5. (I added the corner pin labels to the figure.)

b. Place the chip on top of holes *16-19e* (left side of chip) and *16-19f* (right side of chip), so that you're lining up the corner pins like this: pin 1 into hole *16e*, pin 4 into hole *19e*, pin 5 into hole *19f*, and pin 8 into hole *16f*.

c. Press down slowly on the body of the chip until the pins are snugly inserted into the contact holes. (See Figure 11-6.) Make sure that the underside of the chip is laying flat on the breadboard surface.

Figure 11-5   Figure 11-6

3. Insert a 5/16-inch (minimum) jumper wire into the breadboard.

Plug one end of the jumper wire into hole **16a** and the other end of the jumper wire into the negative power rail to the left of row **16**. (See the orange jumper wire in Figure 11-7.)

4. Insert the 0.1 µF film capacitor into the breadboard.

a. Make sure you're using the correct capacitor. The 0.1 µF capacitor you insert in this step is larger than the 0.01 µF capacitor you insert in a later step.

b. If you'd like to make your circuit neater, bend and trim the capacitor leads so that each lead is about 3/8-inch long below the bend.

c. Plug one lead (either one) into hole **17a** and the other lead into the negative power rail to the left of row **17**. (See Figure 11-8.) Note that this capacitor is nonpolarized, so it doesn't matter which way you orient it in a circuit.

Figure 11-7

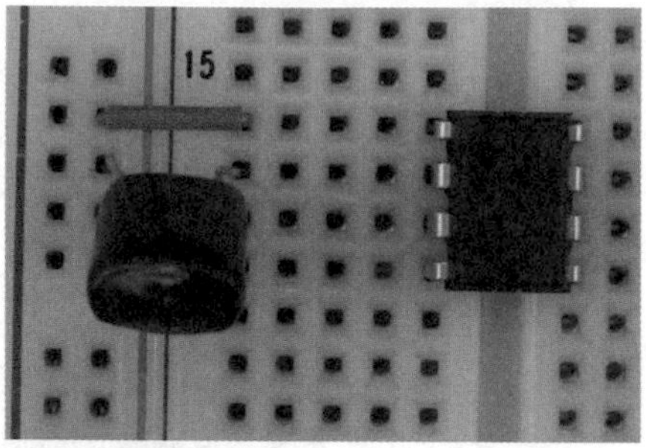

Figure 11-8

5. Insert a 1-inch (minimum) jumper wire into the breadboard.

   This jumper wire connects pins 2 and 6 on the 555 timer IC together. Plug one end of the jumper wire into hole **17d** and the other end of the jumper wire into hole **18g**. (See Figure 11-9.)

6. Insert the 4.7 μF electrolytic capacitor into the breadboard, as shown in Figure 11-10.

   Plug the negative side (identified by a minus sign or black stripe) into hole **12c** and the positive (unlabeled) side into hole **18c**.

Figure 11-9

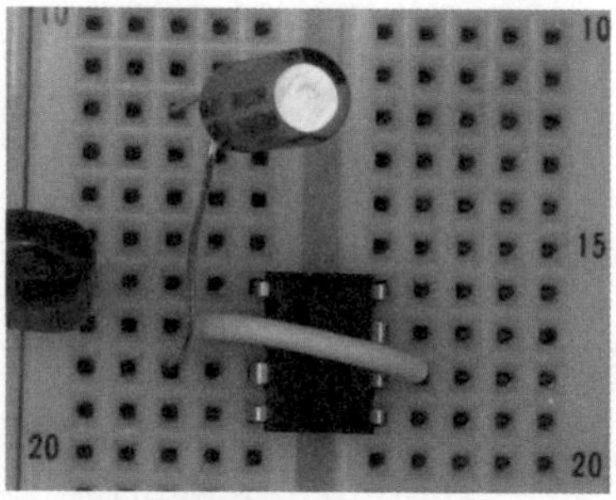

Figure 11-10

7. Insert a 3/8-inch (minimum) jumper wire into the breadboard.

   Plug one end of the jumper wire into hole **19a** and the other end of the jumper wire into the positive power rail to the left of row **19**. (See the yellow jumper wire to the left of the chip in Figure 11-11.)

8. Insert the 0.01 µF film capacitor into the breadboard.

   a. If you'd like to make your circuit neater, bend and trim the capacitor leads so that each lead is about 3/8-inch long below the bend.

   b. Plug one lead of this nonpolarized capacitor into hole **19j** and the other lead into the negative power rail to the right of row **19.** (See Figure 11-12.)

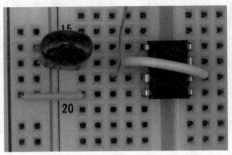 

Figure 11-11   Figure 11-12

9. Insert a 1-inch (minimum) jumper wire into the breadboard.

   Plug one end of the jumper wire into hole **18i** and the other end of the jumper wire into hole **28i**. (See the grey wire in Figure 11-13.)

10. Insert a 10 kΩ resistor (brown-black-orange) into the breadboard.

    a. Bend and trim the resistor leads so that each lead is about 1/4-inch long below the bend.

Figure 11-13

    b. Plug one lead into hole **17h** and the other lead into hole **21h,** as shown in Figure 11-14.

11. Insert a 2.2 kΩ resistor (red-red-red) into the breadboard.

   a. Bend and trim the resistor leads so that each lead is about 1/4-inch long below the bend.

   b. Plug one lead into hole **17j** and the other lead into the positive power rail to the right of row **17,** as shown in Figure 11-15.

Figure 11-14

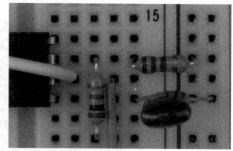
Figure 11-15

12. Insert a 5/16-inch (minimum) jumper wire into the breadboard.

   Plug one end of the jumper wire into hole **16j** and the other end of the jumper wire into the positive power rail to the right of row **16.** (See the orange jumper wire to the right of the chip in Figure 11-16.)

13. Insert the first pushbutton switch — let's call it SW1 (short for switch 1) — into the breadboard.

   a. Orient the switch so that it straddles the center ditch in the breadboard from rows **26** to **28**, and its pins are sitting on top of holes **26e**, **26f**, **28e**, and **28f**, as shown in Figure 11-17. It doesn't matter if you orient the switch right side up or upside-down. Note that the switch's pins should be curved out and to the left or right. (If the pins are curved out toward the top and bottom of the breadboard, you won't be able to insert the switch across the center ditch in the breadboard.)

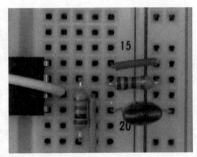

Figure 11-16

Figure 11-17

b. Insert the four switch pins firmly into holes **26e, 26f, 28e,** and **28f.** I found that the best way to insert the switch is to place my thumbnails on either side of the switch and push down evenly on the body of the switch. (See Figure 11-18.)

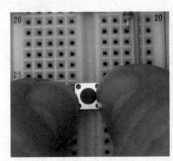

Figure 11-18

c. If the switch isn't going in smoothly, remove it and take a look at its pins. If any pins are bent, use your needle-nose pliers to bend the pin (or pins) back into shape. Then, reinsert the switch into the breadboard.

14. Insert the other seven pushbutton switches (SW2-SW8) into the breadboard as follows (see Figure 11-19):

a. Insert the second switch (SW2) into holes **30e, 30f, 32e,** and **32f.**

b. Insert the third switch (SW3) into holes **34e, 34f, 36e,** and **36f.**

c. Insert the fourth switch (SW4) into holes **38e, 38f, 40e,** and **40f.**

d. Insert the fifth switch (SW5) into holes *42e*, *42f*, *44e*, and *44f*.

e. Insert the sixth switch (SW6) into holes *46e*, *46f*, *48e*, and *48f*.

f. Insert the seventh switch (SW7) into holes *50e*, *50f*, *52e*, and *52f*.

g. Insert the eighth switch (SW8) into holes *54e*, *54f*, *56e*, and *56f*.

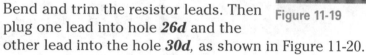

Figure 11-19

15. Insert the 820 Ω resistor (grey-red-brown) into the breadboard.

Bend and trim the resistor leads. Then plug one lead into hole *26d* and the other lead into the hole *30d*, as shown in Figure 11-20.

16. Insert one of the 1.8 kΩ resistors (brown-grey-red) into the breadboard.

Bend and trim the resistor leads. Then, plug one lead into hole *30c* and the other lead into the hole *34c*, as shown in Figure 11-21.

Figure 11-20   Figure 11-21

17. Insert the other 1.8 kΩ resistor (brown-grey-red) into the breadboard.

Bend and trim the resistor leads. Then, plug one lead into hole **34d** and the other lead into the hole **38d**, as shown in Figure 11-22.

18. Insert a 2.2 kΩ resistor (red-red-red) into the breadboard.

   Bend and trim the resistor leads. Then, plug one lead into hole **38c** and the other lead into the hole **42c**, as shown in Figure 11-23.

Figure 11-22   Figure 11-23

19. Insert a 1.2 kΩ resistor (brown-red-red) into the breadboard.

   Bend and trim the resistor leads. Then, plug one lead into hole **42d** and the other lead into the hole **46d**, as shown in Figure 11-24.

20. Insert a 2.7 kΩ resistor (red-violet-red) into the breadboard.

Figure 11-24

   Bend and trim the resistor leads. Then, plug one lead into hole **46c** and the other lead into the hole **50c**, as shown in Figure 11-25.

21. Insert a 3 kΩ resistor (orange-black-red) into the breadboard.

   Bend and trim the resistor leads. Then, plug one lead into hole **50d** and the other lead into the hole **54d**, as shown in Figure 11-26.

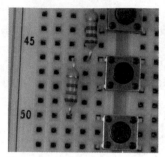

Figure 11-25   Figure 11-26

22. Insert seven 3/8-inch (minimum) jumper wires into the bread-board, as follows (see Figure 11-27):

    a. Insert the first jumper wire into holes **28g** and **32g**.

    b. Insert the second jumper wire into holes **32h** and **36h**.

    c. Insert the third jumper wire into holes **36g** and **40g**.

    d. Insert the fourth jumper wire into holes **40h** and **44h**.

    e. Insert the fifth jumper wire into holes **44g** and **48g**.

    f. Insert the sixth jumper wire into holes **48h** and **52h**.

    g. Insert the seventh jumper wire into holes **52g** and **56g**.

Figure 11-27

23. Insert the 10 kΩ potentiometer into the breadboard, as shown in Figure 11-28.

    Plug one pot lead (either one) into hole **21f** and the other pot lead into hole **26b**.

24. Insert the speaker into the breadboard, as shown in Figure 11-29.

Figure 11-28

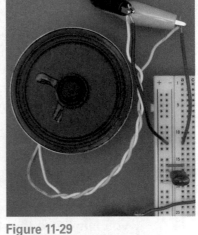

Figure 11-29

Plug one of the leads (either one) into hole **12a** and the other lead into any hole in the negative power rail on the left. (I used the hole to the left of row 12.)

Figure 11-30 shows the completed circuit (except for the battery and the power rail connections at the bottom of the breadboard).

Double-check all your connections and the orientation of the 555 timer IC and the 4.7 µF electrolytic capacitor. Make sure that all the switches are firmly inserted into the breadboard. After you check your circuit, it's time to tune your keyboard and make some music!

Figure 11-30

Test and Tune Your Keyboard

Turn on the power switch. Press any of the pushbutton switches. Do you hear a tone? Try all the other switches.

If you don't hear tones when you press each switch, triple-check all your connections. Pay close attention to the capacitors, making sure you have the 0.01 µF capacitor connected between 555 pin 5 and the negative power rail, and the 0.1 µF capacitor connected between 555 pin 2 and the negative power rail.

Once your circuit is working, you're ready to tune your keyboard.

The values of the resistors in this circuit are designed to create certain frequencies of sound from the speaker when you press each switch. However, resistor values aren't always exact, so you may need to adjust the resistance that creates the tones. (I explain more about how the resistors work together to create the right tones in the optional section, "Examine the Schematic," at the end of this project.)

By turning the knob on the 10 kΩ potentiometer, you alter the resistances associated with all pushbutton switches — which are the keys on your keyboard. And by altering those resistances, you adjust the frequency of the up-and-down voltage that the 555 timer puts out on pin 3 when each key is pressed. That output voltage is what controls the tone emitted by the speaker.

Figure 11-31 shows a sideways view of the keys in your keyboard circuit, with each switch labeled with the note it is designed to play. You need to adjust the pot resistance so that your circuit plays the tones of the eight notes in the C-major scale, from middle C (which is the first note in the C-major octave) to high C, when you press SW8 to SW1 in descending order. But to tune your keyboard, you need to compare one of your keyboard's notes to a known tuned note.

Figure 11-31

Use a tuned piano or other instrument as the source for your known tuned note. If you don't have a tuned piano or other source of a known note, you can search the Internet for a video that plays any one of the notes on your keyboard. I recommend searching for *hear middle C note* to find a YouTube video that plays middle C.

Your goal is to have the speaker emit the middle C tone when you press SW8. Follow these steps to tune your keyboard:

1. Play the known middle C note (using your piano, a video, or something else) while pressing and holding down SW8.

2. As you listen to the sounds of the known note and your circuit's note, slowly turn the pot knob.

   You should hear the tone from your speaker change in frequency as you dial the pot.

3. Keep playing the known note while pressing SW8 and dialing the pot slowly until the tone from your keyboard sounds like the known note.

   Try getting your circuit's tone as close as possible to the known middle-C tone.

Once you've tuned your middle C key, all the other tones will be tuned. (Well, they should be close to the correct tones, but they may not be perfect due to variations in actual resistances.)

You don't have to tune your keyboard using middle C as your known note. You can use any note in the C-major scale. Just be sure to press the key on your keyboard that corresponds to the known note you're playing as you dial the pot knob. For instance, say you have a tuning fork that is tuned to play an A (which is 440 Hz). As the tuning fork plays its A note, you press SW3 (which is the switch that corresponds to the A tone) on your keyboard, and turn the pot knob until your circuit's tone matches the tone from the tuning fork.

After you tune your keyboard, try playing the C-major scale by pressing the pushbutton switches in order starting from SW8 and ending with SW1. Does it sound like the C-major scale you know and love? If it sounds a bit off, try turning the pot knob ever so slightly, and see if that makes you change your tune.

Play Some Tunes!

With the eight notes on your keyboard, you can play a variety of songs, such as the ones shown in Figure 11-32. Note that C in the figure refers to middle C (SW8) while C_{hi} refers to high C (SW1).

The way the notes are grouped should give you an idea of the rhythm of each tune, but you still have to figure out how long to hold each note (by keeping your finger pressed down on a switch) and when to play a *staccato* (very short) note (by briefly pressing down and then quickly releasing a switch).

Now set up some chairs in the room, and invite your family and friends to your electronic keyboard concert!

A Tisket A Tasket

A G   E F G   E F GGGA G   E E FF DD FF DD G F E D E   C

Amazing Grace

C F AFA G F D C C F AFA G C$_{hi}$ A C$_{hi}$ AC$_{hi}$AF C D FFDC C D AFA D C

Another One Bites the Dust (by Queen)

D D D   DDDD F FG   D D D   DDDD F FG A AGGFD A A GGFD   D AAA A AG

London Bridge Is Falling Down

G AG F E F G   C E F   E F G   G AG F E F G   D   G   EC

One Love (by Bob Marley)

E E   D D   F E DC DC E D C

Row, Row, Row Your Boat

C C C DE E DE FG   C$_{hi}$C$_{hi}$C$_{hi}$GGGEEECCC G FE DC

Taps

C CF   C FA   CFA CFA CFA   F AC$_{hi}$ A F C   C CF

The First Noel

EDC DEFG ABC$_{hi}$ B A G   ABC$_{hi}$ B A G A B C$_{hi}$ G F E

This Old Man (or "The Barney Song")

G EG G EG A GF E D E F E F G C CCC CDEFG G D D F E D C

Twinkle, Twinkle, Little Star

CCGGAAG FFEEDDC GGFFEED GGFFEED CCGGAAG FFEEDDC

Figure 11-32

Examine the Schematic

If you want to understand how your keyboard works, start by looking at the schematic. But if you aren't jazzed up about understanding how your keyboard works, feel free to skip this section and move on to another project.

Figure 11-33 shows the schematic for your keyboard circuit. Don't let this schematic scare you. This circuit is similar to the light-controlled sound effects circuit you build in Project 10.

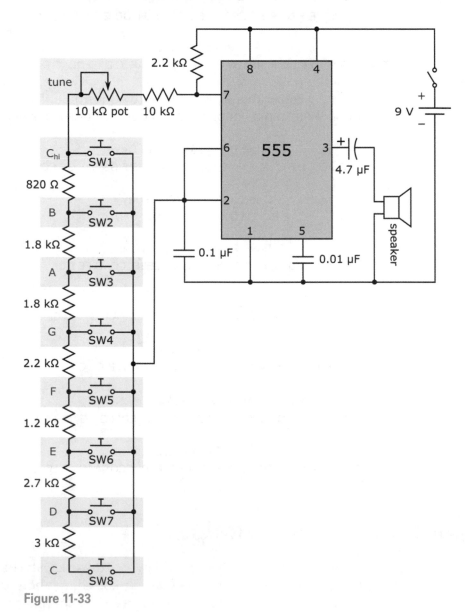

Figure 11-33

Note that the battery is shown on the right side of the schematic instead of the left. I put the battery on the right just to leave room on the left for all those resistors and switches, but the battery connections are the same as those in the other projects in this book that use the 555 timer (Projects 8, 9, 10, 12, and 13).

In the schematic, the switches are labeled SW1-SW8 and the note that each switch represents is shown in red. The potentiometer has the label *tune* next to it, indicating that you tune the notes by dialing the pot knob.

If you ignore the ladderlike set of resistors and switches, the 10 kΩ resistor, and the potentiometer, you may recognize that the structure of this circuit is the same as that of the light-controlled sound effects circuit in Project 10. In that circuit (and in this keyboard circuit, as you soon find out), the timing, or *oscillation rate*, of the output voltage on pin 3 of the 555 timer is determined by three components:

✏ Resistance between pins 7 and 8 (let's call this R1)

✏ Resistance between pins 7 and 2 (let's call this R2)

✏ Capacitance between pins 2 and the negative side of the battery (let's call this C)

The oscillation rate is also known as the *frequency*, which is measured in units called *hertz (Hz)*. The higher the frequency of a tone, the higher the pitch.

The frequency of the tone produced by any 555 timer circuit that is set up as an oscillator can be calculated by plugging the values of R1, R2, and C into the following formula:

$$frequency = \frac{1.44}{(R1 + 2R2) \times C}$$

This frequency equation works for your keyboard circuit, too. Figure 11-34 shows the schematic for your keyboard circuit, with blue labels for the three components that determine the frequency of the output tone. From this figure, you know that R1 is 2.2 kΩ and C is 0.1 µF. But what is R2?

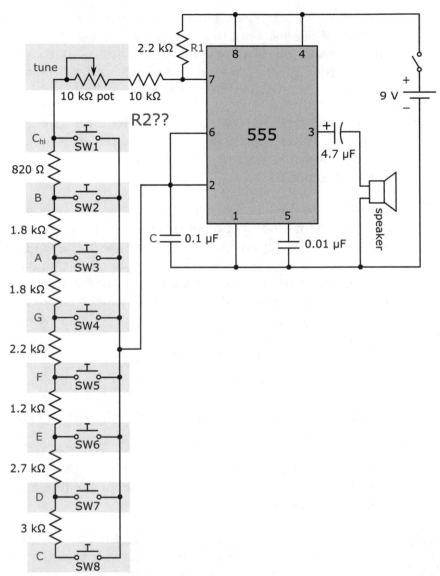

Figure 11-34

In the preceding bulleted list, I told you that R2 is the resistance between pins 7 and 2 of the 555 timer. But in this keyboard circuit, what is between pins 7 and 2 of the 555 timer? A whole bunch of resistors, a potentiometer, and some switches! So how can you determine what the resistance is between pins 7 and 2?

The answer is that you follow the path that the current follows between pins 7 and 2 and figure out the resistance along that path. To figure out the resistance, you need to know one rule about resistors that I haven't told you yet.

Resistors that are in series (connected in a single path) add up. So if you place, say, a 10 kΩ resistor in series with a 2.2 kΩ resistor, the total resistance in that path is 10 kΩ + 2.2 kΩ = 12.2 kΩ.

In your keyboard circuit, the path that the current follows between pins 7 and 2 depends on which switch is pressed. Each switch connects a different set of resistors between pins 7 and 2. So the total resistance between pins 7 and 2 is the sum of the resistors connected in the path when a particular switch is pressed. An example will help explain this total resistance.

Take a look at Figure 11-35, which shows what happens when SW4 is pressed. The path through which current flows between pins 7 and 2 is highlighted in yellow.

Think of the resistor-switch ladder as a maze. Only one path exists for current to flow through this maze from pin 7 to pin 2. If current tries to follow a different path through the maze, it runs into a road-block in the form of an open switch that prevents it from flowing.

The total resistance between pins 7 and 2, or R2, when SW4 is pressed is the sum of the resistors in the highlighted path:

$$R2 = 10 \text{ k}\Omega + R_{pot} + 820 \text{ }\Omega + 1.8 \text{ k}\Omega + 1.8 \text{ k}\Omega$$

In this equation, R_{pot} is the resistance of the potentiometer. If you substitute this total resistance (which depends on the exact resistance of the potentiometer), along with the values for R1 and C, into the equation for frequency, you get the frequency of the tone generated when you press SW4.

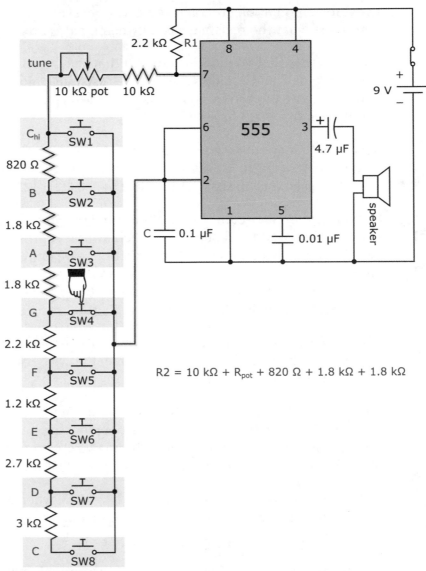

Figure 11-35

Don't worry about the value of R2. The exact resistance is not important for understanding how this keyboard circuit works. What is important is that you understand that pressing a different switch means that the path through the maze changes. A different path means a different amount of resistance (R2) is connected between pins 7 and 2 of the 555 timer, which causes the oscillation rate to change — which produces a different frequency tone from the speaker.

The values of the individual resistors between pins 7 and 2 in your keyboard circuit were selected to produce the frequencies that create the tones of the C-major scale. The exact frequency of each note is well known (for instance, an A note is a 440-Hz tone), so by looking up the frequencies, using a little bit of math, and knowing that resistors in series add up, the values of the resistors needed to produce each tone can be calculated.

But enough about math and resistance. Press some switches, make some music, and have fun!

Part IV
Impress Your Friends: Advanced Projects

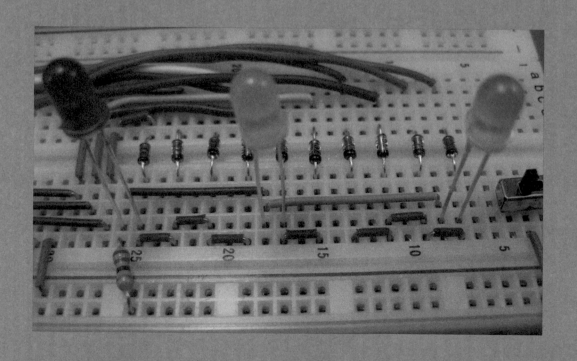

In this part, you'll build

Check out the video of a guess-the-number game that uses a light chaser at www.dummies.com/ extras/electronicsfk.

Roulette (Guess-the-Number) Wheel

Have you ever heard of a roulette wheel? You spin the wheel and a ball travels around the wheel from one numbered compartment to another until the wheel stops spinning and the ball settles into one of the compartments. Roulette wheels are used in games of chance. If you guess the number of the compartment that the ball ends up in, you win a prize.

In this project, you build a circuit that mimics the action of a roulette wheel. The "wheel" in your circuit is actually ten LEDs in a row. The LEDs light up sequentially and repeatedly, at a rate that decreases over time, until just one LED stays lit.

Your roulette circuit uses two integrated circuits (ICs): the 555 timer (which is used in Projects 8–11) and a new (to you) IC — the *4017 decade counter*. Sprinkle in ten LEDs, a few resistors and capacitors, a boatload of jumper wires, a pushbutton switch, and a speaker for sound effects, and you have all the ingredients you need to create a fun electronic game of chance.

Check out the video for this project at www.dummies.com/extras/electronicsfk.

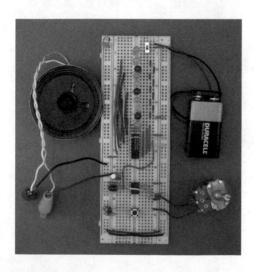

The 4017 Decade Counter IC

Do you remember counting on your fingers when you first learned to count? You start with your fingers closed, like you're making a fist. Then, one at a time, you stick out a finger (or thumb) as you count, "1, 2, 3, 4, 5, 6, 7, 8, 9, 10." In this project, you use a special IC known as a decade counter to count from 1 to 10. (In electronics-speak, the 4017 decade counter counts from 0 to 9, but I refer to the count as 1 to 10 because it's easier to think of the count that way.)

The 4017 decade counter IC, shown in Figure 12-1, is a CMOS chip. *CMOS* stands for *complementary metal oxide semiconductor*, but you don't really need to know that. What you *do* need to know — before you handle your 4017 chip — is that all CMOS chips are very sensitive

Figure 12-1

to static electricity. *Static electricity* is what zaps you when you shuffle your feet across a carpet and touch a doorknob. It doesn't take much static electricity to zap a CMOS chip and transform it into a useless hunk of unattractive plastic. CMOS chips usually come mounted on a piece of antistatic foam, as shown in Figure 12-1, right.

Protect your CMOS chip

You need to free yourself of as much static electricity as you can before handling your 4017 decade counter IC — or any other CMOS chip. And believe me, your body is carrying static electricity, whether you shuffle your feet across a carpet or not. A good way to reduce static electricity is to wear low-static cotton or wool clothing (avoiding all polyester and acetate clothing, which you probably avoid anyway) and wear an antistatic wrist strap while you're working with the chip.

Pictured in Figure 12-2, an *antistatic wrist strap* prevents static electricity from building up by providing a conductive path for static charges to flow from your body to a safe place, known as earth ground. *Earth ground* is any point that is connected to the earth — meaning the ground (yes, the actual dirt) outside your house. Certain items in your house are connected to the earth via piping and

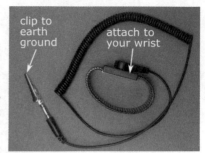

Figure 12-2

wiring behind your walls, so all you have to do is wrap the antistatic wrist strap tightly around your wrist, remove any metal jewelry, and connect the clip on the end of the wrist strap to a grounded item in your house.

So what items are grounded, you ask? The bare (unpainted) metal surface of a computer case (with the computer plugged in), the bare surface of a radiator, and a metal clip nestled snugly against a copper pipe are some examples of proper earth ground connections. Note that if your house contains polyvinyl chloride (PVC) or plastic pipes, your plumbing may not be electrically connected to the earth. Figure 12-3 shows how I connect my antistatic wrist strap when I'm working in my kitchen or in my basement. Be sure to review the instruction sheet that comes with your antistatic wrist strap.

Figure 12-3

Explore the 4017 decade counter

The 4017 decade counter IC has 16 pins. (See the pin diagram in Figure 12-4.) Of these, 10 output pins keep track of the count. You can think of these 10 pins as you do your 10 fingers when you count — er, I mean, when you *used to* count on your fingers. Each time the 4017 increases the count, one of its 10 counting pins goes

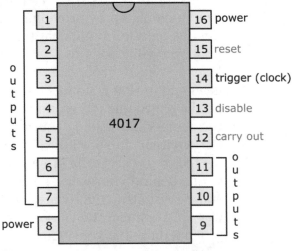

Figure 12-4

high (that is, that pin has the battery voltage applied to it) while all the other counting pins go low (that is, they have no voltage applied to them). So, at any given moment, just one of the 4017 IC's 10 counting pins is high and all 9 other counting pins are low. The high pin tells you the count at that moment.

Another one of the 4017 decade counter's pins is used to control, or *trigger*, the counting process. The count advances only when the trigger pin changes from low to high. You can think of this as a teacher prompting a child who is counting on his or her fingers. When the teacher says, "What number comes next?" the child responds with the next number. Likewise, when the 4017 IC's trigger pin changes from a low voltage to a high voltage, the 4017 IC puts a high voltage on the next counting pin and a low voltage on all the other counting pins.

Inside the 4017 decade counter IC is a cool circuit that makes all this triggering and counting possible. Outside the chip, there are just 16 pins that enable you to control and use the 4017, as follows:

✔ **Pins 8 and 16 are used for power connections.**

You connect the positive terminal of a battery to pin 16 and the negative terminal of a battery to pin 8.

✔ **Pin 14 is the all-important trigger pin (also known as the** *clock* **pin), which is an input.**

When pin 14 goes from low to high, the chip changes the count. This pin is an input pin because whatever voltage is applied to it affects what is happening inside the chip. You find out in the next section where you get the voltage you need to apply to pin 14 for your circuit.

✔ **Pins 1–7 and 9–11 are the counting pins, which are outputs.**

I wish I could tell you that the count follows the order of the pin numbers, but it doesn't. As the chip counts up from 1 to 10, the pins go high in this order: 3, 2, 4, 7, 10, 1, 5, 6, 9, 11. This counting cycle repeats as long as the chip is operating and the trigger pin is, well, triggered.

In this project, you use the ten counting pins to control the voltages across ten LEDs, so that the LEDs light up sequentially (that is, one-by-one in order) and the lighting cycle repeats until you remove power from the circuit.

✔ **Pins 12, 13, and 15 are used for other functions.**

These pins are used to enable or disable counting, to reset the count, and to connect multiple 4017 decade counters together so you can count up to 100, 1,000, or even higher. For this project, you don't use pin 12, and pins 13 and 15 are simply connected to the negative terminal of your battery so that you don't disable or reset the count.

Don't worry if all this information sounds strange or confusing. I show you exactly how to connect the 4017 decade counter in your circuit.

Use the 555 Timer as a Trigger

In Projects 8–11, you use a 555 timer IC to control either the blinking of an LED or the sound coming out of a speaker. In this project, you use the *output* (good ole pin 3) of a 555 timer IC as the trigger *input* to the 4017 decade counter.

As you discover in Project 8, the 555 timer chip is designed to output an alternating up-and-down, high-and-low voltage on its pin 3. Figure 12-5 shows what a graph of that oscillating output voltage looks like. Exactly how long the voltage stays high or low during each *cycle* (meaning the part that repeats) depends on the values of two resistances and one capacitance connected to pins 2, 6, and 7 of the 555 timer chip. (Project 8 explains how to calculate the timing of the output voltage on pin 3 using those resistance and capacitance values.)

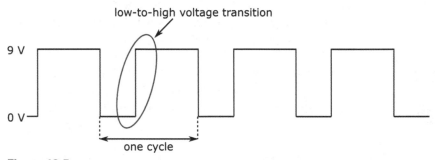

Figure 12-5

Note that during each cycle, the output voltage transitions from low to high (and then back from high to low). That low-to-high voltage transition is exactly what the 4017 decade counter needs to trigger the count to advance.

By connecting pin 3 (output) of the 555 timer chip to pin 14 (trigger input) of the 4017 decade counter IC, you can use the oscillating 555 timer output to trigger the counting process. (Amazing stuff, isn't this?) With that connection in place, every time the 555 timer output goes from low to high (which it does once every cycle), the 4017 decade counter count advances.

Ready to take a spin at building your roulette circuit?

Gather the Parts You Need

This project calls for a lot of jumper wires. In the parts list that follows, I tell you the minimum lengths of the wires you need if you want to keep your circuit as neat as possible. Please don't spend too much time measuring and cutting jumper wires to exact specifications! Your jumper wires don't have to be perfect (mine aren't!) and it's okay if your jumper wires are a little too long and curve upward between contact holes in your breadboard. So use the lengths given as guidelines for preparing your jumper wires. You can always trim a wire a bit more if it's much too long and getting in the way of operating your circuit, or make a new wire if you've cut a jumper wire too short.

Collect all the parts on this list (see Figure 12-6):

- Solderless breadboard, prepared with
  - 9-volt battery with battery clip
  - Power switch and jumper wire
  - Power rail jumper-wire connections
- One 8 Ω speaker, along with the following items attached:
  - Two 2-inch (or so) 22-gauge solid wires with stripped ends
  - Two insulated mini alligator clips
- One LM555 timer IC
- One CMOS 4017 decade counter IC
- One 4-pin pushbutton switch (momentary on, normally open)
- Ten LEDs (clear or diffused, 3 mm or 5 mm, each LED can be any color)

- Capacitors:

    - One 0.01 µF film (nonpolarized) capacitor

    - One 0.1 µF film (nonpolarized) capacitor

    - One 4.7 µF electrolytic (polarized) capacitor

    - One 10 µF electrolytic (polarized) capacitor

    - One 22 µF electrolytic (polarized) capacitor

- Resistors:

    - One 100 Ω resistor (brown-black-brown)

    - One 330 Ω resistor (orange-orange-brown)

    - One 47 kΩ resistor (yellow-violet-orange)

    - One 470 kΩ resistor (yellow-violet-yellow)

- Jumper wires:

    - Ten 3/16-inch (minimum) jumper wires

    - Eight 5/16-inch (minimum) jumper wires

    - Three 3/8-inch (minimum) jumper wires

    - One 9/16-inch (minimum) jumper wire

    - Three 3/4-inch (minimum) jumper wires

    - One 1-inch (minimum) jumper wire

    - Two 1 1/4-inch (minimum) jumper wires

    - One 1 3/8-inch (minimum) jumper wire

    - One 1 1/2-inch (minimum) jumper wire

- One 2-inch (minimum) jumper wire

- Three 2 1/4-inch (minimum) jumper wires

- One 2 1/2-inch (minimum) jumper wire

✔ Optional: One 100 kΩ potentiometer (preferably linear taper) with attached leads

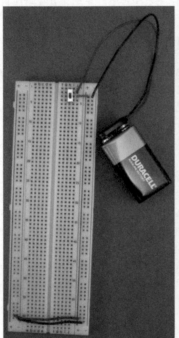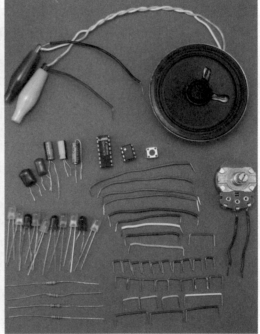

Figure 12-6

I highly recommend that you use an antistatic wrist strap while you're building your circuit. You can still build the circuit without using one, but you may be disappointed if you accidentally zap the 4017 chip.

You also need your wire cutters for trimming leads and your needle-nose pliers for bending leads and inserting components into your breadboard (and, possibly, restoring bent IC pins back to normal). If you need to make some jumper wires (which is highly likely), have your wire strippers handy.

Two-Part Project

You build the roulette circuit in two parts:

✔ In the first part, you build and test a light chaser circuit. The *light chaser* turns each of your ten LEDs on one at a time and repeats the pattern at a constant rate (so it looks like the LEDs are chasing each other). This circuit keeps sequencing through all ten LEDs as long as power is applied to the circuit. Once you complete this light chaser circuit, you test it before moving on to the second part.

✔ In the second part, you make a few changes to the light chaser circuit to alter its timing so that you create the effect of a roulette wheel. The LED lighting pattern slows down over time, and eventually just one LED remains lit. You also add a speaker to mimic the sound of a roulette wheel in this second part.

 The circuit in Project 13 (three-way traffic light) is similar to the roulette circuit in this project. If you intend to tackle Project 13 after you've built your roulette circuit, I recommend keeping the roulette circuit set up. You'll save a lot of time by removing just a few components and reusing the rest of the roulette circuit.

Part 1: Light Chaser Circuit

 The light chaser circuit involves some rather hairy wiring. It's all too easy to get your wires crossed as you build this circuit, so please take your time and be careful when plugging jumper wires and components into your breadboard. Troubleshooting this circuit is not fun, so it's best to take the extra time and care to set up the circuit right the first time.

Part 1 is rather long (Part 2 is much shorter), so if you have to use the bathroom, now's the time to go.

Build the light chaser

Follow these steps to build your light chaser circuit:

1. Double-check your solderless breadboard (see Figure 12-7).

   a. Make sure that the two positive power rails are connected and the two negative power rails are connected.

   b. Check that your power switch and jumper-wire connections are properly installed and that the switch is in the off position.

   c. Verify that the leads from your battery clip are snugly plugged into the correct contact holes in your breadboard.

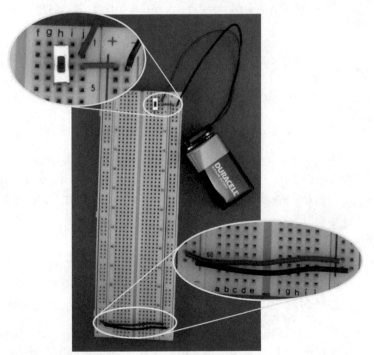

Figure 12-7

2. Insert the 555 timer chip into the breadboard.

   a. Orient the 555 timer IC with the dimple (clocking mark) in the upper-left corner (see Figure 12-8, left). I added the corner pin labels to the figure.

Figure 12-8

b. Place the chip on top of holes **45–48e** (left side of chip) and **45–48f** (right side of chip), so that you are lining up the corner pins like this: pin 1 into hole **45e**, pin 4 into hole **48e**, pin 5 into hole **48f**, and pin 8 into hole **45f**.

c. Press down slowly on the body of the chip until the pins are snugly inserted into the contact holes. (See Figure 12-8, right.) Make sure that the underside of the chip is lying flat on the breadboard surface.

3. Insert a 5/16-inch (minimum) jumper wire into the breadboard.

   Plug one end of the jumper wire into hole **45a** and the other end of the jumper wire into the negative power rail to the left of row **45**. (See the orange jumper wire in Figure 12-9.)

4. Insert the 0.1 μF capacitor into the breadboard.

   a. Make sure you are using the correct capacitor. The 0.1 μF capacitor you insert in this step is a nonpolarized film capacitor, and it is larger than the 0.01 μF nonpolarized film capacitor you insert in a later step.

   b. Bend and trim the capacitor leads so that each lead is about 3/8-inch long below the bend.

   c. Plug one lead (either one) into hole **46a** and the other lead into the negative power rail to the left of row **46.** (See Figure 12-10.) Because this capacitor is nonpolarized, you can orient it either way in the circuit.

Figure 12-9

Figure 12-10

5. Insert a 1-inch (minimum) jumper wire into the breadboard.

   This jumper wire connects pins 2 and 6 on the 555 timer IC together. Plug one end of the jumper wire into hole **46d** and the other end of the jumper wire into hole **47g**. (See Figure 12-11.)

6. Insert a 3/8-inch (minimum) jumper wire into the breadboard.

   Plug one end of the jumper wire into hole **48a** and the other end of the jumper wire into the positive power rail to the left of row **48**. (See the yellow jumper wire to the left of the chip in Figure 12-12.)

Figure 12-11

Figure 12-12

7. Insert the 0.01 µF capacitor into the breadboard.

   a. Bend and trim the capacitor leads so that each lead is about 3/8-inch long below the bend.

b. Plug one lead of this nonpolarized capacitor into hole **48j** and the other lead into the negative power rail to the right of row **48.** (See Figure 12-13.)

8. Insert a 470 kΩ resistor (yellow-violet-yellow) into the breadboard.

   a. Bend and trim the resistor leads so that each lead is about 1/4-inch long below the bend.

   b. Plug one lead into hole **46i** and the other lead into the positive power rail to the right of row **46,** as shown in Figure 12-14.

Figure 12-13

Figure 12-14

9. Insert a 47 kΩ resistor (yellow-violet-orange) into the breadboard.

   a. Bend one of the resistor's leads so that it is parallel to the other lead, as shown in Figure 12-15, left.

   b. Trim both leads so that each lead extends about 1/4-inch beyond the body of the resistor (see Figure 12-15, center).

   c. Plug one lead into hole **46h** and the other lead into hole **47h,** as shown in Figure 12-15, right.

Figure 12-15

10. Insert a 5/16-inch (minimum) jumper wire into the breadboard.

   Plug one end of the jumper wire into hole *45j* and the other end of the jumper wire into the positive power rail to the right of row *45*. (See the orange jumper wire to the right of the chip in Figure 12-16.)

11. Insert five 5/16-inch (minimum) jumper wires into the breadboard, as shown in Figure 12-17.

   a. Plug the first jumper wire into holes *27e* and *27f*.

   b. Plug the second jumper wire into holes *28e* and *28f*.

   c. Plug the third jumper wire into holes *29e* and *29f*.

   d. Plug the fourth jumper wire into hole *30j* and the positive power rail to the right of row *30*.

   e. Plug the fifth jumper wire into hole *37a* and the negative power rail to the left of row *37*.

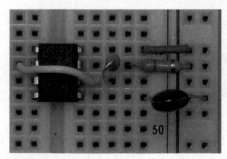

Figure 12-16

Figure 12-17

12. Insert two 3/8-inch (minimum) jumper wires into the breadboard. (See the yellow jumper wires in Figure 12-18.)

    a. Plug the first jumper wire into hole **31j** and the negative power rail to the right of row **31.**

    b. Plug the second jumper wire into hole **33j** and the negative power rail to the right of row **33.**

13. Insert three 3/4-inch (minimum) jumper wires into the breadboard. (See the brown jumper wires in Figure 12-19.)

    a. Plug the first jumper wire into holes **27i** and **35i.**

    b. Plug the second jumper wire into holes **28h** and **36h.**

    c. Plug the third jumper wire into holes **29g** and **37g.**

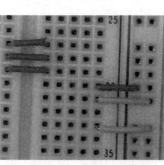 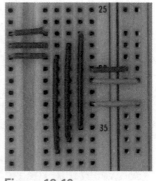

Figure 12-18   Figure 12-19

14. Insert nine 3/16-inch (minimum) jumper wires into the breadboard. (See the red jumper wires in Figure 12-20.)

    a. Plug the first jumper wire into holes **7i** and **9i.**

    b. Plug the second jumper wire into holes **9j** and **11j.**

    c. Plug the third jumper wire into holes **11i** and **13i.**

    d. Plug the fourth jumper wire into holes **13j** and **15j.**

    e. Plug the fifth jumper wire into holes **15i** and **17i.**

f. Plug the sixth jumper wire into holes
   17j and *19j*.

g. Plug the seventh jumper wire into holes
   19i and *21i*.

h. Plug the eighth jumper wire into holes
   21j and *23j*.

i. Plug the ninth jumper wire into holes
   23i and *25i*.

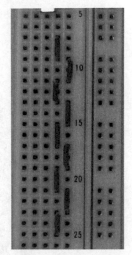

15. Insert the 330 Ω resistor (orange-orange-
    brown) into the breadboard.

    Bend and trim the resistor leads. Then, plug
    one lead into hole *25j* and the other lead
    into the negative power rail to the right of row *25,* as shown in
    Figure 12-21.

Figure 12-20

16. Insert a 3/16-inch (minimum) jumper wire into the breadboard.

    Plug the jumper wire into holes *25d* and *27d.* (See the red wire
    in Figure 12-22.)

Figure 12-21

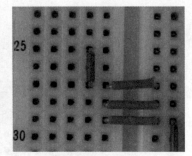

Figure 12-22

17. Insert a 1 1/4-inch (minimum) jumper wire into the
    breadboard.

    Plug the jumper wire into holes *15c* and *28c.* (See the yellow
    wire in Figure 12-23.)

18. Insert a 9/16-inch (minimum) jumper wire into the breadboard.

    Plug the jumper wire into holes **23b** and **29b.** (See the blue wire in Figure 12-24.)

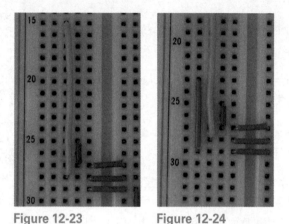

Figure 12-23   Figure 12-24

19. Insert a 1 3/8-inch (minimum) jumper wire into the breadboard.

    Plug the jumper wire into holes **21a** and **35a.** (See the white wire in Figure 12-25.)

20. Insert a 1 1/2-inch (minimum) jumper wire into the breadboard.

    Plug the jumper wire into holes **19b** and **34b.** (See the red wire indicated by the arrows in Figure 12-26.)

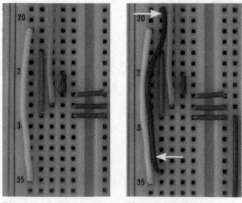

Figure 12-25   Figure 12-26

21. Insert a 1 1/4-inch jumper wire into the breadboard.

    Plug the jumper wire into holes **17d** and **30d.** (See the red wire indicated by the arrows in Figure 12-27.)

22. Insert a 2 1/4-inch jumper wire into the breadboard.

    Plug the jumper wire into holes **11c** and **33c.** (See the red wire indicated by the arrows in Figure 12-28.)

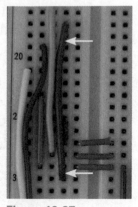

Figure 12-27

23. Insert a 2 1/4-inch jumper wire into the breadboard.

    Plug the jumper wire into holes **13a** and **36a.** (See the orange wire indicated by the arrows in Figure 12-29.)

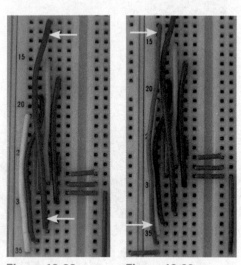

Figure 12-28   Figure 12-29

24. Insert a 2 1/4-inch jumper wire into the breadboard. (It's getting a little hairy now, isn't it?)

    Plug the jumper wire into holes **9b** and **31b.** (See the orange wire indicated by the arrows in Figure 12-30.)

25. Insert a 2 1/2-inch (minimum) jumper wire into the breadboard. (Last one!)

Plug the jumper wire into holes **7b** and **32b.** (See the orange wire indicated by the arrows in Figure 12-31.)

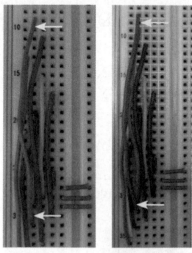

Figure 12-30   **Figure 12-31**

26. Insert the ten LEDs into the breadboard.

I recommend that you do *not* trim the LED leads for this project. It's easier to build the circuit with the LEDs sticking up above the breadboard. Plus the light chaser just looks better with the LEDs sticking up!

Make sure you know which side of each LED is the anode and which is the cathode. (See Figure 12-32.)

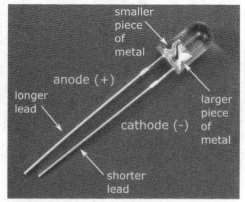

Figure 12-32

TIP

As you follow the next steps to insert the LEDs, note that each of the ten LEDs is oriented the same way: straddling the center ditch of the breadboard, with the anode (positive side, longer lead, smaller piece of metal inside the case) inserted into a hole in column *e,* and the cathode (negative side, shorter lead, larger piece of metal inside the case) inserted into a hole in column *f.*

Here are the details of where to insert the LEDs (see Figure 12-33):

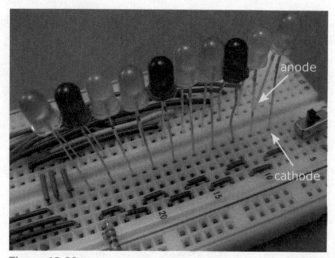

Figure 12-33

a. Plug the anode of the first LED (let's call it LED1) into hole *7e* and the cathode into hole *7f.* (You may choose any of your ten LEDs.)

b. Plug the anode of LED2 into hole *9e* and the cathode into hole *9f.*

c. Plug the anode of LED3 into hole *11e* and the cathode into hole *11f.*

d. Plug the anode of LED4 into hole *13e* and the cathode into hole *13f.*

e. Plug the anode of LED5 into hole *15e* and the cathode into hole *15f.*

f. Plug the anode of LED6 into hole *17e* and the cathode into hole *17f.*

g. Plug the anode of LED7 into hole *19e* and the cathode into hole *19f.*

h. Plug the anode of LED8 into hole *21e* and the cathode into hole *21f.*

i. Plug the anode of LED9 into hole *23e* and the cathode into hole *23f.*

j. Plug the anode of LED10 into hole *25e* and the cathode into hole *25f.*

27. Insert the 10 µF electrolytic capacitor into the breadboard.

a. Clip the leads so that they are both the same length (about 1/2-inch long).

b. Insert the negative side (indicated by a black stripe or minus sign) into the negative power rail to the left of row *3.* Insert the positive side into the positive power rail to the left of row *3.* (See Figure 12-34.)

28. Insert a 2-inch (minimum) jumper wire into the breadboard.

Plug one end of the wire into hole *32j* and the other end into hole *47c.* If you'd like a neater circuit, use your fingers to press the wire down against the surface of the breadboard and shift the wire towards the right side of the breadboard, as shown in the figure. (See the orange wire indicated by the arrows in Figure 12-35.)

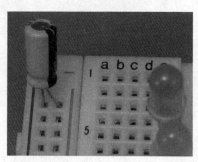

Figure 12-34

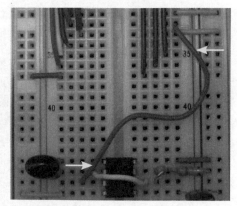

Figure 12-35

29. Insert the 4017 decade counter IC into the breadboard.

Because this CMOS chip is sensitive to static discharge, you insert it last so you reduce the risk of zapping the chip as you build your circuit. If you have an antistatic wrist strap, make sure you put it on and connect it to an earth ground connection.

a. If the pins are angled outward, give them a squeeze to make them as straight as possible. (See Figure 12-36.)

b. Orient the 4017 decade counter IC with the notch (clocking mark) on the upper edge,

Figure 12-36

as shown for the two 4017 decade counters (from different manufacturers) in Figure 12-37. (I added corner pin labels to the figure.) Some chips also have a dimple in the upper-left corner (see Figure 12-37, left). But be careful! Some chips have a dimple on the lower edge (see Figure 12-37, right). The notch in the plastic case is what to look for to determine which pin is pin 1.

c. Place the chip on top of holes **30–37e** (left side of chip) and **30–37f** (right side of chip), so that you are lining up the corner pins like this: pin 1 into hole **30e**, pin 8 into hole **37e**, pin 9 into hole **37f**, and pin 16 into hole **30f**.

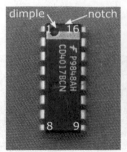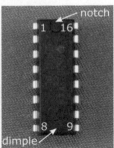

Figure 12-37

d. Press down slowly on the body of the chip, applying even pressure across the top of the chip, to insert the pins into the contact holes. As you press down, look at all the pins to make sure they are going into the holes. If any pin is not going in, stop pressing down, gently guide the pin into the hole, and then press down on the chip again until the pins are snugly inserted. (See Figure 12-38.)

Figure 12-38

Figure 12-39 shows the completed light chaser circuit (except for the battery and the power rail connections), turned on its side so that the LEDs light from left to right.

Double-check all your connections. Make sure that both ICs are oriented correctly, with the notch of the 4017 chip in the upper-left corner and the dimple of the 555 timer IC in the upper-left corner. Verify that the 10 μF electrolytic capacitor is inserted properly, with the negative side in the negative power rail and the positive side in the positive power rail. Check that each LED is inserted correctly, with the anode (longer lead) in column *e* and the cathode (shorter lead) in column *f*.

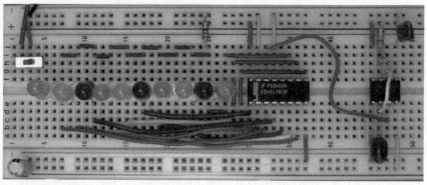

Figure 12-39

Do your best to check all the crazy jumper-wire connections. After you check your circuit, it's time to chase some lights!

Operate your light chaser

Turn on the power switch. Do the LEDs light up one at a time, as if they are chasing one another? You should see the LEDs light up in order from LED1 (row 7) to LED10 (row 25), and the pattern should repeat itself.

If your light chaser is working properly, congratulations! If not, read on!

Troubleshooting the light chaser circuit

If none of the LEDs is lighting, turn off the power switch and check all your connections again. Here are some things to look for:

✔ Is your battery fresh? Are its leads connected to the board properly? Is the power switch inserted firmly into the correct holes in the breadboard?

✔ Is the wire connecting the left and right positive power rails at the bottom of your breadboard inserted firmly into the breadboard? How about the wire connecting the left and right negative power rails?

✔ Are both ICs (the 555 timer and the 4017 decade counter) oriented properly? Are any of the pins bent or not inserted

properly into the contact holes? Are the chips inserted firmly
in the correct contact holes?

✔ Is the 10 μF capacitor inserted firmly into the positive and
negative power rails at the top-left corner of your breadboard?
Is the negative side of the capacitor inserted into the negative
power rail?

✔ Is pin 16 of the 4017 IC connected (through a jumper wire) to
the positive power rail? Are pins 8, 13, and 15 connected
(through jumper wires) to the negative power rail?

✔ Is pin 8 of the 555 timer IC connected (through a jumper wire)
to the positive power rail? Is pin 1 connected to the negative
power rail?

✔ Is the 47 kΩ resistor connected between pins 6 and 7 of the
555 timer? Is the 470 kΩ resistor connected between pin 7 of
the 555 timer and the positive power rail?

✔ Is the cathode (negative side) of each LED connected to a
short red jumper wire? Is LED10 (the one closest to the 4017
IC) connected to both a short red jumper wire and the 330 Ω
resistor? Is the other side of the 330 Ω resistor connected to
the negative power rail?

✔ Is there a jumper wire connecting pin 3 of the 555 timer IC to
pin 14 of the 4017 IC?

✔ Are all jumper wires inserted firmly into the correct contact
holes?

If some, but not all, of the LEDs are lighting, or the LEDs are lighting but not in the correct order, focus your troubleshooting on
the LEDs and the jumper wires that connect to the LEDs. Here are
some things to look for:

✔ Are neighboring LEDs spaced two rows apart? Are the LEDs
inserted into columns *e* and *f* of the odd rows starting with
row *7* and ending with row *25?*

✔ Are all the LED leads inserted firmly into the contact holes?

✔ Is each of the LEDs oriented correctly, with its anode inserted in a hole in column *e* and its cathode inserted in a hole in column *f*?

✔ Look at the little red jumper wires to the right of the LEDs. Is one side of each jumper wire connected in the same row as one side of its neighboring jumper wire? Is the last (lowest) jumper wire connected in row **25** to one side of the 330 Ω resistor? Is the other side of the 330 Ω resistor connected to the negative power rail?

✔ Look at the jumper wires to the left of the LEDs. Are they all inserted firmly into the correct contact holes? (I know, it's hard to tell!)

If you still can't figure out the source of your problem, ask a friend or family member to assist you. Sometimes having another pair of eyes triple-check the connections is what you need to get your circuit working.

Part 2: The Roulette Wheel

In this part, you move one resistor and add three components to change the timing of the light chaser so that the circuit behaves like a roulette wheel. Then you have the option of adding a potentiometer to improve the randomness of the roulette outcome. Finally, you add a capacitor and a speaker for sound effects.

Change the timing

Leave your light chaser circuit in place, but turn off the power switch. Then follow these steps to alter the timing of the 555 timer output to transform your light chaser circuit into a roulette (guess-the-number) game.

1. Relocate the 470 kΩ resistor in your breadboard.

If the 0.01 µF capacitor (in hole **48j** and the negative power rail) is in your way as you relocate the 470 kΩ resistor, just take the capacitor out until you finish relocating the resistor, and then plug the capacitor back in.

a. Remove the 470 kΩ resistor from hole **46i** and the positive power rail. Your needle-nose pliers may help make removal easier. (See Figure 12-40, left.)

b. Insert the 470 kΩ resistor into holes **46i** and **50i.** (See Figure 12-40, right.)

Figure 12-40

2. Insert a 5/16-inch (minimum) jumper wire into the breadboard.

Plug one end of the jumper wire into hole **50j** and the other end of the jumper wire into hole **53j**. (See the lower orange jumper wire in Figure 12-41.)

3. Insert the pushbutton switch into the breadboard.

a. Orient the switch so that it straddles the center ditch in the breadboard from rows **53** to **55**, and its pins are sitting on top of holes **53e**, **53f**, **55e**, and **55f**, as shown in Figure 12-42. Note that the switch's pins are curved out and to the left or right when you have the switch oriented properly. (If the pins are curved out toward the top and bottom of the breadboard, you won't be able to insert the switch across the center ditch in the breadboard.) You can still orient the switch right-side-up or upside-down — it doesn't matter which way you do it.

Figure 12-41

Figure 12-42

b. Insert the four switch pins firmly into holes *53e*, *53f*, *55e*, and *55f*. I find the best way to insert the switch is to place my thumbnails on either side of the switch and push down evenly on the body of the switch. (See Figure 12-43.)

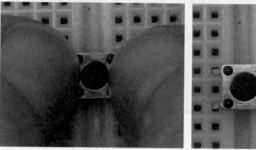

Figure 12-43

c. If the switch isn't going in smoothly, remove it and take a look at its pins. If any pins are bent, use your needle-nose pliers to bend the pin (or pins) back into shape. Then, reinsert the switch into the breadboard.

4. Insert the 100 Ω resistor (brown-black-brown) into the breadboard.

Bend and trim the resistor leads. Then, plug one lead into hole *55a* and the other lead into the positive power rail to the left of row *55,* as shown in Figure 12-44.

5. Insert the 22 µF electrolytic capacitor into the breadboard.

Figure 12-44

a. Bend one of the capacitor's leads so that it is parallel to the other lead, as shown in Figure 12-45, left.

b. Trim both leads so that each lead extends about 1/2-inch beyond the body of the capacitor (see Figure 12-45, center).

Figure 12-45

c. Insert the negative side (indicated by a black stripe or negative sign) into the negative power rail to the left of row **53.** Insert the positive side into hole **53a.** (See Figure 12-45, right.)

Figure 12-46 shows the altered section of your circuit. Double-check these new connections. When you think you're ready, it's time to give your roulette circuit a whirl!

Figure 12-46

Play the guess-the-number game

Turn on the power switch. Just one of the LEDs should light. Now press and release the pushbutton switch. Do the LEDs chase each other as before? Does the pace of the chase slow down over time? (It should.) After about 15 seconds, is just one LED lit? If so, press the pushbutton switch again and try to guess which LED will remain lit.

If the circuit isn't working — but the light chaser from Part 1 was working — go back through the steps in Part 2 and triple-check your connections.

Add a potentiometer (optional)

The game is more fun if the outcome of the roulette wheel is unpredictable. With your roulette circuit, you may find that there's a pattern to which LED stays lit on each successive play of the game. For instance, if LED2 remained lit after one round of the game, the next two rounds may result in LED4 and then LED6 remaining lit. Players may catch on to such a pattern.

To increase the randomness of the outcome, you need to make one simple change: Replace the jumper wire in holes **50j** and **53j** with a 100 kΩ potentiometer (see Figure 12-47). Then (with the power switch on again) each time you start a new game, before you press the pushbutton switch, turn the knob of the potentiometer a bit. This action changes the timing of the 555 timer output slightly and ensures a more random outcome than before.

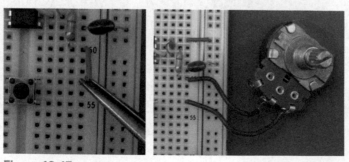

Figure 12-47

Add sound effects

Now for the most fun part of this project: the sound effects. You need a 4.7 µF electrolytic capacitor and a speaker with leads and alligator clips attached. (Refer to Project 10 for details on connecting lead wires and alligator clips to your speaker.)

Turn off the power switch and follow these steps to add sound effects:

1. Insert the 4.7 µF electrolytic capacitor into the breadboard, as shown in Figure 12-48.

   Plug the negative side (identified by a minus sign or black stripe) into hole *42b* and the positive (unlabeled) side into hole *47b*.

2. Insert the speaker into the breadboard, as shown in Figure 12-49.

   Plug one of the leads (either one) into hole *42a* and the other lead into any hole in the negative power rail on the left (I used the hole to the left of row *39.*)

Figure 12-48

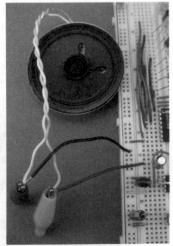

Figure 12-49

Now turn on the power switch and press the pushbutton switch. Do you hear clicking at the same rate as the lighting of the LEDs? Does it sound like a real roulette wheel? Pretty cool, isn't it?

Schematics and Circuit Explanation

In this section, I show you the schematic for the light chaser and a partial schematic for the roulette wheel (just the part of the light chaser that was altered to create the wheel). Then I explain how these circuits work. There will not be a quiz on this material, so feel free to skip this section and move on to another project if you want.

Light chaser

Figure 12-50 shows the schematic for Part 1 of this project, the light chaser circuit, with some helpful (I hope) labels.

On the left side of the schematic is the 555 timer. The 470 kΩ resistor, 47 kΩ resistor, and 0.1 μF capacitor to the left of the 555 timer control the timing of the output voltage on pin 3. That output voltage is used to trigger the 4017 decade counter, so pin 3 of the 555 timer is connected to pin 14 (trigger input) of the 4017 IC.

On the right side of the schematic is the 4017 decade counter. Its ten counting outputs are all connected to LEDs. The cathodes of the LEDs are connected together and to one side of the 330 Ω resistor. That 330 Ω resistor limits the current that passes through each LED. (Note that you need only one current-limiting resistor for the LEDs because only one LED is lit at any time.) The other four pins (8, 13, 15, and 16) are connected to either the positive or the negative side of the battery.

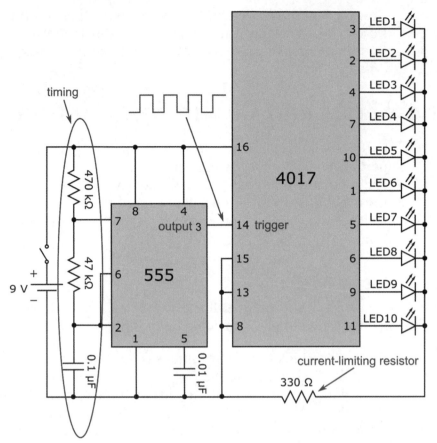

Figure 12-50

Roulette wheel

The roulette wheel circuit is nearly the same as the light chaser circuit. The only differences are in the left side of the circuit, with the 555 timer and the components that control the timing.

Figure 12-51 shows just the left side of the schematic for the roulette wheel circuit with sound effects, including the Part 2 alterations except for the optional potentiometer. The 9 V battery is shown on the right side of the schematic.

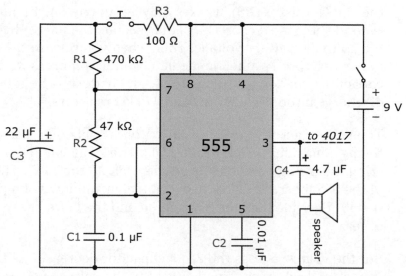

Figure 12-51

Note that the 470 kΩ resistor is not connected directly to the positive side of the battery, as it is in the light chaser circuit. Instead, the 470 kΩ resistor is connected to the pushbutton switch and to the 22 µF capacitor. The other side of the pushbutton switch is connected to the positive side of the battery through the 100 Ω resistor.

When the power switch is turned on, but before the pushbutton switch is pressed, the 555 timer chip is powered up (through pins 1 and 4). However, the timing components — the 470 kΩ resistor (R1), the 47 kΩ resistor (R2), and the 0.1 µF capacitor (C1) — aren't doing their timing job because no power is applied to them. As a result, just one LED is lit, and it remains lit because there is no variation in the 4017 trigger input (which comes from the 555 timer output).

Note that the 22 µF capacitor (C3) is connected across the three timing components. This capacitor is the key to the new timing of the roulette wheel. When you press the pushbutton switch, this 22 µF capacitor charges up quickly to the battery voltage through the 100 Ω resistor (R3). It takes only about one one-hundredth of a second (because $5 \times R3 \times C3 = 0.011$) second to charge that capacitor up to the battery voltage. Then when you release the pushbutton switch (pretty much immediately after you press it), the 22 μF capacitor is no longer connected to the battery — so it begins to discharge through the 47 kΩ and 470 kΩ resistors.

The voltage across the 22 μF capacitor is applied across the 555 timing components (R1, R2, and C1). The 22 μF capacitor is powering the timing components so they can do their job. The output of the 555 timer oscillates between a high and low voltage — so the 4017 decade counter is triggered and the LEDs chase each other.

But the voltage across the 22 μF capacitor decreases as that capacitor discharges. The decrease in the voltage powering the timing components (R1, R2, and C1) causes the timing to slow down. As the voltage decreases, the oscillation rate of the output voltage on pin 3 of the 555 timer decreases. (The details of why the rate decreases involve a more technical explanation of how a 555 timer works.) Because the output of the 555 timer (pin 3) is connected to the trigger input of the 4017 decade counter (pin 14), the rate of the 4017 counting process decreases as the oscillation rate of the 555 timer decreases. A slower count means a slower LED chase — so you see the rate of the LED lighting pattern slow down.

Eventually, the 22 μF capacitor discharges so much that the voltage across the 555 timing components is too low to produce an oscillating output voltage on pin 3. At that point, the 4017 is no longer triggered, and whichever LED is lit at that time — the winning LED — stays lit.

Reward yourself

If you followed the schematics and the explanation of how the roulette wheel works, go tell a grownup. Then ask that grownup to take you out for ice cream, or zip lining, or something else you really enjoy. You deserve a reward!

Three-Way Traffic Light

Project 4 shows you how to use a single switch to control two LEDs, so that when one LED is on, the other is off, and vice versa. If you use a red and a green LED, you can use that circuit as a two-way manual traffic light.

In this project, you use two integrated circuits (ICs) — a 555 timer and a 4017 decade counter — to automate the on/off switching and timing of three LEDs. If you use a red, yellow, and green LED, you can use this circuit as a three-way automated traffic light.

In addition to the LEDs and the two ICs, you need a few resistors and capacitors, a bunch of jumper wires, and a handful of plain, ordinary diodes — the kind that don't emit light.

This circuit is similar to the roulette circuit in Project 12, so if you have that circuit set up on your breadboard, don't take it apart just yet!

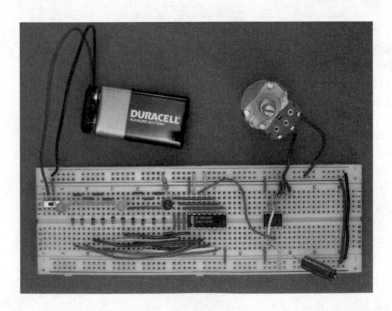

Meet the 1N4148 (or 1N914) Diode

Diodes do a simple but important job: They allow current to flow in just one direction. In many projects in this book (including this project), you use a special kind of diode — a light-emitting diode, or LED — for the purpose of, well, lighting up. You have to be careful to orient the LED the correct way, or current won't flow at all.

In this project, you use another kind of diode to perform the important task of preventing current from flowing the wrong way in your circuit. The type of diode you use in this project — a 1N4148 (or 1N914) diode — doesn't light up. It just does its job as a one-way valve for current without calling attention to itself.

Pictured in Figure 13-1, the 1N4148 diode is a signal diode. A *signal diode* is designed to handle relatively small currents and voltages, such as the ones you use in the projects in this book. Diodes that can handle large current and voltages are known as *power diodes*, but you won't need to use them.

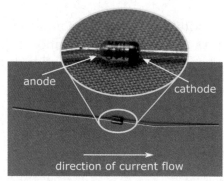

Figure 13-1

The black band at one end of the 1N4148 diode indicates the cathode (negative side). Current flows from the anode (positive side) to the cathode, but not the other way. (Some types of diodes have a silver band instead of a black band to indicate the cathode.)

The 1N914 diode is considered equivalent to the 1N4148 diode, so either type is fine. You use ten of these little diodes in this project to prevent current from flowing *into* the ten *outputs* of a 4017 decade counter integrated circuit (IC). Each diode allows current to flow out of but not into the 4017 chip. You find out why you need to use these diodes for this project later.

Reuse and Save Time

If you built the roulette circuit in Project 12 and still have it set up, you can reuse quite a bit of it to get a head start on the three-way traffic light. By removing certain components and jumper wires, you can leave the reusable sections of your roulette circuit in place — and skip through many of the circuit-building steps in this project.

Here are the parts to remove from your roulette circuit:

✔ All ten LEDs (you need three LEDs for this project, but they go in different contact holes than those in the roulette circuit)

✔ All four resistors (but hold on to the 330 Ω and 100 Ω resistors for use in different places in this project)

✔ The speaker

✔ The pushbutton switch

✔ The 4.7 µF capacitor (holes *42b* and *47b*)

✔ The 10 µF capacitor (top row of positive and negative power rail on the left)

✔ The 0.1 µF capacitor (hole *46a* and the negative power rail to the left of row *46*)

✔ The 22 µF capacitor (hole *53a* and the negative power rail to the left of row *53*)

✔ The nine 3/16-inch jumper wires in rows *7–25,* columns *i* and *j* (but hold on to seven of them for this project)

✔ The 5/16-inch jumper wire in holes *50j* and *53j* (keep this jumper for this project)

Leave the rest of the roulette circuit in place. For this project, you reuse most of the 555 timer IC section of the roulette circuit (all but the timing components), and you reuse the 4017 decade counter IC and all those spaghetti-like jumper wires that make connections to the 4017's pins.

If you built the roulette circuit but have taken it apart already, you're still ahead of the game! You can reuse many of the roulette circuit components — and the jumper wires.

Get Your Parts Ready

In the parts list that follows, the lengths of jumper wires are guidelines for preparing your jumper wires. You can always trim a wire a bit more if it's much too long and getting in the way of operating your circuit, or make a new wire if you've cut a jumper wire too short. In other words, don't tear your hair out worrying about the exact lengths of your jumper wires.

Collect all the parts in this list (see Figure 13-2):

✔ Solderless breadboard, prepared with

 • 9-volt battery with battery clip

 • Power switch and jumper wire

 • Power rail jumper-wire connections

✔ One LM555 timer IC

✔ One CMOS 4017 decade counter IC

✔ Ten 1N4148 (or 1N914) diodes

✔ Three LEDs (clear or diffused, 3 mm or 5 mm, each LED can be any color; I used 5mm diffused LEDs in red, yellow, and green)

✔ Capacitors:

- One 0.01 µF film (nonpolarized) capacitor

- One 47 µF electrolytic (polarized) capacitor

- Optional: One 100 µF electrolytic (polarized) capacitor

✔ Resistors:

- One 100 Ω resistor (brown-black-brown)

- One 330 Ω resistor (orange-orange-brown)

- One 22 kΩ resistor (red-red-orange)

✔ One 100 kΩ potentiometer (preferably linear taper) with attached leads

✔ Jumper wires:

- Eight 3/16-inch (minimum) jumper wires

- Seven 5/16-inch (minimum) jumper wires

- Three 3/8-inch (minimum) jumper wires

- One 9/16-inch (minimum) jumper wire

- Four 3/4-inch (minimum) jumper wires

- Two 1-inch (minimum) jumper wires

- Two 1 1/4-inch (minimum) jumper wires

- One 1 3/8-inch (minimum) jumper wire

- One 1 1/2-inch (minimum) jumper wire

- One 2-inch (minimum) jumper wire

- Three 2 1/4-inch (minimum) jumper wires

- One 2 1/2-inch (minimum) jumper wire

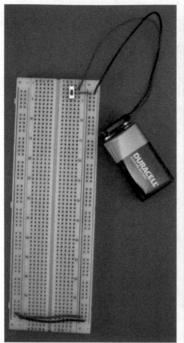
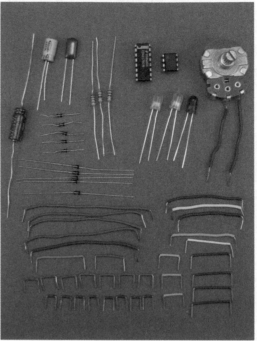

Figure 13-2

TIP

I highly recommend that you use an antistatic wrist strap while you are building your circuit to avoid accidentally zapping the static-sensitive 4017 chip. (Project 12 explains what an antistatic wrist strap is and why it's recommended.)

You need your wire cutters for trimming leads and your needle-nose pliers for bending leads, inserting and removing components, and (possibly) straightening out bent IC pins. If you need to make some jumper wires, you also need your wire strippers.

Build the Three-Way Traffic Light

Follow these steps to build your three-way traffic light circuit:

1. Double-check your solderless breadboard (see Figure 13-3).

   a. Make sure that the two positive power rails are connected and the two negative power rails are connected.

b. Check that your power switch and jumper-wire connections are properly installed and that the switch is in the off position.

c. Verify that the leads from your battery clip are snugly plugged into the correct contact holes in your breadboard.

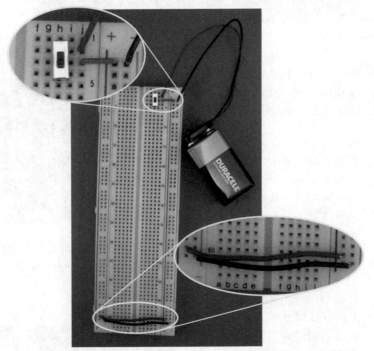

Figure 13-3

2. Insert the 555 timer chip into the breadboard.

a. Orient the 555 timer IC with the dimple (clocking mark) in the upper-left corner (see Figure 13-4, left).

b. Place the chip on top of holes **45–48e** (left side of chip) and **45–48f** (right side of chip), so that you are lining up the corner pins like this: pin 1 into hole **45e**, pin 4 into hole **48e**, pin 5 into hole **48f**, and pin 8 into hole **45f**.

c. Press down slowly on the body of the chip until the pins are snugly inserted into the contact holes. (See Figure 13-4, right.)

Figure 13-4

3. Insert a 5/16-inch (minimum) jumper wire into the breadboard.

   Plug one end into hole **45a** and the other end into the negative power rail to the left of row **45**. (See the orange jumper wire in Figure 13-5.)

Figure 13-5

4. Insert the 47 µF electrolytic capacitor into the breadboard.

   Trim the capacitor leads if you'd like a neater circuit (I didn't). Then plug the negative lead (indicated by a stripe, an arrow, or a minus sign) into the negative power rail on the left (any hole) and the positive (unlabeled) lead into hole **46b**. (See Figure 13-6.)

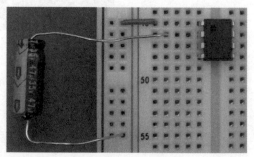

Figure 13-6

5. Insert a 1-inch (minimum) jumper wire into the breadboard.

   This jumper wire connects pins 2 and 6 on the 555 timer IC. Plug one end of the jumper wire into hole **46d** and the other end of the jumper wire into hole **47g**. (See Figure 13-7.)

6. Insert a 3/8-inch (minimum) jumper wire into the breadboard.

   Plug one end of the jumper wire into hole **48a** and the other end of the jumper wire into the positive power rail to the left of row **48**. (See the yellow jumper wire to the left of the chip in Figure 13-8.)

Figure 13-7   Figure 13-8

7. Insert the 0.01 µF film capacitor into the breadboard.

   a. Bend and trim the capacitor leads so that each lead is about 3/8-inch long below the bend.

   b. Plug one lead of this nonpolarized capacitor into hole **48j** and the other lead into the negative power rail to the right of row **48**. (See Figure 13-9.)

8. Insert a 100 Ω resistor (brown-black-brown) into the breadboard.

   a. Bend and trim the resistor leads so that each lead is about 1/4-inch long below the bend.

   b. Plug one lead into hole **46i** and the other lead into hole **50i**, as shown in Figure 13-10.

Figure 13-9

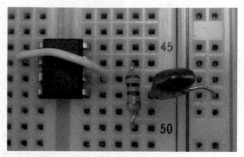

Figure 13-10

9. Insert a 100 kΩ potentiometer into the breadboard, as shown in Figure 13-11.

Plug one of its attached leads into hole **50j** and the other lead into the positive power rail on the right (I used the hole to the right of row **53**).

Figure 13-11

10. Insert a 22 kΩ resistor (red-red-orange) into the breadboard.

 a. Bend one of the resistor's leads so that it is parallel to the other lead, as shown in Figure 13-12, left.

 b. Trim both leads so that each lead extends about 1/4-inch beyond the body of the resistor. (See Figure 13-12, center.)

 c. Plug one lead into hole **46h** and the other lead into hole **47h**, as shown in Figure 13-12, right.

11. Insert a 5/16-inch (minimum) jumper wire into the breadboard.

Plug one end of the jumper wire into hole **45j** and the other end of the jumper wire into the positive power rail to the right of row **45**. (See the orange jumper wire to the right of the chip in Figure 13-13.)

Figure 13-12

12. Insert five 5/16-inch (minimum) jumper wires into the breadboard. (See the orange wires in Figure 13-14.)

a. Plug the first jumper wire into holes **27e** and **27f**.

b. Plug the second jumper wire into holes **28e** and **28f**.

c. Plug the third jumper wire into holes **29e** and **29f**.

d. Plug the fourth jumper wire into hole **30j** and the positive power rail to the right of row **30**.

e. Plug the fifth jumper wire into hole **37a** and the negative power rail to the left of row **37**.

Figure 13-13

Figure 13-14

13. Insert two 3/8-inch (minimum) jumper wires into the breadboard. (See the yellow jumper wires in Figure 13-15.)

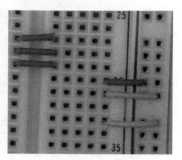

   a. Plug the first jumper wire into hole **31j** and the negative power rail to the right of row **31**.

   b. Plug the second jumper wire into hole **33j** and the negative power rail to the right of row **33**.

Figure 13-15

14. Insert four 3/4-inch (minimum) jumper wires into the breadboard. (See the brown jumper wires in Figure 13-16.)

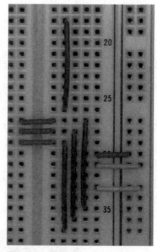

   a. Plug the first jumper wire into holes **18g** and **26g**.

   b. Plug the second jumper wire into holes **27i** and **35i**.

   c. Plug the third jumper wire into holes **28h** and **36h**.

   d. Plug the fourth jumper wire into holes **29g** and **37g**.

Figure 13-16

15. Insert a 1-inch (minimum) jumper wire into the breadboard. (See the grey jumper wire in Figure 13-17.)

   Plug the jumper wire into holes **8h** and **18h**.

16. Insert seven 3/16-inch (minimum) jumper wires into the breadboard. (See the red jumper wires in Figure 13-18.)

   a. Plug the first jumper wire into holes **7j** and **9j**.

   b. Plug the second jumper wire into holes **9i** and **11i**.

c. Plug the third jumper wire into holes *11j* and *13j.*

d. Plug the fourth jumper wire into holes *13i* and *15i.*

e. Plug the fifth jumper wire into holes *19j* and *21j.*

f. Plug the sixth jumper wire into holes *21i* and *23i.*

g. Plug the seventh jumper wire into holes *23j* and *25j.*

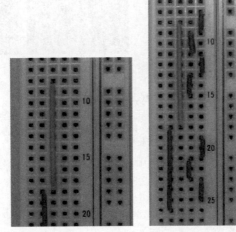

Figure 13-17   Figure 13-18

17. Insert the 330 Ω resistor
    (orange-orange-brown) into
    the breadboard.

    Bend and trim the resistor
    leads. Then, plug one lead into
    hole *26j* and the other lead
    into the negative power rail to
    the right of row *25,* as shown
    in Figure 13-19.

Figure 13-19

18. Insert ten jumper wires (of various minimum lengths) into the breadboard.

    Figure 13-20, left, shows the first six of these jumper wires. Figure 13-20, right, shows all ten jumper wires. For detailed photos of each substep, refer to Figures 12–22 to 12–31 in Project 12.

    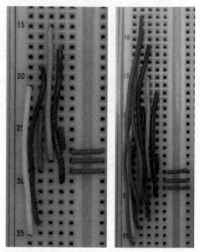

    Figure 13-20

    a. Plug the first (3/16-inch) jumper wire into holes **25d** and **27d**.

    b. Plug the second (1 1/4-inch) jumper wire into holes **15c** and **28c**.

    c. Plug the third (9/16-inch) jumper wire into holes **23b** and **29b**.

    d. Plug the fourth (1 3/8-inch) jumper wire into holes **21a** and **35a**.

    e. Plug the fifth (1 1/2-inch) jumper wire into holes **19b** and **34b**.

    f. Plug the sixth (1 1/4-inch) jumper wire into holes **17d** and **30d**.

    g. Plug the seventh (2 1/4-inch) jumper wire into holes **11c** and **33c**.

    h. Plug the eighth (2 1/4-inch) jumper wire into holes **13a** and **36a**.

    i. Plug the ninth (2 1/4-inch) jumper wire into holes **9b** and **31b**.

    j. Plug the tenth (2 1/2-inch) jumper wire into holes **7b** and **32b**.

19. Bend and trim the ten 1N4148 (or 1N914) diodes.

Trim each lead so that it is about 1/4-inch below the bend (see Figure 13-21).

20. Insert the ten trimmed 1N4148 (or 1N914) diodes into the breadboard.

Figure 13-21

As you follow the upcoming steps to insert the diodes, note that each of the ten diodes is oriented the same way: straddling the center ditch of the breadboard, with the anode (positive side) inserted into a hole in column *e* and the cathode (negative side, black stripe) inserted into a hole in column *f*.

Here are the details of where to insert the diodes (see Figure 13-22):

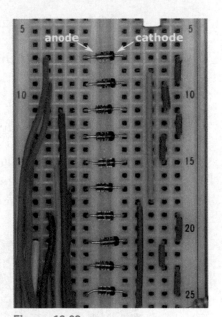

a. Plug the anode of the first diode (let's call it D1) into hole **7e** and the cathode (black stripe) into hole **7f**.

b. Plug the anode of D2 into hole **9e** and the cathode into hole **9f**.

c. Plug the anode of D3 into hole **11e** and the cathode into hole **11f**.

d. Plug the anode of D4 into hole **13e** and the cathode into hole **13f**.

Figure 13-22

e. Plug the anode of D5 into hole **15e** and the cathode into hole **15f**.

f. Plug the anode of D6 into hole **17e** and the cathode into hole **17f**.

g. Plug the anode of D7 into hole **19e** and the cathode into hole **19f**.

h. Plug the anode of D8 into hole **21e** and the cathode into hole **21f**.

i. Plug the anode of D9 into hole **23e** and the cathode into hole **23f**.

j. Plug the anode of D10 into hole **25e** and the cathode into hole **25f**.

21. Insert the three LEDs into the breadboard.

Make sure you know which side of each LED is the anode and which is the cathode. (See Figure 13-23.)

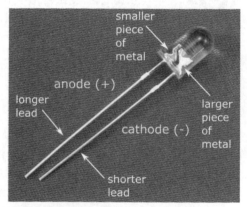

Figure 13-23

a. Plug the anode of the green LED (let's call it LED1) into hole **7i** and the cathode into hole **8i**. (See Figure 13-24.)

Figure 13-24

b. Plug the anode of the yellow LED (LED2) into hole **17i** and the cathode into hole **18i.** (See Figure 13-24.)

c. Plug the anode of the red LED (LED3) into hole **25i** and the cathode into hole **26i.** (See Figure 13-24.)

22. Insert a 2-inch (minimum) jumper wire into the breadboard.

Plug one end of the wire into hole **32j** and the other end into hole **47c**. (See the orange wire indicated by the arrows in Figure 13-25.)

23. Insert the 4017 decade counter IC into the breadboard.

Because this CMOS chip is sensitive to static discharge, you insert it last so you reduce the risk of zapping the chip as you build your circuit. If you have an antistatic wrist strap, make sure you put it on and connect it to an earth ground connection.

a. If the pins are angled outward, give them a squeeze so they are as straight as possible. (See Figure 13-26.)

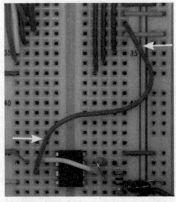

Figure 13-25   Figure 13-26

b. Orient the 4017 decade counter IC with the notch (clocking mark) on the upper edge, as shown for the two 4017 decade counters (from different manufacturers) in Figure 13-27. (I added the corner pin labels to the figure.)

c. Place the chip on top of holes **30–37e** (left side of chip) and **30–37f** (right side of chip), so that you are lining up the corner pins like this: pin 1 into hole **30e**, pin 8 into hole **37e**, pin 9 into hole **37f**, and pin 16 into hole **30f**.

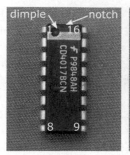

Figure 13-27

d. Press down slowly on the body of the chip, applying even pressure across the top of the chip, to insert the pins into the contact holes. As you press down, look at all the pins to make sure they are going into the holes. If any pin is not going in, stop pressing down, gently guide the pin into the hole, and then press down on the chip again until the pins are snugly inserted. (See Figure 13-28.)

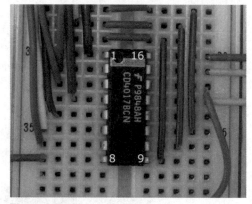

Figure 13-28

Figure 13-29 shows the completed three-way traffic light circuit (except for the battery and the power rail connections), turned on its side so that the LEDs light from left to right.

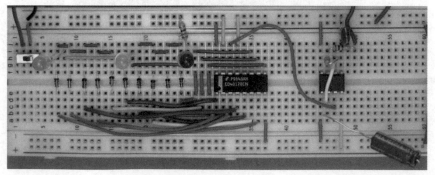

Figure 13-29

Operate Your Traffic Light

Turn on the power switch. Does one of the LEDs light up? It should. If it doesn't, check all your connections and the orientation of all ten diodes and the three LEDs. Also make sure that the two chips are oriented correctly and that their pins are inserted into the correct contact holes. Still not working? Then check all your jumper-wire connections, the orientation of your 47 µF capacitor, and the values of your resistors.

You should see each LED light one at a time, with LED1 (green) staying on the longest, then LED3 (red), and then LED2 (yellow). One entire cycle of the three LEDs lighting should take 14 to 47 seconds, depending on the position of your potentiometer knob.

Change the Timing

You can make small adjustments to your circuit to change the overall timing of the lighting sequence as well as the relative timing of the individual LEDs.

Alter the overall timing

You can control how quickly the three lights go through an entire sequence in two ways:

✔ **Turn the knob on the potentiometer.**

Adjusting the pot changes the timing of the output voltage on pin 3 of the 555 timer IC, which in turn changes the input trigger on pin 14 of the 4017 decade counter IC. By adjusting the pot, you can vary the timing of one cycle between about 14 and 47 seconds.

✔ **Swap out the 47 µF capacitor for a 100 µF capacitor (an optional component in your parts list).**

By replacing the 47 µF capacitor with a 100 µF capacitor (oriented with its negative side in the negative power rail and its positive side in hole **46b**, as shown in Figure 13-30), you slow down the green-yellow-red lighting sequence by about a factor of two (because the capacitance is roughly doubled).

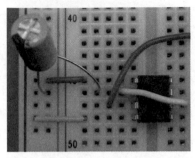

Figure 13-30

With this 100 µF capacitor in place, adjusting the pot knob varies the timing of one cycle between about 31 and 100 seconds. (To understand how this timing change happens, check out the next section, "Understand Your Traffic Light Circuit.")

Alter the relative timing

You can lengthen the duration of the yellow light and shorten the duration of the green light by making one small change: Move the jumper wire in holes **13i** and **15i** to holes **15j** and **17j**. Figure 13-31 shows a section of the circuit after this jumper has been moved.

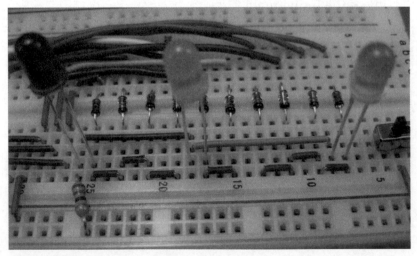

Figure 13-31

Understand Your Traffic Light Circuit

If you'd like to understand how this circuit works (especially why you need ten diodes), this section is for you! Don't feel like you have to read this section, though, just to make me (or anyone else) happy. Totally up to you!

Explore the schematic

Figure 13-32 shows the schematic for the original three-way traffic light circuit. (By *original,* I mean with the 47 µF capacitor and the jumper wire that affects the relative timing in its original location, holes *13i* and *15i*.)

On the left side of the schematic is the 555 timer. The 100 kΩ potentiometer, 100 Ω resistor, 22 kΩ resistor, and 47 µF capacitor to the left of the 555 timer control the timing of the output voltage on pin 3. (Refer to Project 8 for details about this.) That output voltage is used to trigger the 4017 decade counter, so pin 3 of the 555 timer is connected to pin 14 (trigger input) of the 4017 IC.

In an earlier section, you have the option of swapping out the 47 µF capacitor for a 100 µF capacitor. That action roughly doubles the capacitance, which halves the frequency of the 555 timer output. So, roughly doubling the capacitance slows down the triggering of the 4017 decade counter by about a factor of two.

On the right side of the schematic is the 4017 decade counter. (For detailed information on how the 4017 decade counter IC works, check out Project 12.) Its ten counting outputs are all connected to diodes. The cathodes of D1–D5 are connected, and those diodes are connected to LED1 (green). The cathode of D6 is connected to LED2 (yellow). The cathodes of D7–D10 are connected, and those diodes are connected to LED3 (red).

The sole purpose of diodes D1–D10 is to prevent current from flowing back into the 4017 chip. They allow current to flow out of the chip but not back in. As you soon find out, there's a good reason why you need these diodes.

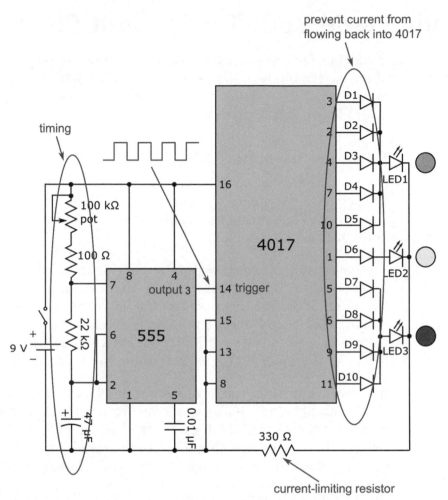

Figure 13-32

The cathodes of the three LEDs are connected to each other and to one side of the 330 Ω resistor. That 330 Ω resistor limits the current that passes through each LED. (Note that you need only one current-limiting resistor for the LEDs because only one LED is lit at any time.) The other four pins (8, 13, 15, and 16) are connected to either the positive or the negative side of the battery.

As the 4017 decade counter counts from 1 to 10, its ten output pins go high one at a time. Because the first five output pins (pins 3, 2, 4, 7, and 10) are all connected (through diodes D1–D5) to LED1 (green), all five of those outputs cause LED1 to light. So LED1 lights for five counts. The sixth output pin (pin 1) is connected (through diode D6) to LED2 (yellow), so LED2 lights for one count. The last four output pins (pins 5, 6, 9, and 11) are all connected (through diodes D7–D10) to LED3 (red), so LED3 lights for four counts. Then the cycle repeats itself.

So what role are the diodes (D1–D10) playing? Read on!

The importance of being a diode

Let's pretend for a minute that you don't have any of the diodes (D1–D10) in place, and you simply connect the output pins directly to the LEDs. (See Figure 13-33.) When, say, output pin 3 goes high, current flows out of the 4017 chip via pin 3, *and then it splits and flows back into the 4017 IC via pins 2, 4, 7, and 10,* in addition to flowing through LED1. Sending current *into* the *outputs* of the 4017 IC is a big no-no.

Because you are connecting multiple 4017 IC output pins together to control a single LED, you have to find a way to prevent current coming out of the 4017 IC via one pin from flowing back into the chip via another pin.

The solution is to connect a diode to each of the ten output pins. This way, current can flow only *out* of the chip via each output pin. So when, say, pin 3 goes high, current flows out of the chip via pin 3 and then current flows only through LED1. Current can't flow from the cathode to the anode of a diode, so diodes D2–D5 prevent current from flowing back into the 4017 IC via pins 2, 4, 7, and 10.

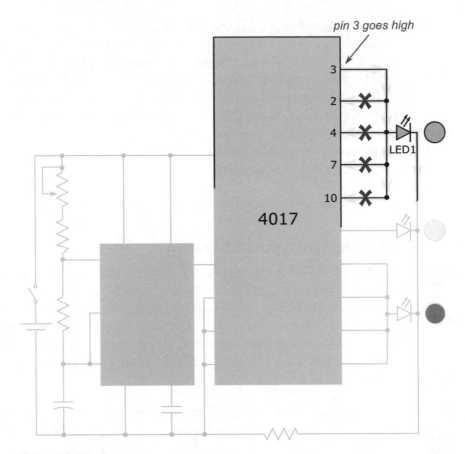

Figure 13-33

You may realize that you don't really need D6, because pin 1 is the only output pin connected to LED2. However, using a diode at pin 1 gives you the flexibility to change the relative timing of the LED lighting, say, to have the yellow LED light for two counts instead of one, while the green LED lights for four counts instead of five. By moving one jumper wire, you can make that change. (See the section "Alter the relative timing," earlier in this project.)

Those lowly little diodes play a big part in your traffic light circuit — and in many other circuits in electronics you use every day.

Radio and Amplifier

Do you enjoy listening to music?

In this project, you use just four components to build a radio receiver and another handful of components to construct an audio amplifier so you can hear the radio signal over a speaker.

Then, if you want, you can hack a cheap set of headphones and hook up its wires to the input of your amplifier. That way, you can listen to music from your iSomething or other music player.

What Is Radio?

This section helps you understand why the project you are about to build works. You don't need to understand it to build the project, so feel free to skip ahead to the next section if you'd like.

In scientific terms, *radio* is the transmission of a certain kind of electromagnetic energy through the air. *Electromagnetic energy* is energy that is radiated (meaning emitted) by an object and travels in waves, similar to the way sound is transmitted. X-rays, microwaves, visible light, and ultraviolet light (think sunburn) are other types of electromagnetic energy.

One way in which X-rays, microwaves, light, and radio waves differ is in the length of their waves. Picture yourself throwing a rock into a calm lake. When the rock hits the lake, the water on the surface begins to ripple, which means that little waves have been created that emanate in an expanding circle around the center (where the rock hit). The distance between the peaks of neighboring ripples is the *wavelength* of the ripple. Different forms of electromagnetic energy are radiated at different wavelengths, which is how we tell them apart.

The frequency of electromagnetic energy is closely related to the wavelength. *Frequency* is a measure of how many complete up-and-down waves pass a given point in space each second. The longer the wavelength, the lower the frequency, and vice versa.

Commercial radio stations are commonly identified by their transmission frequencies. For instance, 1010 WINS is an AM radio station in New York City. The *1010* in its name refers to 1010 kilohertz (kHz), which is the frequency at which the radio waves are transmitted from the station's antenna. Another NY-based radio station, 95.5 WPLJ, is an FM station that transmits at 95.5 megahertz (MHz).

The radio frequency (RF) spectrum (that is, range of frequencies) spans 3 kHz to 300 GHz (gigahertz) and is used for TV, shortwave, cellphone, GPS, and other types of transmissions in addition to radio station transmissions. Each AM radio station transmits at a frequency between 535 kHz and 1700 kHz, and each FM radio station transmits at a frequency between 87.5 MHz and 108 MHz.

Radio transmitters send *information*, which can be music or speech, over RF waves by modifying the pattern of the RF waves in a way that is related to the electrical pattern, or *signal*, representing the music or speech. This process is known as *modulation*. The RF waves are *carriers* of the actual signal (for instance, music). At the receiving end, a radio receiver *demodulates* the RF waves, separating the signal from the carrier. The signal can then be amplified through an electronic circuit and played through a speaker or headphones.

Although this radio transmission and reception process sounds complicated, building a basic radio receiver is fairly simple.

Plan Your Mission

Your job in this project is to pull a single radio signal out of the air, amplify the signal, and send it to a speaker so you can hear it. Sounds simple enough, doesn't it? As long as there is at least one reasonably strong AM radio station near your location, you should be able to detect and amplify a radio signal.

If you live in an area that is far from a radio station, you may not be able to detect a radio signal. It's worth a try to see if you can, but if you can't, you can switch to Plan B. Plan B involves building the audio amplifier and doing the optional part at the end of the project: cutting off an earpiece from a cheap set of headphones and using the headphone wires to input sound from an iPod, an iPhone, or other music player into your amplifier.

To pull a single radio signal out of the air, you need:

✔ An *antenna* to collect all the electromagnetic energy from the air. The antenna you use in this project is just a long wire connected to a large metal object, such as a coffee can or the spokes of a bicycle wheel.

✔ A *tuner* to select just one radio frequency. Your tuner consists of an *inductor* (just a coil of wire) and a *variable capacitor* (a capacitor that can be adjusted to store different amounts of electric charge). In the next section, you find out how to make your own inductor and variable capacitor.

✔ A radio wave *detector* to extract the signal (the music or talk show) from the selected frequency. Your detector is a specific kind of diode made from germanium.

One way to amplify the signal is to use a special integrated circuit (IC) known as an LM386 audio power amplifier, plus a few resistors, some capacitors, and a battery. And, of course, you need a speaker to hear the amplified signal. Figure 14-1 is a block diagram of your game plan.

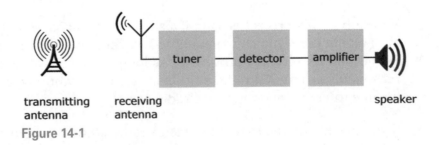

transmitting antenna   receiving antenna   speaker

Figure 14-1

Homemade Tuner

In this section, you make your own inductor and variable capacitor. These parts work together to tune in a specific frequency. Here are the supplies you need:

- A spool of 24-gauge magnet wire (50 feet minimum)

  Magnet wire is copper wire with a very thin enamel coating that serves as insulation (see Figure 14-2). Don't be fooled by the appearance of magnet wire; it is not bare copper wire, even though it looks as shiny as metal.

Figure 14-2

- Two 12-inch jumper wires

- One empty toilet paper (TP) roll, free of all paper

- One empty paper towel roll, free of all paper

- One small piece of medium or coarse (40–80 grit) sandpaper

- Aluminum foil

- One plain white sheet of paper (such as printer paper)

- Transparent tape (the kind you use to wrap gifts)

Make an inductor

All you need to make your own inductor is the TP roll, magnet wire, sandpaper, some tape — and a lot of patience. Follow these steps to make your inductor:

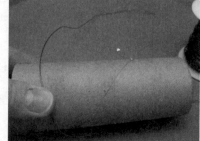

1. Start about 1 inch from one end of the TP roll.

2. Use your thumb to hold the magnet wire against the TP roll, leaving about 10 inches of magnet wire free. (See Figure 14-3.)

Figure 14-3

3. Wind the magnet wire around the roll, holding it in place with your thumb and counting the number of turns. (See Figure 14-4.)

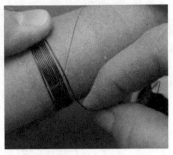

Make sure that each turn of the wire lies flat against the TP roll and is as close as possible to the previous turns. Avoid kinking the wire or overlapping turns.

Figure 14-4

4. When you've wound 5–10 turns of wire, use some tape to secure the wire in place against the TP roll. (See Figure 14-5.)

5. Continue to wind the wire, as shown in Figure 14-6, until you've counted 100 turns.

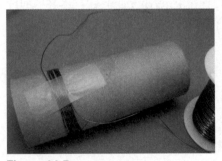

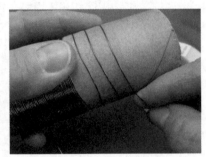

Figure 14-5

Figure 14-6

You may need to periodically adjust the wire to ensure that the turns are wound close together without any overlap or kinks.

6. Use tape to secure the 100 turns of wire against the TP roll.

7. Cut the end of the wire about 10 inches after the last turn.

You should have about 10 inches of free wire on each end of the 100 turns. (See Figure 14-7.)

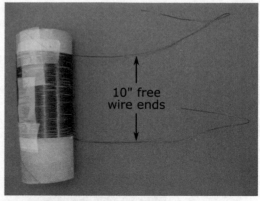

8. Sand about 1 inch of the enamel coating off each of the two ends of your coil.

Fold your sandpaper over one end of the wire and move the

Figure 14-7

sandpaper back and forth, squeezing it against the wire, until the copper underneath the enamel is exposed. Repeat the sanding process for the other end of the wire. (See Figure 14-8.)

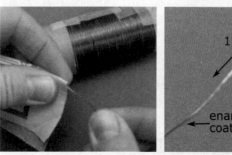 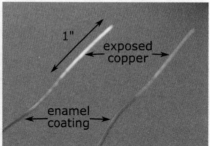

Figure 14-8

Exposing the copper core at each end of the wire enables you to connect your inductor to your circuit. Leaving the enamel on the rest of the wire prevents the individual turns of the wire from making electrical contact with each other.

This simple coil of wire plays an important part in tuning your radio.

Make a variable capacitor

The other component of your radio tuner is a variable capacitor. Grab the paper towel roll, aluminum foil, paper, two 12-inch jumper wires, and tape. Then follow these steps to make your variable capacitor:

1. Carefully cut two pieces of aluminum foil roughly 5 1/2 inches by 6 1/2 inches each. (See Figure 14-9.)

Figure 14-9

The foil should be as smooth as possible.

2. Tape the 5 1/2-inch side of one piece of foil to one end of the paper towel roll, as shown in Figure 14-10.

Figure 14-10

3. Wrap the foil around the paper towel roll and tape the free end down.

   Smooth the foil as you wrap it. The two ends should overlap. (See Figure 14-11.)

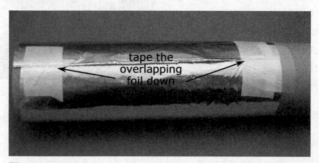

Figure 14-11

4. Cut a piece of plain paper 5 3/4 by 6 inches.

5. Lay the second piece of foil on top of the paper as follows:

   a. On three sides, make sure that the paper is visible under the foil.

   b. On the fourth side, make sure that the foil hangs over the edge of the paper by about 1/2 inch.

   c. Tape the foil to the paper on three sides.

   d. Make sure that one end of the foil sticks out over the edge of the paper. (See Figure 14-12.)

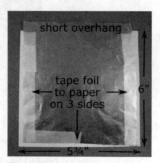

Figure 14-12

6. Wrap the foil-paper combination around the paper towel roll:

a. Do not tape the foil-paper combination to the paper towel roll. Instead, wrap the foil-paper combination around the paper towel roll so that it overlaps the inner foil. (See Figure 14-13.)

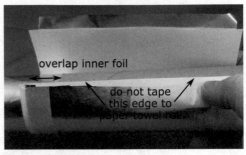

Figure 14-13

b. Leave the foil-paper combination a little loose so that you can slide it up and down along the length of the paper towel roll.

c. Tape the overhanging foil edge down. (See Figure 14-14.)

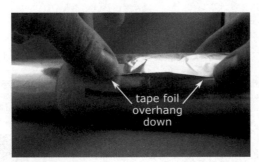

Figure 14-14

Make sure you can slide the foil-paper combination up and down, but be careful to avoid sliding it too far. If it slides beyond the inner foil, you might tear the inner foil when you slide the foil-paper combination the other way. The two layers of foil should always overlap at least a little.

7. Attach jumper wires to the two ends of the variable capacitor, as shown in Figure 14-15 (my jumper wires are scrunched up so they can fit in the picture).

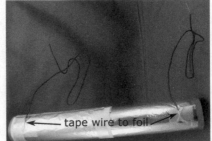

Figure 14-15

a. Tape the stripped end of a 12-inch jumper wire to one end of the capacitor, so the bare wire makes contact with the foil.

b. Tape the stripped end of another 12-inch jumper wire to the other end of the capacitor.

Together, your inductor and your variable capacitor will play the role of the tuner in your radio circuit. You may want to hot-glue your inductor and your variable capacitor to a piece of cardboard or a large plastic lid to make them easier to work with as you build your radio amplifier circuit. (See Figure 14-16.)

Figure 14-16

Meet Your Radio Signal Detector

The 1N34A germanium diode shown in Figure 14-17 serves as the detector in your radio receiver.

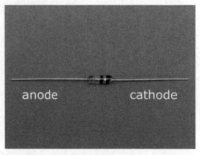

Like all diodes, the 1N34A allows current to flow in just one direction (from anode to cathode) and needs a certain amount of voltage applied to it to conduct current. Because it is made of germanium, it doesn't need as much voltage as do the diodes you use in Project 13, which are made of silicon.

Figure 14-17

The tiny radio signal oscillates up and down around 0 volts. The 1N34A diode blocks the lower part of each oscillation because current can flow only one way through the diode. So as the tiny radio signal passes through the diode, only the top half makes it through. That part of the signal carries the important speech or music information transmitted from the radio station.

The LM386 Audio Amplifier

Figure 14-18 shows an 8-pin IC known as the LM386 low-voltage audio power amplifier. Does it look just like the 555 timer IC you use in Projects 8–13? Well, the two chips may look alike, but they function differently. The LM386 amplifies, or boosts, audio (that is, sound) signals.

Figure 14-18

To use the LM386, you connect an audio signal between its input pins (pins 2 and 3), add battery power to pins 4 and 6, and connect a few resistors and capacitors to other pins. The result: a larger version of the input signal at the output (pin 5). By connecting a speaker at the output, you can hear the amplified sound. It's really that simple.

In this project, you use the LM386 to boost your radio signal so you can hear it. You also add a potentiometer near the input to the chip for volume control.

Gather Parts

Collect all the parts on this list:

- Solderless breadboard, *completely bare*
- 9-volt battery with battery clip
- One single-pole, double-throw (SPDT) switch
- Homemade variable capacitor (with leads)
- Homemade inductor
- One LM386 audio power amplifier IC

✔ One 1N34A germanium diode

✔ Capacitors:

- One 0.047 ceramic disc (nonpolarized) capacitor

- One 2200 picofarad (pF) ceramic disc (nonpolarized) capacitor

- One 0.1 µF film (nonpolarized) capacitor

- Two 10 µF electrolytic (polarized) capacitors

- One 220 µF electrolytic (polarized) capacitor

✔ One 10 Ω resistor (brown-black-black)

✔ One 10 kΩ resistor (brown-black-orange)

✔ One 100 kΩ potentiometer (preferably audio or logarithmic taper, but linear is okay too) with three attached leads

✔ One 8 Ω speaker, along with the following items attached:

- Two 2-inch (or so) 22-gauge solid wires with stripped ends

- Two insulated mini alligator clips

✔ Four 5/16-inch (minimum) jumper wires

✔ One 3/8-inch (minimum) jumper wire

✔ One 6-inch jumper wire

✔ Two long (roughly 5 feet) wires with stripped ends

✔ One 14-inch jumper lead with alligator clips

Figure 14-19 shows all parts except the breadboard and the 5-foot long jumper wires.

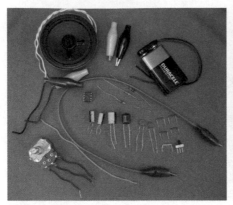

Figure 14-19

Once you have collected all your parts, you'll be ready to build your radio and amplifier. You start by building the amplifier on a solderless breadboard. Then you connect your antenna, tuner, and detector to the input of your amplifier.

Choose a Good Work Space

For your radio receiver to work, you need to connect your circuit to earth ground, so you should build your circuit within 5 feet or so of an earth ground connection. Certain objects inside your house, such as metal radiators, metal faucets, and copper pipes, are electrically connected to the ground outside your house. Such objects serve as earth ground connections.

My circuit-building space is in an unfinished room in my basement. Copper pipes run across the ceiling in this room, with copper brackets holding the copper pipes in place. It's easy for me to attach an alligator clip to one of the copper brackets, and use the clip to connect a wire to my circuit.

Build Your Amplifier

Follow these steps to build your audio amplifier circuit:

1. Add a power switch connection to your solderless breadboard (see Figure 14-20).

Figure 14-20

For this project, you connect just the positive side of the battery to the power switch. You do not use the negative power rail for connections to the negative side of the battery because of the sensitivity of the circuit. (You'll connect both sides of the battery to the circuit in a later step.)

a. Start with a completely bare solderless breadboard.

b. Insert an SPDT switch into holes *2h*, *3h*, and *4h* of the breadboard.

c. Insert a 5/16-inch (minimum) jumper wire between hole *3j* and the positive power rail to the right of row *3*.

d. Turn off the power switch (slider positioned toward row 60).

2. Insert the LM386 audio amplifier chip into the breadboard.

a. Orient the LM386 IC with the dimple (clocking mark) in the upper-left corner (see Figure 14-21, left).

b. Place the chip on top of holes *15–18e* (left side of chip) and *15–18f* (right side of chip), so that you are lining up the corner pins like this: pin 1 into hole *15e*, pin 4 into hole *18e*, pin 5 into hole *18f*, and pin 8 into hole *15f*.

c. Press down slowly on the body of the chip until the pins are snugly inserted into the contact holes. (See Figure 14-21, right.)

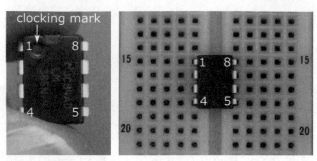

Figure 14-21

3. Insert a 10 µF electrolytic capacitor into the breadboard.

   Trim the capacitor leads so that they are about 5/8 inch long. Then plug the negative side (minus sign or black stripe) into hole **15g** and the positive side into hole **15d**. (See Figure 14-22.)

   By connecting this capacitor between pins 1 and 8 of the LM386 chip, you boost the gain of the amplifier from 20 to 200.

4. Insert the 2200 pF ceramic disc capacitor into the breadboard.

   Trim the capacitor leads to about 1/4 inch in length. Then plug one side into hole **16d** and the other side into hole **17d**. (See Figure 14-23.)

Figure 14-22

Figure 14-23

5. Insert a 5/16-inch (minimum) jumper wire into the breadboard.

   Plug one end of the jumper wire into hole **16a** and the other
   end of the jumper wire into the negative power rail to the left
   of row **16**. (See the orange wire in Figure 14-24.)

   You use the negative power rail to connect several points in
   your circuit, but you do not connect these points to the
   battery.

6. Insert a 10 kΩ resistor (brown-black-orange) into the
   breadboard.

   Trim the resistor leads. Then plug one side of the resistor into
   hole **13c** and the other side into hole **17c**. (See Figure 14-25.)

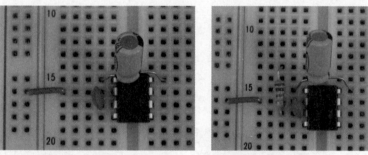

Figure 14-24   Figure 14-25

7. Insert a 0.1 µF film capacitor into the breadboard.

   Trim the capacitor leads to about 5/8 inch in length. Then plug
   one side into hole **18d** and the other side into hole **17g**. (See
   Figure 14-26.)

8. Insert a 3/8-inch (minimum) jumper wire into the breadboard.

   Plug one side into hole **18c** and the other side into hole **22c**.
   (See Figure 14-27.)

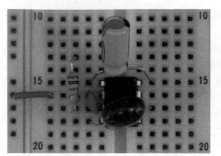

Figure 14-26   Figure 14-27

9. Insert a 5/16-inch (minimum) jumper wire into the breadboard.

   Plug one end of the jumper wire into hole **22a** and the other
   end of the jumper wire into the negative power rail to the left
   of row **22**. (See the lower orange wire in Figure 14-28.)

10. Insert the 0.047 µF ceramic disc capacitor into the breadboard.

   Trim the capacitor leads to about 3/8 inch in length. Then plug
   one side into hole **22e** and the other side into hole **22f**. (See
   Figure 14-29.)

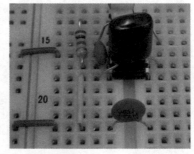

Figure 14-28   Figure 14-29

11. Insert a 220 µF electrolytic capacitor into the breadboard.

   Trim the capacitor leads so that they are about 5/8 inch long.
   Then plug the negative side (minus sign or black stripe) into
   hole **20g** and the positive side into hole **18g**. (See Figure 14-30.)

12. Insert a 10 Ω resistor (brown-black-black) into the breadboard.

Trim the resistor leads. Then plug one side of the resistor into hole **18i** and the other side into hole **22i**. (See Figure 14-31.)

Figure 14-30

Figure 14-31

13. Insert a 5/16-inch (minimum) jumper wire into the breadboard.

Plug one end of the jumper wire into hole **17j** and the other end of the jumper wire into the positive power rail to the right of row **17**. (See the orange wire on the right in Figure 14-32.)

14. Insert a 10 µF electrolytic capacitor into the breadboard.

Trim the capacitor leads so that they are about 1/2 inch long. Then plug the negative side (minus sign or black stripe) into hole **11d** and the positive side into hole **8d**. (See Figure 14-33.)

Figure 14-32

Figure 14-33

15. Insert the 100 kΩ potentiometer into the breadboard.

    For this project, you use both ends and the center tap of the potentiometer, so make sure you have leads attached to all three pot terminals. Try to make your leads fairly short, say 1 1/2 inches or even 1 inch. (See Figure 14-34.) (Refer to Project 8 for details about potentiometers and how to attach leads.)

    This potentiometer will enable you to control the volume of your audio amplifier.

    Plug the terminal 3 (right) lead into hole **11a**, the terminal 2 (center) lead into hole **13a**, and the terminal 1 (left) lead into the negative power rail to the left of row **17**. (See Figure 14-35.)

 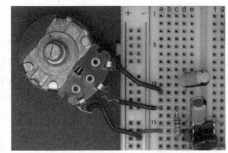

Figure 14-34   Figure 14-35

16. Insert the speaker into the breadboard.

    Plug one of the leads (either one) into hole **22d** and the other lead into hole **20j**. (See Figure 14-36.)

17. Connect the 9 V battery to the breadboard.

    Verify that the power switch is in the off position (slider toward row 60). Then plug the positive battery lead into hole **2j** and the negative battery lead into hole **22b**. (See Figure 14-37.)

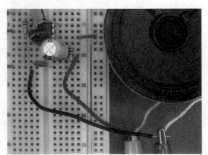

Figure 14-36

Figure 14-37

The circuit you just built is an audio amplifier that is ready and waiting for an input signal. Before you move on, please check all your connections. Make sure that the LM386 chip and the three electrolytic capacitors are oriented correctly. Check that your potentiometer leads are making good contact with the pot terminals, and that the speaker leads going into your breadboard are connected securely with alligator clips to the wires coming from the speaker. Check your battery connections.

The next step is to add the radio to the input of your amplifier.

If you would rather not build the radio but would like to try connecting your music player to your audio amplifier, you can skip ahead to the section "Tap into a Headphone Set," later in this project.

Connect the Radio

The radio consists of your homemade inductor, your homemade variable capacitor, the 1N34A germanium diode, a 5-foot wire antenna, and a 5-foot wire connection to earth ground. You also need two alligator clips and an alligator clip lead. Wiring these components is somewhat challenging, but if you are careful and an AM transmitter is within range, you should be able to hear the signal.

Follow these steps to hook up the radio:

1. Insert the 1N34A germanium diode into the breadboard.

   Trim the diode's leads. Then plug the cathode (black striped side) into hole **8e** and the anode (unmarked side) into hole **4e**. (See Figure 14-38.)

Figure 14-38

2. Insert one side of the inductor into the breadboard.

   Plug one of the inductor leads (either one) into hole **4a**. (See Figure 14-39.)

3. Insert one side of the variable capacitor into the breadboard.

Figure 14-39

   Plug one of the leads (either one) into hole **4b**. (See Figure 14-40.)

4. Insert one side of a 5-inch (minimum) jumper wire into the breadboard.

   Plug one side of the wire into the negative power rail to the left of row **25**. (See Figure 14-41.)

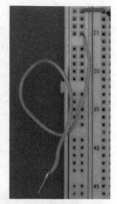

Figure 14-40   Figure 14-41

5. Use an alligator jumper lead to hold three wires together.

   a. Twist the following three wires together: the unconnected end of the 5-inch jumper wire you inserted in the previous step, the unconnected variable capacitor lead, and the unconnected inductor lead. (See Figure 14-42, left.)

   b. Use the alligator clip at one end of the jumper lead to hold the three twisted wires together securely. (See Figure 14-42, right.)

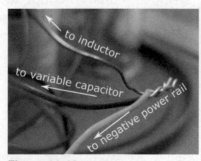

Figure 14-42

6. Connect your circuit to earth ground.

   Use a long wire (at least 5 feet), or a spool of wire, with 1/2 inch to 1 inch of insulation stripped off each end. Attach one end to a copper pipe, metal faucet, or metal radiator fin in your house, using an alligator clip to secure the wire to the object. These objects are electrically connected to the ground outside your house, so they enable you to make a connection to earth ground.

Figure 14-43, left, shows one side of my earth ground connection. I used an alligator clip to connect one (stripped) end of a spool of 22-gauge insulated wire to a copper bracket holding a copper pipe in place in the ceiling of my basement workshop.

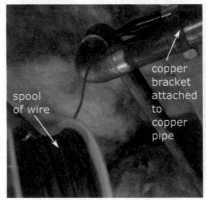

Figure 14-43

Connect the other (stripped) end of the long wire (or spool of wire) to the other side of the alligator jumper lead you used in the preceding step to hold the three twisted wires together. (See Figure 14-43, right.)

7. Connect an antenna to your breadboard.

Plug one stripped end of a 5-foot (or longer) wire into hole **4c**. Use an alligator clip to connect the other end to a large metal object (but not an object connected to earth ground). I used a large metal coffee can. (See Figure 14-44.)

Figure 14-44

The spokes of a bicycle, a large disposable aluminum pan, or an unplugged metal lamp are some other possibilities. Place the metal object so that the antenna is stretched out but not tight.

Check all your connections thoroughly. Once you have checked everything, you'll be ready to turn on your radio.

Operate Your Radio

Turn on the power switch. If you don't hear anything from the speaker, try adjusting your variable capacitor by sliding the moveable foil-paper combination up and down along the length of the paper towel roll. Be careful not to move it too far, or you may rip the underlying foil. If a strong enough AM radio signal is in your area, you should be able to tune it in.

If you still don't get a signal, use the fingers on one hand to hold on to the far end of the antenna and hold your other arm out but don't touch anything with your second hand. Your body will act like an extension of the antenna, which may be enough to pull in a radio signal.

If you get a signal, turn the knob on the potentiometer to adjust the volume. Turning the knob to the left turns the volume down; turning the knob to the right turns the volume up. Try adjusting your variable capacitor to see if you can pick up another radio station. I got two AM stations, but I live near a big city, so my area has lots of stations.

No luck? Check all your connections again, including the wires taped to the variable capacitor. If you still can't get a signal, you may want to move on to the next section, which guides you through disconnecting the radio part of your circuit and connecting a hacked headphone to the input of your circuit so you can play music through your audio amplifier.

Tap into a Headphone Set

Your audio amplifier can boost a radio signal or an audio signal from another source. By chopping off the earpiece of a cheap set of headphones, you can wire a connection from your iPhone, iPod, or other music player into your audio amp, and listen to music from your music player over your 8 Ω speaker.

Gather parts

Here are the parts you need (see Figure 14-45):

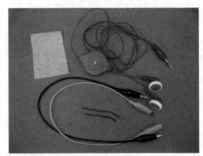

Figure 14-45

- One inexpensive 3.5 mm audio headphone set

- Two 2-inch jumper wires

- Two 14-inch jumper leads with alligator clips

- A small piece (2-inch square or so) of fine-to-medium (100–180 grit) sandpaper

In addition, you need your wire cutter or strippers. You may also find a magnifying glass helpful (it was essential for me).

Hack the headphones

It's easy (and fun) to chop off the earpiece of headphones. The challenging part of hacking headphones is identifying and preparing the two different sets of wires — audio signal and audio ground — that lead to the earpiece. You'll connect those wires to the input of your audio amplifier.

Here's how your hack your headphones:

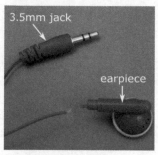

1. Cut off one of the earpieces.

   Use your wire cutters to slice through the wire leading to one earpiece, as shown in Figure 14-46.

2. Carefully strip about an inch of insulation from the headphone wire.

Figure 14-46

Use your wire strippers, but be very careful not to cut through the wires underneath the insulation. (See Figure 14-47.)

Figure 14-47

If you accidentally cut through the wires — which is easy to do — just strip another inch of insulation. (I had to restrip insulation two or three times.)

3. Identify the audio signal and audio ground wires.

   It may be hard to believe, but there are two separate sets of wires underneath the insulation. The wiring in audio jacks can vary widely depending on the manufacturer. If you see bare copper stranded wire, that's the audio ground wire.

   The audio signal wire is insulated, but the insulation may be just a thin layer of enamel (like the magnet wire you use earlier in this project to make the inductor). The insulation is colored (often red, white, or blue).

Figure 14-48 shows what the wires in my audio headphone set look like. I used my magnifying glass to help distinguish the stranded copper ground wire from the red enameled signal wires. My wires also contain thin white nylon strands that provide support for the delicate audio wires.

4. Remove roughly 1/4 inch of insulation (or enamel) from the signal wire.

   If your signal wire has rubber insulation, use your wire strippers to carefully cut the insulation. If your signal wire is coated with enamel as mine was, gently sand the enamel off the stranded wires using fine sandpaper. I placed my wire on a tabletop, held the wire in place with my finger, and gently rubbed the sandpaper over the wire in one direction repeatedly. (See Figure 14-49.)

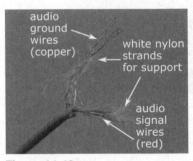

Figure 14-48

Figure 14-49

 It is difficult to remove the enamel without breaking some or all of the wires. Just take your time, be patient, and sand the wires very gently. You don't have to remove the enamel from the entire section of signal wire. You just need to expose some of the copper wire inside, and then (in a later step) adjust the connection between this signal wire and an alligator clip until you hear sound from your amplifier.

5. Attach alligator jumper leads to each set of audio wires, keeping track of which is signal and which is ground. (See Figure 14-50.)

Figure 14-50

a. Attach an alligator clip at the end of a 14-inch jumper lead to the audio ground wire or wires. Don't worry if you also clip some white nylon strands.

b. Attach an alligator clip at the end of another 14-inch jumper lead to the audio signal wire or wires. This jumper lead is separate from the jumper lead you use to connect to the audio ground wire or wires.

6. Attach 2-inch jumper wires to the alligator clips at the other ends of the alligator jumper leads.

Your hacked headphone set should look similar to the set shown in Figure 14-51.

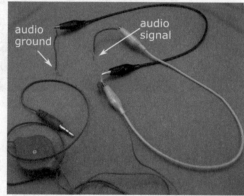

Figure 14-51

Remove the radio inputs

If you built the radio, you need to remove the radio components before you can connect the audio inputs from your headphones to your amplifier. Here's how:

1. Remove the earth ground connection (negative power rail to the left of row **25**).

2. Remove the 1N34A germanium diode (holes *4e* and *8e*).

3. Remove the inductor lead (hole *4a*), the variable capacitor lead (hole *4b*), and the antenna input (hole *4c*).

Figure 14-52 shows the audio amplifier without any audio inputs.

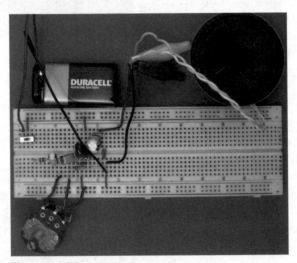

Figure 14-52

Connect your audio inputs to your amplifier

Connecting your headphone inputs to your amplifier is simple. Follow these steps (see Figure 14-53):

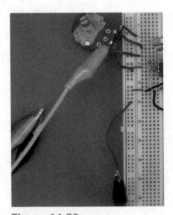

1. Connect the lead wire from the audio signal wires to hole *8a*.

2. Connect the lead wire from the audio ground wires to the negative power rail on the left. (I used the hole to the left of row *25*.)

Figure 14-53

Play your music player through your amplifier

Connect the 3.5 mm audio jack to your iPod, iPhone, or other music player and turn on the power switch on your bread-board. (See Figure 14-54.)

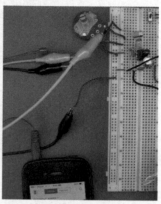

Figure 14-54

Do you hear music? If not, try turning up the volume on your music player, your audio amp (potentiometer knob), or both. If you still don't hear any sound, try fid-dling with the alligator clips that connect to the headphone wires to improve the electrical contact between the clips and the audio wires. If that doesn't work, you may need to rework those tiny audio headset wires.

Add a Selector Switch

If you were successful with both the radio and the audio head-phone inputs, you may want to connect both inputs to a switch so that you can choose between the two inputs without rewiring your amplifier. You need to add an SPDT switch, move your head-set audio input lead, and reconnect your radio.

Follow these steps to add a selector switch:

1. Turn off the power switch.

2. Move the headphone audio input signal lead from hole **8a** to hole **9a**. (See Figure 14-55.)

3. Insert the SPDT switch in holes **7b, 8b,** and **9b**. (See Figure 14-56.)

Figure 14-55

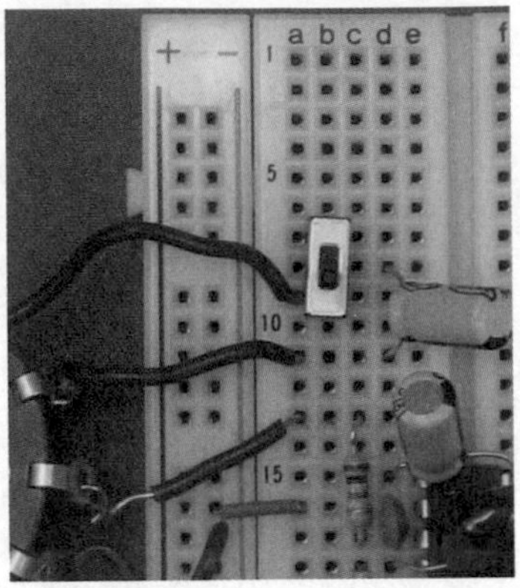

Figure 14-56

4. Insert the anode of the 1N34A germanium diode in hole **3e** and the cathode (black stripes) in hole **7e**. (See Figure 14-57.)

5. Plug the earth ground connection from the radio into the negative power rail on the left. I used the hole to the left of row **30**. (See Figure 14-58.)

Figure 14-57

Figure 14-58

6. Reconnect the free ends of the inductor (hole **3a**), variable capacitor (hole **3b**), and the antenna (hole **3c**). (See Figure 14-59.)

Figure 14-59

Check all your connections. Then turn on the power switch. The SPDT switch you just added controls which input signal — the radio or the music player — is connected to your audio amplifier.

Try moving the slider on the SPDT switch to choose between the two inputs. If you're successful in switching between radio and music player, give yourself a huge pat on the back!

Index

About the Author

Cathleen Shamieh is an electrical engineer and high-tech writer with extensive engineering and consulting experience in the fields of medical electronics, speech processing, and telecommunications.

Dedication

To all kids — young and old — who are happy to put down their electronic devices to tinker with electronic circuits.

Author's Acknowledgments

Thanks to the wonderful team at Wiley for all their hard work and support throughout this project. I'm grateful to Katie Mohr for giving me the opportunity to write an electronics book for kids and for helping to shape the vision for the book. This was such a fun project to work on!

I was thrilled to work on another book with the inimitable Susan Pink, project and copy editor extraordinaire, and technical wizard Kirk Kleinschmidt. Susan is a master at rewording awkward sentences, issuing gentle reminders, and instilling peace and calm during times of stress as deadlines approach (and pass). Kirk's attention to detail is amazing! If it weren't for him, kids that dutifully follow the circuit-building steps in this book would be scratching their heads wondering what's wrong, when the problem was a mistake in one (or more) instructions. Thank you, Susan and Kirk!

I'm very grateful to Debbye Butler for her thorough proofreading of the book. Debbye's sharp eyes identified a few nonexistent transistor models, in addition to many other mistakes. I'd also like to acknowledge Matthew Lowe, Cherie Case, Kumar Chellappan, and all the other Wiley folks who contributed their time and talents to this project.

Thank to my sons, Kevin, Peter, Brendan, and Patrick, for accepting frozen pizza in lieu of real food on many a night. Special thanks to Brendan for running to RadioShack for me and to Patrick, my budding engineer, who tried out the projects and let me know when something I wrote didn't make sense to him.

Last but not least, I'd like to thank my husband, Bill, for always being patient and kind, and for taking on more than his fair share of the family responsibilities during the closing weeks of this project.

Publisher's Acknowledgments

Acquisitions Editor: Katie Mohr

Project Editor: Susan Pink

Copy Editor: Susan Pink

Technical Editor: Kirk Kleinschmidt

Editorial Assistant: Matthew Lowe

Sr. Editorial Assistant: Cherie Case

Production Editor: Kumar Chellappan